D1482326

*If Only We Could Know!*

# If Only We Could Know!

<hr />

*An Interpretation of Chekhov*

## VLADIMIR KATAEV

<hr />

*Translated from the Russian and Edited by*

HARVEY PITCHER

<hr />

IVAN R. DEE
*Chicago 2002*

Library of Congress Cataloging-in-Publication Data:
Kataev, V. B. (Vladimir Borisovich)
   [Selections. English. 2002]
   If only we could know : an interpretation of Chekhov / Vladimir Kataev ;
translated from the Russian and edited by Harvey Pitcher.
      p. cm.
   Includes bibliographical references and index.
   ISBN 1-56663-448-2 (alk. paper)
      1. Chekhov, Anton Pavlovich, 1860–1904—Criticism and interpretation.
I. Pitcher, Harvey J. II. Title.

PG3458.Z8 K38213 2002
891.72'3—dc21                                              2002024613

*To Mariana*

# Contents

# Introduction

I ASKED a friend of mine who had recently gone to live in America what his impressions were of the country and its people.

"One thing I've noticed," he replied, "is how many Chekhov characters there are living in the world. Only they don't realize it."

His observation unwittingly confirms once again what Tolstoy said immediately after Chekhov's death: that Chekhov's works and his characters are close not only to every Russian but to people everywhere, and that this universal quality is the most important thing about him.

It will soon be a hundred years since the physical death of Anton Pavlovich Chekhov. Immortality, he was apt to remark, is rubbish, but what has happened to his creative legacy during that time matches all the metaphors ever created by man to express the idea of immortality. It is a process that is still going on, overcoming boundaries of time and space, and taking a different form in different countries.

In his Introduction to *Chekhov on the British Stage*, Patrick Miles writes: "The progress of Chekhov's plays in Britain . . . is a remarkable phenomenon, especially in a theater traditionally so insular. . . . Actors, audiences, and directors have gradually taken Chekhov to their heart, and his interaction with the British stage has been subtle, all-pervading, and durable. It has amounted to a massive inter-

vention in our theater."[1] The comparison between Chekhov's influence on world drama and that of Shakespeare has become a commonplace of literary criticism. On the American stage Chekhov is
now the most popular foreign dramatist, and Edward Albee has
long held the view that Chekhov had a greater influence than anyone else on the course of twentieth-century drama. Until the mid-
1950s, German theorists still refused to accept Chekhov as a
genuine dramatist, but now no serious work on the theory of drama
could fail to take him into account.[2] Many similar examples can be
offered, changing the names of countries and continents.

These two circumstances—that Chekhov is recognized as a cultural figure of world status, and that he continues to exert a considerable influence on contemporary art and literature—present his
critics with special kinds of problems.

In his own country the measures and parameters of studying
Chekhov were set by several (partly paradoxical) definitions of Tolstoy's: "Chekhov is Pushkin in prose"; "Shakespeare's plays are
dreadful, but yours are even worse"; "he created completely new
forms of writing, quite unlike anything I have ever met elsewhere."[3]

As early as the mid-1880s some of Chekhov's contemporaries
had already begun speaking of a "revolution in literature" that he
was carrying out.[4] Interpretation of his work began during his lifetime, but for many years the assessment of this contemporary criticism offered in 1967 by Kornei Chukovsky seemed patently true:
*"Twenty years of incomprehension."*[5] Only the productions of the
Moscow Art Theater, it was considered, adequately interpreted
Chekhov's plays. In spite of the fact that Chekhov's own response to
two of their four productions had been sharply critical,[6] it was these

  1. Patrick Miles, ed., *Chekhov on the British Stage* (Cambridge, 1993), p. 1.
  2. See Bernhard Brehmer, "Tvorchestvo Chekhova v nemetskom literaturovedenii i
teorii dramy" in *Chekhov v Germanii* (Moscow, 1996), pp. 252–271.
  3. See *Literaturnoye nasledstvo*, vol. 68 (Moscow, 1960), pp. 660, 875.
  4. See *Pis'ma A. P. Chekhovu yego brata Aleksandra Chekhova* (Moscow, 1939), p. 149.
  5. Kornei Chukovsky, *O Chekhove* (Moscow, 1967), p. 89.
  6. On Chekhov's differences of opinion with the Moscow Art Theater over their
productions of *The Seagull* and *The Cherry Orchard*, see *Perepiska A. P. Chekhova*, 3 vols.
(Moscow, 1996), vol. 3.

productions that for decades, right up to the mid-twentieth century, determined how Chekhov should be treated on the Soviet stage.

During the Soviet period as a whole, the attitude to Chekhov can best be summed up by another formula taken from Vasily Grossman's novel *Life and Fate*, where the characters say: "*Chekhov is allowed here, because they don't understand him.*"[7] Even though Gleb Struve called his article on the twenty-volume *Collected Works* of the 1940s "Chekhov in Communist Censorship,"[8] and pointed to dozens of cuts, mainly ideological in character, that the editors had made in Chekhov's letters, it is true that in regard to editions of his works, productions of his plays, and the creation of museums, Chekhov as a whole fared well during the Soviet years. But as to the function that was assigned to this *state-approved Chekhov* in the general system of ideological directives, and the extent to which the approach of Chekhov scholars became biased or distorted as a result—those are different questions.

From the mid-1940s, Vladimir Yermilov and his school of critics consciously and deliberately complied with the directive to create an image of "our" Chekhov. G. P. Berdnikov went further, and in his book published in the 1980s and awarded all manner of prizes because of the author's official position, offered as the highest praise of Chekhov the following formula: that as a result of his searchings the author had raised himself to the level of "social realism"[9]—although the heights of Socialist Realism remained inaccessible to him. Chekhov's "seagull," it was wittily remarked, had been painted to look like Gorky's "stormy petrel": this was the price to be paid for official approval of Chekhov and even reverence toward him.

Ilya Ehrenburg, rereading Chekhov and the literature on him in the late 1950s, during the period of Khrushchev's "thaw," accurately noted how depressingly monotonous were the conventional formulas that had now penetrated everywhere, even into school textbooks

---

7. Grossman's novel, *Zhizn' i sud'ba*, was written in 1961 and published in the USSR in 1988.

8. *Slavonic and East European Review*, vol. 20 (1961), pp. 327–341.

9. G. P. Berdnikov, *A. P. Chekhov. Ideinye i tvorcheskiye iskaniya*, 3rd ed. (Moscow, 1984), p. 398.

and encyclopedias: Chekhov was said to have "unmasked," "accused," "anticipated," "greeted." But articles were being written in literally the same terms about Saltykov-Shchedrin and Gleb Uspensky as about Chekhov.[10] A vast distance, however, separated this official Chekhov scholarship from the lively interest that readers and audiences had never stopped showing in him. Individual works by A. B. Derman, A. P. Skaftymov, and G. A. Byaly struck a dissonant note; but they did not call the tune.[11]

The turning point came in the 1970s. Largely as a result of growing international interest in Chekhov and international criticism of earlier Soviet editions of his works, the Institute of World Literature in Moscow began work on a thirty-volume scholarly edition of Chekhov's complete works and letters. The "Chekhov group" brought together highly qualified literary specialists and textologists, and attracted younger scholars at the start of their careers. A. P. Chudakov, myself, and other literary specialists of our generation first had our attitudes to Chekhov shaped by the university seminars conducted by V. V. Vinogradov and S. M. Bondi. They inculcated in their students the habits of "honest reading," of seeking to understand an author's meaning and paying attention to the text. I joined the group at the last moment. My task was to write the commentaries on Chekhov's story "The Bishop" and on his letters devoted to the Dreyfus Affair. Since religion and anti-Semitism were politically sensitive subjects, the person invited to write the commentaries had turned the commission down as too risky. Taking that risk fell to me, a very junior Chekhov scholar.

At that time we certainly did not restrict ourselves to questions of textology and annotation but were absorbed by serious problems that demanded a new approach to Chekhov. During the 1970s direct confrontation with the problems of Chekhov's poetics and the interpretation of his works provided a refreshing new approach, which challenged pseudo-sociological schemes of interpretation.

---

10. See Ilya Ehrenburg, *Perechityvaya Chekhova* (Moscow, 1960), pp. 8–9.
11. A. B. Derman, *O masterstve Chekhova* (Moscow, 1959); A. P. Skaftymov, *Nravstvenniye iskaniya russkikh pisatelei* (Moscow, 1972: the articles on Chekhov); G. A. Byaly, *Chekhov i russkii realizm* (Leningrad, 1981).

The challenge was felt by adherents of the official school of Chekhov studies; the old guard was not prepared to tolerate liberties. Chudakov's book on Chekhov's poetics was severely criticized in the semi-official monthly *Voprosy literatury* (Problems of Literature), while a favorable review in the same journal of my book on interpreting Chekhov was withdrawn at the last moment, when the piece was already in type. Fortunately, times changed, and expressing unorthodox views on Chekhov long ago ceased to be regarded as the equivalent of undermining the foundations of society.

But the questions that seemed vital to me twenty years ago, when I was writing my first book on Chekhov, seem the same today. Chekhov is loved everywhere, but how correctly is he understood? And what does a "correct" understanding mean in this instance?

It is obvious, after all, that specifically "Soviet" interpretations are no more than particular examples of misinterpreting Chekhov. When you consider all the changing images of him in literary criticism during the past century, you realize that they are not simply a reflection of changing social and cultural paradigms or directives. Chekhov has been seen in all manner of ways: as a social writer and chronicler of his times, an exponent of the ideology of the Russian intelligentsia, a writer-psychologist, a cold ironist, or an exponent of humanist values. He has been proclaimed as the writer who brought the Golden Age of Russian realism to a close, or conversely, as the writer who ushered in the literary avant-garde, the literature of the absurd, and now even postmodernism. All these kinds of interpretations can be found in the literature on Chekhov in different languages.

What critics regard as central to his work may be a particular theme, such as "moral awakening" or "culture," "universal alienation" (or, in contrast to that, "the religious theme" or "the theme of sexual relations"); a feature of his mental makeup ("Chekhov's powers of observation," "his interest in the diverse phenomena of life"); some driving force, such as the "protest against vulgarity, philistinism, or small-mindedness"; or a distinctive feature of his poetics ("fortuitousness," "compression," etc.).

One is struck by the colorful variety of theories underlying these

dominant principles. Very often, notwithstanding the critic's declarations, a selective approach is evident: those works or fragments of
works that support the chosen concept are analyzed while others
contradicting it are set aside and declared to be atypical.

Today not only traditional cultural-historical or structuralist
methods are applied to Chekhov. The latest winds of change in literary criticism—deriving from the concepts of deconstructionism,
elimination of the author, and any number of arbitrary reader's
strategies for interpreting a text—have not passed him by. I am not
convinced of the fruitfulness of interpretations of Chekhov that demand, for example, that the meaning of his "Lady with a Little
Dog" be linked with the fact that the Hebrew word *gur* (which
strikes a chord with the hero's surname, Gurov) means a "puppy" or
"little dog"; or that one can present *Three Sisters* as a geopolitical
fantasy on the theme of obtaining sovereignty for the three Baltic
republics. Such contemporary approaches (both in literary criticism
and on the stage) may be ingenious, but they tell us more about the
interpreter than about Chekhov.

In this book the reader will find an interpretation, or attempted
interpretations, of individual works by Chekhov. But it is in no way
my intention to offer a list or catalogue of previous interpretations.
What interests me most are the *problems* of interpretation: its possibilities, limits, and principles, what is open to interpretation, and
what is relevant to the interpretation of Chekhov's works.

Like the world itself, a work of literature is open-ended in
meaning, and for that reason "definitive" interpretations are inconceivable. But we can apply the criterion of correct/incorrect to the
interpreter's activities; an objective basis for correct interpretation is
built into the text, and it is placed there by the author (by virtue of
his artistic purpose and the organization of his material in line with
that purpose).

One may agree with those who claim that in a text it is not the
author speaking so much as the words themselves, and that consequently each reader works out his own "strategy" for assimilating
the text, seeing in it meanings that were not foreseen by the author.

But should we make this "elimination" of the author a compulsory starting point? Especially an author like Chekhov, who most certainly had something to say? Is it not better and more interesting at the start to try to hear what that particular author wishes to say to us?

Attempting to grasp what an author was setting out to achieve does not exclude different ways of studying a work, but it precedes and underlies them. How can one adequately argue with an author, refute him or judge him or, conversely, see in him an ally who shares one's point of view, unless one has established the genuine meaning of his works? "There's no harm in understanding something in one's own way," as Chekhov commented in his article "*Hamlet* on the Stage of the Pushkin Theater," about the play's latest production— "but one should do so without giving offense to the author."[12]

The problem of the unity of Chekhov's artistic world has come more and more to the forefront. There is a growing understanding that the distinctive features of Chekhov's content, style, and poetics are based on a definite concept of life, which deserves special attention. The organizing principle of Chekhov's artistic world is often defined as its "leading line," to be traced either "vertically" (through the different levels of language, plot, characterization, idea, etc.) or "horizontally" (in different works). But this kind of model works better if one thinks not of a single line but of a system of coordinates. The model can become multi-dimensional if each work is understood as the outcome of an interaction between several dominant principles, and if the whole of Chekhov's artistic world is seen as a system developing in time.

To define Chekhov's dominant principles by deriving them from some separate, "special" theme, problem, or situation, or simply from his method of presenting life's material, either narrows down and trivializes Chekhov's originality or concentrates on effects instead of causes. It is vital to understand Chekhov as the representative of a particular type of artistic thinking and creativity, vital to

12. *Works*, 16:20. The abbreviations *Works* and *Letters* refer to the thirty-volume Chekhov *Collected Works* (Moscow, 1974–1983), consisting of eighteen volumes of *Works* and twelve of *Letters*.

perceive that the actual artistic forms he uses are themselves important. This book attempts to concentrate on what may be called Chekhov's "conception of the world," his angle of vision on reality, which predetermines his unique treatment of a whole range of diverse themes, motifs, and situations.

I cannot fail to recall with gratitude the man in whose company some of the ideas for this book were first discussed and took shape: Sergei Mikhailovich Bondi, whose lifelong love of Pushkin was matched only by his love of Chekhov.

The book has been further enriched by analysis, discussion, debate, sometimes argument, but in general collaboration with the students and postgraduates who participated in the Chekhov seminar in the Philological Faculty of Moscow University.

Finally, I wish to express my profound thanks to Harvey Pitcher, without whom this English-language translation could not have appeared. Himself the author of several original works on Chekhov, and the translator into English of perhaps Chekhov's most difficult texts, the early comic stories, Harvey generously offered to take on the task of choosing and translating those parts of my books on Chekhov that would be of greatest interest to American and British readers. Our correspondence on the subtleties and complexities of the translation opened up new horizons in my own understanding of Chekhov.

To Ivan Dee we offer our joint thanks for reading the text with great care and suggesting a number of improvements.

# Editor's Note

VLADIMIR KATAEV'S *Proza Chekhova: problemy interpretatsii*
(Chekhov's Prose: Problems of Interpretation) was published in
1979. Of its twenty-five chapters, nineteen are included here,
though sometimes considerably shortened (to exclude, for example,
comparisons with Russian writers unlikely to be well known in the
West). Ten years later Kataev published *Literaturnye svyazi Chekhova*
(Chekhov's Literary Connections). This included long chapters on
four of Chekhov's plays: *Ivanov*, *The Seagull*, *Three Sisters*, and *The
Cherry Orchard*. These have been shortened and adapted for this
book by the author, who has also added a new chapter on *Uncle
Vanya*. Finally, the essay on "Kashtanka" (comic and serious at the
same time), which became the present Chapter 1, is taken from
*Slozhnost' prostoty* (The Complexity of Simplicity), which appeared
in 1998. All three volumes were published by Moscow State University.

*Proza Chekhova* contained all of the author's main ideas on
Chekhov. Its reception among specialists in the West was warmer
than its official reception in the Soviet Union, but it never reached
the wide general audience it deserved. It was praised not so much
for its obvious erudition as for its uncompromising honesty—to
echo the kind of vocabulary that Kataev himself uses about
Chekhov. This was all the more remarkable because of the ideologi-

cal climate in which it was written. With his careful arguments, Kataev quietly undermines many conventional (and still persistent) approaches to Chekhov, Western as well as Russian, and sets up a radically new position of his own. As Tolstoy pointed out, Chekhov is universal property—and rightly so—but it is important nonetheless for those of us in the West to see how Chekhov is interpreted by a Russian who has devoted so much of his time and thought to him.

*If Only We Could Know!*

# I

# A Cautionary Tale: "Kashtanka" (1887)

You will not find a reading of "Kashtanka" among the most brilliant or famous pages of Russian literary criticism. Yet this story about a dog, transparently clear and easily understood by children, offers a good example of how different and sometimes diametrically opposed meanings may be ascribed to a work of literature as a result of shifts in ideology and even politics.

Differences of interpretation are not, of course, the product of ideologies alone. There are as many interpretations as there are readers with different tastes and temperaments, different powers of imagination, different degrees of sympathy and compassion. Just as each playgoer has his own Hamlet, so each Russian reader has his own Kashtanka.

What kind of story is it? Junior arts students, unaffected by jargon and ignorant of what has been written on the subject, give their own kinds of answers.

"For a long time I couldn't get to the bottom of it. Was it just a story about a dog, about seeing the world through a dog's eyes? Or did it have other meanings?"

"I suppose it's a lot more complicated than one thinks. . . ."

"What about the cat? Is *he* meant to be significant?"

"No, he's just a fat, lazy cat. . . ."

"When I was a child, it used to annoy me that the dog goes back to her tormentors. This seemed cruel to the dog, and I felt sorry for her. Now I think it may be a story about going back to your own environment. . . ."

"I always felt sorry for Kashtanka's new master, the circus artist. In the film versions he's left on his own and *he's* the one you feel sorry for. . . ."

This is how today's students and yesterday's children, the readers of "Kashtanka," move the question of "What is this story about?" or "What is the guy trying to say?" (the worst question, in Vladimir Nabokov's opinion, that "Teachers of Literature" are capable of devising) onto a different plane by asking: "Who do we feel most sorry for at the end when Kashtanka leaves her new master to return to her old ones?" In answering that question in different ways, they are offering different interpretations of the story.

But the same Nabokov—after poking fun at donnish questions of the "What is the author trying to achieve?" variety—goes on to talk about "certain points, byroads, favorite hollows that one evokes more eagerly and enjoys more tenderly than the rest of one's book," and of "the subliminal coordinates by means of which the book is plotted."[1] What else is this if not an invitation to speculate about the meaning an author attaches to his work and about its interpretation?

Chekhov's story consists of two interwoven and superimposed systems of episodes and descriptions. First, of course, it is a story about a dog, about her habits, way of life, and one particular overriding instinct—the instinct of attachment to her master, even though he torments her. A veterinarian or a dog breeder might explain this instinct in technical terms; what the artist does is to illustrate it in practice. Second, it is a representation of the world refracted through a particular prism—the world as seen by a dog (the kind of task that was evidently of special interest to Chekhov

---

1. Vladimir Nabokov, "On a Book Entitled Lolita" in *The Annotated Lolita* (London, 1993), pp. 311, 315, 316.

in 1886, when he wrote many stories from the point of view of a child).

This gives rise to the story's comic elements and fresh descriptions: the elephant that Kashtanka sees as a fat face with a tail instead of a nose, the circus top like an inverted soup tureen; her division of the human race into cabinetmakers and customers; and the chicken leg that she hides from her master behind the cupboard. This is what children love about "Kashtanka." And this is what the story was like in its original version, entitled "In Learned Society." But then Chekhov adds Chapter 6, "A Troubled Night," which is no longer meant only for children: lines about loneliness and how those we are attached to go away for good. Here are those "favorite hollows," in Nabokov's words, those "subliminal coordinates" (I should prefer to say, conscious coordinates) to which an interpreter should look for the author's meaning.

But now our students begin to find out what the critics have had to say about "Kashtanka."

In a 1976 monograph for teachers of literature, entitled *Chekhov the Artist*, M. L. Semanova, having listed in detail the "visible or hidden signs of Kashtanka's spiritual condition," addresses the significance of the story's conclusion, which she interprets thus: "The ending shows the triumph of such feelings as attachment, love, and loyalty, which prove stronger than material comforts, vainglory, and the bright lights of fame."

This must be taken to mean that Kashtanka acquires the first set of values in the home of the poor cabinetmaker, and turns her back on the second set when she escapes from the rich artist. That is how "the author's sympathies and predilections, his social and moral criteria for evaluating what he describes," are expressed in the story. In Semanova's opinion, Chekhov "was trying to remind the reader of the simplest unchanging values, overlooked by 'bourgeois civilization'—naturalness, a healthy moral outlook, humaneness, freedom from prejudice and superstition, calculation, and self-interest—and to express his vision of a different world, a world of happiness, harmony, and human unity."

This line of reasoning can be said to derive from the critic's desire to show or confirm once again that Chekhov was a "progressive" writer, "a writer-democrat" who was on the side of the poor and against the rich. The only problem is that none of this bears even the remotest relation to the text of "Kashtanka":

"Naturalness, a healthy moral outlook" (Semanova); "The cabinetmaker was as drunk as a lord . . ." (Chekhov). "Humaneness" (Semanova); "Once . . . he had even got hold of her foxlike ear in his fist, pulled it, and said very deliberately: 'Why-don't-you-just-drop-dead!' " (Chekhov). "Freedom from prejudice and superstition" (Semanova); "He was waving his arms about, sighing deeply and muttering: 'Here we are walking along the street looking at these little lamps, but once we die, we shall all burn in fiery Hyena [the cabinetmaker's garbled version of Gehenna] . . .' " (Chekhov).

In a word, whatever virtues Semanova may attribute to the "representatives of the people," you will not find them in the real heroes of the story (which does not mean that Luka the cabinetmaker and his son Fedyushka are not sympathetic in their own way).

The critic does not draw her arguments from the text—which flatly contradicts them—but from another interpretation. She recalls that when the celebrated Moscow Art Theater actor V. I. Kachalov took the part of the author in a radio production of "Kashtanka," "he put special emphasis on the life-affirming humanism of the story, on Chekhov's defense of the 'simple' life."[2]

That was the value system in the "years of stagnation" [roughly 1965–1982]: a "simple" person (a worker, craftsman, or peasant) embodied the moral virtues while a rich person was in essence depraved—this morality was exclusively class-based. At least we can be grateful that the critic did not interpret the thought that enters Kashtanka's head, "No, life is intolerable!" as a call by Chekhov to revolution. That, after all, was the meaning given to a similar phrase from the story "Gooseberries" by V. V. Yermilov (see the chapter "Life Has Become Intolerable!" in his book on Chekhov).[3]

The mythologized image of Chekhov in the Soviet epoch was

2. M. L. Semanova, *Chekhov-khudozhnik* (Moscow, 1976), pp. 42, 46.
3. V. V. Yermilov, *A. P. Chekhov* (Moscow, 1954), pp. 290–294.

more broadly based, of course, but the technique of making a story yield a required ideological message is fully demonstrated even in interpretations of "Kashtanka."

Then came a new epoch, that of *perestroika*. With it came a new treatment of "Kashtanka," one based on making literary connections. "Kashtanka and Sharik" is the title of a 1990 paper by Yu. A. Bogomolov juxtaposing Chekhov's character with the hero of Bulgakov's *The Heart of a Dog*, which was tremendously popular in those years. The critic supposes that "these two famous literary dogs might have met at one of the circus performances, Chekhov's Kashtanka as an artiste and Bulgakov's Sharik (Sharikov) as a spectator."

Here the plus and minus signs are reversed in accordance with the spirit of the times. Kashtanka's story is to be understood thus: only after exchanging her proletarian surroundings for a life of security and plenty did it become possible for her to be introduced to the higher moral and spiritual values. In her new master's house, Kashtanka experienced a course of "humanization"; Chekhov "tells how a sympathetic creature of reflexes can have spiritual refinement injected into her, and how gleams of consciousness can penetrate a life of reflex reactions."[4] This would be the evolutionary, not the revolutionary, path, and Chekhov's story is called upon to show the advantage of evolution over revolution.

Bogomolov does not take issue with Semanova and may not even have seen her monograph. Times, simply, have changed, and with them the appropriate ideological and political guidelines, the reigning value systems; what called forth hosannas yesterday is today regarded with contempt. But has the essential technique of interpretation also changed? Are the interpretations to which the epoch of *glasnost* gave rise any less arbitrary than those of totalitarianism?

There have been even more extreme interpretations of "Kashtanka."

Edgard Broide's book *Chekhov: Thinker and Artist* was published

---

4. Yu. A. Bogomolov, "Kashtanka i Sharik" in *A. P. Chekhov v kul'ture XX veka. Tezisy dokladov konferentsii* (Moscow, 1990), p. 6.

in "tamizdat" in 1980, when *perestroika*, let alone the collapse of communism, empire, totalitarianism, and the Soviet regime, was still a long way off. In it the author challenged the whole of that still mighty, many-headed hydra, and turned Chekhov into someone who shared his own views.

Here the plus and minus signs are once again completely reversed. Whereas Yermilov and his followers had depicted Chekhov as a herald of the revolution, welcoming the bright (i.e., Soviet) future, Broide set out to show that all of Chekhov's work was dedicated to combating the impending revolutionary catastrophe, that it was filled with prophecies about Russia's dire future and openly or covertly discredited those who were related to the revolution or the future regime. To be specific, if *Three Sisters* contains an unsympathetic character called Solyony ("salty" in Russian), then in Broide's opinion Chekhov must be having a go at Gorky ("bitter") for his revolutionary sympathies. If there is a character in "The Bishop" called Sisoi who gets on the hero's nerves, this is obviously a prophetic hint at the insufferable Stalin, who was known in his youth as Soso. "Kashtanka" does not escape, either. In his story Chekhov apparently stigmatized totalitarian thinking, class-consciousness, and the exploitation by "The Party" of animal instincts. "Armed with 'doctrine,' The Party knew how to make use of *herd feelings*: hatred, envy, greed, fear, 'faith,' unanimity, 'national traditions,' idiocy."

As in the case of Semanova, scarcely any connection can be discovered between this list and the text of "Kashtanka," the only evidence offered being a single quotation with italics added by the author: "Kashtanka divided the human race into *two* very unequal classes, *masters* and *customers*." Kashtanka, Broide concludes, "has a firm grasp of *class-consciousness*," and he sums up with bitter irony: "In the Circus of ideas she would have gone a long way." Another character who embodies totalitarian psychology is the goose, Ivan Ivanovich, who "arched his neck and began talking fast about something, *passionately* but completely *unintelligibly*." Broide takes this to

be a devastating satirical attack by Chekhov on eloquent dema-
gogues, i.e., the future orators of the Communist party.[5]

Broide confirms once again that no ideology, however tri-
umphant or persecuted it may be, can guarantee an honest, ideolog-
ically unbiased reading of literary texts.

But even this is by no means the most extreme case. Artificial or
forced interpretations do not arise only from their authors' political
and ideological obsessions. Ideas based on perfectly scientific prem-
ises, when applied to the understanding of specific texts, may sometimes yield astonishing results.

The American Slavist Savely Senderovich, in the chapter entitled "Fighting the Dragon" from his monograph *Face to Face with
Chekhov* (1994), isolates no less than three dozen of Chekhov's
works that, he argues, are built on an interpretation or transformation of one of the basic Christian myths, the miraculous story of St.
George, the Dragon, and the Maiden. Senderovich concludes that
"by following in the footsteps of St. George the Dragonslayer we
can plumb Chekhov's creative work to previously unimagined
depths."[6]

Any attempt to see what different texts have in common and to
uncover the deep cultural and mythological roots of Chekhov's
work would seem to be fully justified. But what happens when this
approach is applied to specific cases?

For a particular work to belong to the "St. George cycle," it is
only necessary that its characters bear the name George, Yegor, or a
derivative (in the last resort, even the patronymic Yegorovich); that
the presence of some knightly attribute be detectable in the text;
and that the plot be interpreted as the rescue of a maiden from the
dragon.

Senderovich is aware, of course, that the correspondences he
finds may seem unconvincing, but he offers the following explana-

5. Edgard Broide, *Chekhov: myslitel', khudozhnik* (Frankfurt, 1980), p. 103.
6. S. Senderovich, *Chekhov—s glazu na glaz. Istoriya odnoi oderzhimosti A. P. Chekhova* (St. Petersburg, 1994), p. 267.

tion: the myth of St. George and the dragon "is so *deeply rooted* in the writer's consciousness that it *involuntarily* takes possession of his imagination and makes its appearance *spontaneously* in the picture he is creating" (italics added).[7] You can "prove" and "interpret" anything you like that way.

Our "Kashtanka" is one of the stories assigned to the cycle; it too reflects the myth of St. George. The evidence? That is no problem. Kashtanka's new master, the circus artist, is called M. Georges! There does not seem to be a maiden in the story, but—predictably—there is a "substitute": though the likeness to the myth is admittedly "veiled," the investigator removes the veil to show that the place of the mythical princess is occupied by the dog. And the dragon? No prizes for guessing—it is the goose Ivan Ivanovich again, described in the story "advancing with its neck and head bent toward the ground, spreading its wings wide and hissing," while M. Georges is the stranger and rescuer. For good measure Senderovich also discovers in Kashtanka's memories of the torments inflicted upon her by the boy Fedyushka a hidden erotic motif.[8]

Enough! Here we leave the story of the adventures of Chekhov's little dog in the world of literary criticism. How differently this good-natured mixture of dachshund and mongrel has been presented by her learned interpreters during the century and more since her birth: as expressing class-consciousness and the totalitarian mentality, as the embodiment of first the revolutionary and then the evolutionary path of development, even as a secret erotomaniac. . . .

Except that too often these attempts to interpret "Kashtanka" take us away from the story's meaning rather than bringing us closer to it. Perhaps we may better achieve that by asking the simple question heard from our students: Who do we feel most sorry for in the story? Better a direct response and unclouded vision than the preconceptions imposed by the social and critical fashion of the day.

7. Op. cit., pp. 166, 167.
8. Op. cit., pp. 202–212.

2

---

# The Story of Discovery

Let us depart from the usual chronology and enter Chekhov's artistic world not with his stories of 1880 but halfway through his first decade as a writer. In the transitional period leading up to the publication of "The Steppe" in March 1888, Chekhov wrote a number of stories that bear a particular inner resemblance.

One of the first of these is "The Hired Pianist" (1885). The story still reflects much of the early Chekhov's usual aim of making the reader laugh by any means. Its plot is anecdotal: Petya Rublyov, a hired pianist, has a hysterical fit at a merchant's wedding and is thrown out. Its comic names and turns of phrase are in keeping with the spirit of the humorous journals of the time: "There's this retired lieutenant-colonel living on the Arbat by the name of Shpitsky . . . he's giving his daughter away to Eskimosoff, the merchant's son. . . . This Eskimosoff . . . is a pig in a nightcap and *mauvais ton*, but Papa and his daughter have to *manger et boire*, so bad taste doesn't come into it," etc.

But "The Hired Pianist" is not just another comic Chekhov story. Chekhov focuses attention on Petya's psychology. A former student at the conservatory, he earns money by playing the piano at evening parties. At the wedding he forgets himself: he begins talking freely in student fashion to the daughter of the house, as if she were his equal. He is then given a coarse reminder that he is a servant, nothing more, a waiter who knows how to play the piano. "It's quite natural after all," he says later, "it's even funny, but it makes me sick. . . . I ask myself, what kind of a people are we? While you're free or studying or loafing about, you can have a drink with a Russian, pat him on the stomach, and pay court to his daughter, but as soon as you're in the slightest degree subordinate to him, you've got to know your place. . . . I'm trying to stifle the thought, but it keeps making my gorge rise."

The appearance of this "thought," which has been suddenly revealed to Petya, is the main event in "The Hired Pianist." It is a story about a shift in someone's consciousness, about a discovery that destroys a previously held, superficial conception of life. Chekhov returns persistently to this theme in a number of stories written in 1885–1887: "Unemployed," "A Commotion," "A Nightmare," "Her Man Friend," "The Chorus Girl," "A Trifling Occurrence," "His Sister" (retitled "Good People"), "The Magistrate," "His First Love" (retitled "Volodya"), and "Bad Weather." In spite of their varied plots and characters, these stories are similar in subject matter and construction, and form a distinct subgroup within Chekhov's prose in the latter 1880s. They are *stories of discovery*.

The story of discovery consists of a definite set of structural elements and is plotted according to definite rules. Its hero, an ordinary person absorbed in everyday life, is given some kind of jolt, usually through a trivial event or "trifling occurrence." Then follows the main event of the story: the discovery. The result is that a previous conception of life—whether naive, idealistic, stereotyped, habitual, unthinking, or ingrained—is overturned. Life appears in a new light: its "natural" order—confused, complicated, and hostile—is revealed. The denouement is the same in each case: for the first time the hero begins to think.

The discoveries made by the main characters in this group of stories are as varied as the characters themselves.

In "Unemployed" (1885), Perepyolkin, a law graduate, has read and heard, of course, about the existence of bribery, but he is unprepared for the discoveries he makes after his first attempts to find a job. "You warned me," he writes to his uncle, "that I wouldn't get a job for nothing and I'd have to pay, but you never let on that this filthy selling and buying would be conducted in public, in such a loud, barefaced way . . . with ladies present! It makes me feel ashamed, painfully ashamed!"

The theme of "The Hired Pianist" recurs in "A Commotion" (1886), where a young governess is also confronted for the first time with the coarse reality of life. Here too a previous conception of life is overturned. Mashenka Pavletskaya's naive confidence that she can always stand on her dignity and prove her respectability, like her naive schoolgirl habit of taking after-dinner sweets up to her room, and collecting small coins and old stamps—all this is blown sky-high. The true, essentially hostile, nature of life is embodied for Mashenka in the image of her employer's wife, "a haughty, obtuse, happy woman," who has made a search of her belongings. The threat revealed to the heroine—that her sense of identity may be violated at any moment—not only generates a feeling of outrage and wounded self-respect; it also instills a persistent irrational fear. The hero of "Ward No. 6," Ivan Dmitrich Gromov, will later make the same discovery and go mad from it.

In "A Nightmare" (1886) the hero suddenly has his eyes opened to the plight of country priests, doctors, and teachers, and is filled with "an overwhelming sense of shame, both on his own account and at the thought of the invisible truth."

Less serious (though unusually important to him!) is the discovery made by the hero of "The Magistrate" (1887). After a chance conversation during a journey, it suddenly becomes clear to him what a high price he has paid for his thoughtless infidelity to his wife. "The new thought communicated to him by the doctor seemed to have stunned and poisoned him": an ending that is typical of Chekhov's new type of denouement.

Vera Semyonovna in "His Sister" (1886) will never regain her previous faith in her brother. She sees that the brother whom she worshiped was a narrow-minded, limited man; at first this makes her think, "think in a new kind of way, for herself," and later she leaves home for good. Uncle Vanya will later have the scales removed from his eyes in similar fashion, when he is cured of worshiping his former idol, the "dried-up old academic trout" Serebryakov.

The story of eight-year-old Alyosha, deceived by the grown-ups in "A Trifling Occurrence" (1886), ends with the words: "He was trembling, stammering, and crying; it was the first time in his life that he had come face to face with such crude deception; previously he had not known that apart from juicy pears, pies, and expensive wristwatches there are many things in the world that children have no name for."

"Her Man Friend" (1886) would seem to be another anecdotal story in which "the delectable Vanda" (plain Nastasya Kanavkina on her passport) loses her nerve at the dentist's and allows a good tooth to be pulled out instead of a bad one. But once again the anecdote is used as a means of developing the same theme of knowing your own place, and a new, suddenly revealed perception of life is contrasted with an old habitual one: "She walked along the street spitting blood, and each time she saw the red color it reminded her of her difficult, unsatisfactory life, and of the insults she had received and would go on receiving tomorrow, in a week's time, and in a year from now—until the day she died."

Interestingly, this "story of discovery" denouement then appears to give way to a different, happy ending: "But next day she was at the 'Renaissance' again, dancing. . . . And a young merchant from Kazan treated her to supper." This is like an expert variation on the theme: the second, "happy" ending does not upset the composition of the story of discovery but strengthens it, for what the heroes of these stories discover is that life hides its true nature—which is complicated and terrible—behind a misleading and often cheerful exterior.

The story of discovery makes its appearance in Chekhov's work when he himself, like the central characters of "The Hired Pianist," "Unemployed," and "A Commotion," had ceased to be a student

(Chekhov graduated in 1884) and was in a new relationship to the outside world. But the origins of his new attitude to writing and his new type of story go back further. Scholars have pointed to a number of factors apart from his graduation that influenced Chekhov's deeper involvement "in the realm of the serious."[1] From 1883 he was permanent correspondent in Moscow for the St. Petersburg magazine *Fragments*, contributing a regular column, "Fragments of Moscow Life," and this put him, in A. B. Derman's words, "in the position of a professional observer of life."[2] In the summer of 1884 he was already working independently in the hospitals at Voskresensk and Zvenigorod, where he not only treated patients but traveled to postmortems and was called as an expert witness in court, etc.—thereby coming up against a much wider range of phenomena than the usual student.

Moreover, Chekhov's huge arsenal of observations from his early life in Taganrog could now be exploited in a new way, in line with his first properly conceived writing program.

For it is in this group of stories that Chekhov first consciously expresses the theme, the approach to life, that will define the whole of his work. This is the turning point where he begins to converge with his predecessors and contemporaries, only to diverge from them again. Examining these links with the past can help us better understand Chekhov's originality.

Around this time Maupassant—a writer who had made it impossible, in Chekhov's opinion, "to write in the old way"[3]—published several stories with a theme and principle of composition similar to Chekhov's. In stories like "Clair de lune," "Une aventure parisienne," "Promenade," "Garçon, une chope de bière!" and "L'Ermite" (all written in 1882–1886), the central characters—an abbé, the wife of a provincial lawyer, an old bookkeeper, a hard drinker, and a Paris *rentier*—make certain discoveries: their previous ideas

1. *Letters*, 1:67.
2. A. B. Derman, *Anton Pavlovich Chekhov* (Moscow, 1939), p. 64.
3. See *Chekhov v vospominaniyakh sovremennikov* (Moscow, 1986), p. 531.

and convictions are overturned, and life is revealed to them from a new and previously hidden perspective.

It is doubtful that Chekhov knew all these stories in the mid-1880s. What is important is the typological similarity. Both writers' stories have a similar type of event and principle of construction: they belong to the same genre. But in the varied panorama of Maupassant's prose, stories of this kind occur only occasionally and leave no discernible trace, for example, in his novels; whereas the line started by Chekhov in his stories of discovery will continue, as we shall see, without interruption, right up to his very last works.

The discoveries that Chekhov's characters make differ from those to be found in the stories of his contemporary, Vsevolod Garshin. Because of their spiritual makeup, Garshin's heroes, whether it be the civil servant Nikitin in "An Incident" or the artist Ryabinin in "The Artists," are predisposed from the outset to confront social falsehood once they discover it, to go mad as a result, and to commit physical or spiritual suicide. In Garshin, discoveries occur only in the case of a particular kind of "Garshin hero"; only that kind of personality really interests him.

Chekhov, on the other hand, does not concentrate on a single psychological type. His heroes, who begin to think after their confrontation with life, are of different social backgrounds, ages, professions, temperaments, and characters. The stories about the discoveries made by the singer Pasha in "The Chorus Girl" or "the delectable Vanda" in "Her Man Friend" are similar in theme and composition to the stories about the discoveries made by eight-year-old Alyosha in "A Trifling Occurrence," the schoolboy Volodya, the well-to-do magistrate, or the governess Mashenka Pavletskaya.

"The Hired Pianist" has attracted a fair amount of critical attention. A. I. Roskin saw in it a story of unrealized talent. "He dreamed of becoming a composer, but finished up as a hired pianist": for Roskin this is the sort of conclusion the young Chekhov might have reached when thinking about his artist-brother Nikolai, or about his own fate. "The Hired Pianist" is bracketed with stories like "The Horse and the Quivering Hind" ("he dreamed of becoming a writer, but finished up as a reporter").[4] Z. S. Paperny and M. Ye. Yelizarova assign the story to a different thematic group. Like "The Chorus Girl" and "Enemies," they see it as the story of how a "little man," a toiler and pauper, comes into conflict with "gentlemen" and "kind sirs," and how he is cruelly insulted by the boorish attitude of "the boss."[5]

But to say of Chekhov that he is addressing the theme of the "little man" is as inadequate as it would be in the case of Dostoevsky, whose work is so firmly linked with the "little man" theme. Dostoevsky introduced a particular psychological element into this traditional theme, concentrating on anomalies in the "little man's" consciousness or behavior. His poor man is "ambitious," as Dobrolyubov put it, and his conflict with the world—rebellion or madness—is quite distinctive; and in that unique form the theme of the "little man" in Dostoevsky's early works became the kernel of his future great novels.

Chekhov also concentrates on a particular element of the theme. The "little man" in the "stories of discovery" cycle is always captured at a specific moment: he is preoccupied with making sense of life and his position within it, he is moving from one set of conceptions to another, and in this way he emerges as a cognitive subject.

Whether one gets to know life speculatively, discovering new aspects of it for oneself ("The Post"), or orienting oneself within it through action or attempted action ("Volodya"); consciously testing one's previous conceptions ("Good People") or stumbling on a "new thought" by chance ("The Magistrate"); drawing moral conclusions and feeling a sense of shame at the thought of "the invisible truth" ("A Nightmare"), or forgetting about it the next day ("Her Man

4. A. Roskin, *Antosha Chekhonte* (Moscow, 1940), pp. 124, 126.

5. Z. Paperny, *A. P. Chekhov. Ocherk tvorchestva* (Moscow, 1954), pp. 24–31; M. Ye. Yelizarova, *Tvorchestvo Chekhova i voprosy realizma kontsa XIX veka* (Moscow, 1958), pp. 36–37.

Friend"); whether one's eyes are opened to how things are in general ("A Commotion," "A Trifling Occurrence") or to an individual person ("Bad Weather")—in every instance the characters are preoccupied with becoming conscious of the real world and their place in it. All these stories are about seeing life in a new way, rejecting an old approach to life, trying to understand its essential nature. Most often that nature turns out to be impossibly complicated, incomprehensible, and hostile to the individual.

Chekhov puts various members of very different social groups in the same situation (and the discoveries they make also vary in social significance). His rejection of social, psychological, and similar "specialization," his evenhanded treatment of characters in relation to the same process of becoming conscious of the real world and orienting oneself in it—all this will have far-reaching consequences for the treatment of conflict in Chekhov's final works.

The stories of discovery in the latter 1880s build a picture of life that is generally hostile to the heroes, to their desires, dreams, and ideal conceptions. But this hostility always takes exactly the same distinctive form. Life is hostile primarily because it is incomprehensible. The ideas of the stories' heroes are shown to be simplified, or turn out to be illusory. This is what gives a universal and distinctive quality to the picture of the real world that Chekhov is beginning to construct: regardless of who they are, each person comes into the same kind of conflict with life, and finds it inscrutable and incomprehensible.

There is another important qualification to be noted in relation to these discoveries. In both the early stories and the later ones, the new way in which the heroes come to see life is sometimes characterized by concepts like "revelation" and "enlightenment." How does Chekhov's "story of discovery" correspond to Tolstoy's "tale of revelation"? A clear answer is provided by Chekhov's later work, but certain decisive contrasts can be seen in the early stories.

Tolstoy in his tales and novels about "revelation," and Turgenev in his works about "moral enlightenment," lead their characters to certain philosophical or moral discoveries of a final, unconditional, and general character: to "the light" or to "eternal truths." In Chekhov, discoveries do not complete or round off the heroes' searchings. They do not signal that the heroes have arrived at a new philosophical or religious outlook, or acquired a new system of moral criteria. The new vision may come and go ("Her Man Friend," "Bad Weather"); most often, however, it brings not tranquillity but a new sense of unrest.

Two elements are important to Chekhov in the new outlook to which he leads his hero: that it should refute a previously held incorrect view, and that it should present the hero with new problems. It is not the poetry of acquiring final truths that is developed in the stories of discovery, but the poetry of the endless searching for answers to questions to which no answer is given (and none perhaps exists). Words like "revelation" or "enlightenment" can be applied to the changes that happen to Chekhov's heroes only in a conditional sense, not in the way that Tolstoy or Turgenev used them.

# 3

# Chekhov the Writer-Thinker

How the Chekhov hero comes to acquire a new vision of life and a new attitude can be pinpointed with the help of a pair of opposites: *kazalos'* ("it seemed") and *okazalos'* ("it turned out that").

Chekhov makes frequent use of this contrast to move his heroes from one conception of life to the next. To show, for example, in "The Duel" how the main characters' judgments change over the course of time, he uses a variety of constructions such as: "Two years ago it seemed to him that...."; "now he was certain that...."; "When they were traveling to the Caucasus, it seemed to her that...," "but it turned out that...," etc. Dozens of similar examples are to be found in Chekhov's other works.

In the stories of discovery, it seemed to Petya Rublyov in "The Hired Pianist" that it was all right for a poor but educated person like himself to talk to the daughter of the house on equal terms, but it turned out that.... To Perepyolkin ("Unemployed") it seemed that if bribes were given, it would be done secretly, with a sense of shame, whereas it turned out that.... You would have to be involved "in some dreadful business," it seemed to Mashenka Pavletskaya in "A Commotion," to be subjected to a search, whereas it turned out that.... It seemed to the student in "The Post" that everyone round him ought to share his cheerful view of life, but it turned out that. . . . To Alyosha ("A Trifling Occurrence") it seemed that when grown-ups gave a child their word, this was sacred and could not be broken, but it turned out that. . . . In all these instances *okazalos'* ("it turned out that") is directly opposed to *kazalos'* ("it seemed").

The story of discovery was an experimental, transitional form for Chekhov. He wrote no stories after 1888 on the pattern of "The Hired Pianist" or "A Commotion," in which everything boils down to the single basic event of the hero's discovery. Chekhov will describe the same situation on many occasions, but in his later work it is part of a broader picture of life. The "two-dimensional" form of the story of discovery is incorporated into the more complicated structures of Chekhov's later tales and stories.

Jumping a long way ahead, the *kazalos'-okazalos'* situation plays a very significant part in Chekhov's last prose work, "The Fiancée."

In the opening chapters the change from "it seemed" to "it turned out that" defines the whole development of the plot. Nadya Shumina's previous views of the people surrounding her are overturned by one discovery after another.

About her mother: "Nadya felt that her mother did not and could not understand her, she felt this for the first time in her life, and it even made her scared . . ."; "And however much she thought about it, Nadya could not imagine how she could have seen anything special and unusual about her mother, or failed to notice that she was an ordinary, unhappy woman"; "Nadya recalled how until quite recently she had thought of her mother as an unusual woman and had listened to the words she uttered with pride, whereas now she could not bring a single word of hers to mind."

About her fiancé: "It was already clear to her that she had fallen out of love with Andrei Andreyich, or perhaps had never loved him anyway; but how to say this, to whom and for what reason, she did not and could not understand, although she thought about it night and day."

Then about Sasha: "she burst into tears because Sasha no longer seemed so novel, intelligent, and interesting to her as in the previous year."

Nadya not only moves on to a new perception of the people close to her; "everything" seems different to her, the whole of her life in Granny's house. "It seemed" constructions—"The light flickered in the icon lamp, and everything, it seemed, was peaceful and secure . . ."; "And for some reason it seemed that it would be like this now for the whole of her life, never changing, never ending!"— are later reversed: "That's how it feels in the midst of an easy carefree life, when the police suddenly swoop down one night and conduct a search, and it turns out that the head of the house has been embezzling and counterfeiting"; "By now it was clear to her that she would definitely be leaving home . . ."; "She saw clearly that her life had been turned upside down."

This is the same situation of discovery, the same change in the hero from "it seemed" to "it turned out that," which Chekhov had first developed in his cycle of stories in the mid-1880s. It becomes one of his most stable themes and situations, though it acquires new functions in stories like "The Fiancée," no longer rounding off the plot but being followed by a new type of denouement.

Numerically speaking, the stories of discovery occupy a comparatively small place among the stories written in 1885–1887: a dozen or so stories out of more than three hundred works composed after Chekhov's graduation and before the publication of "The Steppe." Pictures of customs, character sketches, psychological and social studies—taken together they make up an exceptionally colorful panorama of Russian life in the 1880s. But selecting out this relatively small group of stories enables us to see that by the mid-1880s Chekhov's work already has an inner conceptual unity.

The story of discovery was designed to refute the hero's simplified conception of life and to protest against interpreting life in a banal (doctrinaire or idealistic) way. But it is true of *most* of the 1885–1887 stories that while they lack the formal element of refutation and the stripping away of illusion, they nonetheless represent a challenge (by virtue of their themes, plots, and depiction of human beings) to literary stereotypes and a protest against conventional views of how literature should depict the real world. Even before "The Steppe," Chekhov's artistic vision and depiction of reality are assuming forms that represent a milestone in Russian literature.

The situation of discovery and change from "it seemed" to "it turned out that," with which this chapter began, is a particular though highly characteristic feature of a wider pattern. It is connected, as we shall try to show later, with one of the main coordinates of Chekhov's world. In the stories of discovery our *perception of life*, our *orientation in the world around us*, are of central importance in their own right. This perspective on the real world will define all of Chekhov's later work.

We call this perspective "epistemological," because in his approach to depicting life in the stories of discovery, the author is basically interested not so much in phenomena *per se* as in our conceptions of them—the possibility of different conceptions of the same phenomena, how these conceptions come to be formed, and the nature of illusion, delusion, and false opinion.

A similar epistemological approach to portraying people, their opinions and conceptions, may be found in literature before and after Chekhov.

Take this extract from *War and Peace*: "After the Austerlitz and 1807 campaigns, Rostov knew from his own experience that when people are telling war stories, they always lie, as he himself did; secondly, he was experienced enough to know that in war everything happens quite differently from how we can describe and relate it. And so he did not like Zdrzhinsky's tale."[1] Here the attention of author and hero is directed not at the actual events surrounding the battle for the Saltanovsky Dam, but at whether a truthful account of those events is possible.

There is a similar passage in *The Kreutzer Sonata*. In a railway compartment the author is listening to an argument between a

---

1. L. N. Tolstoy, *Collected Works* in 90 vols. (Moscow, 1928–1957), vol. 11, p. 56.

woman and an old merchant about the family. The author adds his own commentary to the woman's pronouncements: ". . . she continued, not answering what the old merchant had said, but, as many women are in the habit of doing, answering what she thought he would say . . ."; "she said, addressing me and the lawyer, and completely ignoring the old man . . ."; "the woman was in a great hurry to come out with her judgments, which probably seemed very novel to her," etc. All these comments direct our attention not so much to the woman's actual argument as to the conditional, relative nature of her opinions.

These and similar examples show that the question of distinguishing between knowledge "according to truth" and knowledge "according to opinion," of how opinions may depend on attendant conditions, and similar epistemological questions were touched on by Tolstoy and other writers. But what for them was a peripheral matter acquires a position of exceptional importance in Chekhov's artistic world, and becomes one of his guiding principles. The epistemological point of view becomes one of the components of a new kind of artistic thinking.

A qualification is needed here. In speaking of Chekhov's epistemological approach to life and the epistemological problems in his work, we are aware that philosophical terminology may be applied to literature only in a very conditional sense. No more than an analogy can be drawn between Chekhov's role in relation to Russian literature, and the role played in European philosophy by thinkers who were primarily concerned with problems of the theory of knowledge. In their constant search for truth, thinkers like Socrates subjected all kinds of fixed, traditional, and current ideas to criticism and analysis, challenging those who considered themselves wise but were not so; or, like Kant, they strove to inspect the foundations of those towers erected by human reason. Our analogy is valid, naturally, only within certain limits.

Nevertheless, that the basis of Chekhov's work was philosophical is vital to an understanding of his work. Chekhov was a writer-thinker.

It is true, of course, that in the work of every major writer, or in every great work of literature, you can find philosophical problems, in so far as the work touches on problems of life and death, of love and human relationships, and is a reflection of a particular world-view. But Chekhov's work not only incorporates the whole of that age-old spectrum of philosophical problems in literature; it is uniquely connected with making philosophical sense of the world.

Throughout his career Chekhov consciously posed and shed light on problems to do with the generation, truth, and demonstrability of human knowledge, ideas, and points of view; how they correlate with life; and how their soundness might be tested. We shall have frequent opportunity to see that Chekhov regarded the processes of getting to know the world, and the forms that our knowledge and comprehension take, as of paramount importance.

All these problems are close to those that epistemology—the theory of knowledge—studies as a branch of philosophy. But it would be absurd, of course, to search in his work for an illustration of any particular philosophical thesis. Chekhov is not addressing the special problems of the theory of knowledge as a philosopher; he is writing as an artist about human fates and man's social existence in late-nineteenth-century Russia. What we are saying is this: underlying Chekhov's artistic world is a conceptual philosophical base; in his writings Chekhov tried to offer an integrated picture of the world in light of his "conception of life"; his work is "philosophical" in a different sense from that of other great artists such as Tolstoy and Dostoevsky.

Frequently the philosophical basis of Chekhov's work is denied completely. "In Chekhov's prose the 'philosophical theme' does not and cannot have any independent meaning"[2]: this kind of statement is typical. But "philosophical theme" is used here in a completely pre-Chekhovian sense.

When contemporary critics spoke of "the absence of any kind of unifying idea" in Chekhov, what they had in mind was an idea, doc-

---

2. I. Gurvich, *Proza Chekhova (Chelovek i deistvitel'nost')* (Moscow, 1970), p. 49.

trine, or problem of a finite, dogmatic order: the "immense influence of love on the fate of human beings and human affairs" that Goncharov wrote about;[3] "self-perfection in the religious sense" that preoccupied Dostoevsky's creative consciousness,[4] and "humanizing the teaching of the gospel," which Leskov regarded as "the most noble and immediately relevant task."[5] The absence in Chekhov of any such unifying idea (and the list could be extended) does indeed distinguish him from most of his predecessors and contemporaries. He considered straight theorizing in literature even less acceptable: "To hell with the philosophy of the great ones of this world! With its half-witted 'afterwords' and 'letters to the Governor's wife,' it's not worth the filly in 'Strider.' "[6]

Chekhov's lack of interest in philosophy would seem to be confirmed by his indifference or extreme skepticism toward the ideas of contemporary professional philosophers. To pigeonhole him within any philosophical school or tendency, or to find in his work a substantiation or defense of any of the numerous philosophical ideas that were current in his day, is impossible. Finally, there is a particular feature of Chekhov's heroes that stands in the way of seeing him as a philosopher. Whereas the heroes of Tolstoy and especially Dostoevsky are often intellectual giants, Chekhov's characters, as Dr. Ragin puts it in "Ward No. 6," are "philosophical small fry."

These indisputable facts—that Chekhov has no philosophical allegiance and that his characters do not stand on their own philosophical feet—are adduced as proof of the absence of any philosophical theme in Chekhov. But the lack of independence of Chekhov's philosophizing heroes (which, as we shall see, was part of his artistic plan), and the absence of any pretensions on Chekhov's part to uncover the "eternal secrets" of the soul or the laws govern-

---

3. I. A. Goncharov, *Collected Works* in 8 vols. (Moscow, 1955), vol. 8, pp. 208–209.
4. F. M. Dostoevsky, *Collected Works* in 30 vols. (Leningrad, 1984), vol. 26, p. 166.
5. N. S. Leskov, *Collected Works* in 11 vols. (Moscow, 1958), vol. 11, p. 456.
6. *Letters*, 4:270. Tolstoy had added an "Afterword" to *The Kreutzer Sonata* for an 1891 edition of his works; Gogol's "What Is a Governor's Wife?" is part of his *Selected Passages from Correspondence with Friends* (1847); and "Strider," published in 1885, is Tolstoy's imaginative story of the life and death of a horse.

ing human existence, ought not to obscure the essentially philosophical character of his work. Chekhov's "conception of life,"
which gives meaning to his artistic world, cannot be reduced to
philosophical judgments or logical propositions. That his work is
steeped in a philosophical outlook cannot, however, be doubted.
Chekhov always presents us with a vivid and integral picture of the
real world; and that authorial viewpoint—an interest in the problems of how we know the world and orient ourselves in it—is always
there in the picture's depths. It is expressed in his principles for selecting events and details, in how the plot and the fates of the characters are logically worked out, and in a whole series of other
elements. Without taking it into account, it is impossible to interpret the major part of Chekhov's work.

Having identified one of the coordinates of Chekhov's artistic
world, it is time to trace its expression in the living fabric of specific
works.

# 4

# An Experiment with Time: "Lights" (1888)

The stories of discovery lead straight to the works of 1888. This was an important year for Chekhov, which he himself recognized as a watershed, the beginning of a new creative period. His debut as a writer of serious works in the pages of the "thick" journals, the end of his active association with the "small press," and the award of the Pushkin Prize from the Academy of Sciences—these were the outward signs of this new stage ("I doubt if I'll ever go back to the newspapers again! Farewell, old life!").[1] From now on, Chekhov's characters will be more and more concerned with important problems of ethics, philosophy, and worldview. "I'm writing about matters intellectual," "I'm learning how to convey people's ideas," was how Chekhov himself referred to these new themes.[2]

A typical work in this respect and a difficult one to interpret is "Lights," the long story written immediately after "The Steppe."

What has provoked much debate is the comment that occurs twice in the story's concluding paragraphs: "You can't make any-

1. *Letters*, 2:203.
2. *Letters*, 2:13; 3:79.

thing out in this world! . . . No, you can't understand anything in this world!" Refusing to accept this assertion as it stands, most critics argue that it compromises Chekhov, "flatly contradicting" the "fundamental characteristics" of his work, and they go on to make various attempts to explain how a work with such a conclusion could have come to appear.

But it was quite natural for Chekhov to write a tale with such a conclusion; and it was part of his artistic scheme to express an authorial position that could not be identified either with that of a character or of the narrator—these propositions are beyond dispute.

Chekhov spent two months working on "Lights," longer than on "The Steppe." The tale is experimental, and its structure gives the strong impression of Chekhov performing a technical feat, but here too it is Chekhov the artist who leads the reader to certain conclusions. It is wrong to think of "Lights" as illustrating a particular kind of moral through the story of Kisochka, to see it as a thesis tale; its structure is far removed from such fablelike simplicity.

It is true that Ananyev tells his story with a didactic purpose ("An object lesson! Ah, what a lesson!"). But the story within the story is only part of a complex artistic structure, and the untidiness of the argument is contained within a work of artistic order. The final conclusion derives from an interaction between the hero's story within the story, the correcting observations of the narrator, and the author's artistic techniques, which are in overall command.

Chekhov was later to place an argument between characters at the center of a number of his works: "The Duel," "Three Years," "The House with a Mezzanine," "My Life," and almost all his plays. But in "Lights" there is a crucial difference. This is the first occasion on which Chekhov introduces into a story about wrongly posed questions and wrongly conceived judgments the element of *time*. Taking time into account as an essential factor in conceptions of life is the story's distinguishing feature; the conclusion, "you can't make anything out . . .", is arrived at after analyzing various temporal yardsticks that can be applied to life.

That the element of time enters Chekhov's world with "Lights" is no accident. Ananyev describes how after an interval of seven years he revisited his hometown and found the avenues where he had once strolled with his friends filled with high school boys and young women who were complete strangers to him. And only then, "for the first time in my life did I see with my own eyes how greedily one generation hastens to replace another and what a fateful difference even seven or eight years can make in a person's life." No doubt it was during the young Chekhov's visit to Taganrog in the spring of 1887, which resulted in "The Steppe" and "Lights," that the part played by time in a person's outlook first struck him so palpably and personally.

"Lights" portrays a clash between the moral positions held by Ananyev, a middle-aged engineer, and von Shtenberg, a young student. For Shtenberg, as for Ananyev when he was his young opponent's age, time is associated with eternity. The endless lights along the railway embankment make him think of life thousands of years ago, of the Amalekites and Philistines, and of how in two thousand years' time "not a speck of dust will remain" of the embankment and all those now building it. Seen from this perspective, present-day morality seems very conditional and relative, and any immoral behavior, though it may not be justified, does not at any rate deserve severe censure.

Pessimism leads to immorality and is generated by a particular view of time and fate. Ananyev thought that way in his youth, and after seducing Kisochka, abandoned her, while Shtenberg, who is now passing through the same stage of life as Ananyev earlier, is not prevented by "high-quality thoughts" from making "Don Juan forays" into nearby Vukolovka.

Ananyev has come to accept a different measure of time. Last year, he says, the building site was "bare steppe," whereas now construction of the railway has brought with it "life and civilization," and "in a hundred or two hundred years' time the good people will build factories, schools, and hospitals here—and everything will be in full swing!" While one's age and strength allow, he maintains, one should do practical things and bear in mind their moral or immoral consequences ("to rack one's brains and be inventive, to rise above stereotypes, to take pity on working people, to steal or not to steal," to work for the progress of science and art, not to dismiss as "absurd rubbish" the works of Shakespeare and Darwin simply because geniuses are mortal like everyone else, not to shrug one's shoulders in response to life's accursed questions, etc., etc.). In other words, one should make morality commensurate with the duration of human life and with visible sections of time.

Ananyev had arrived at this view of things on the train, on the night of his flight from Kisochka: "I was already clearly aware of having committed an evil act that was the equivalent of murder. . . . My conscience drove me back to N. and without any sophistry I made my confession, begged Kisochka like a child to forgive me, and wept alongside her." From that discovery, he believes, his "normal way of thinking" began.

In bringing these two logics, these two measures of time and two moralities into conflict, to what conclusions does Chekhov lead the reader? Or what techniques should the reader appreciate in reaching conclusions that adequately reflect the author's intention?

Ananyev is a persuasive speaker, his way of thinking is attractive, and he has acquired his logic and his right to instruct through his own suffering. In other artistic systems this is usually enough to indicate to the reader that the author is in agreement with his hero. Ought one not, therefore, to decide that Ananyev's conclusions, based on his life experience, are the real point of the story? It is certainly tempting to see this advocate of the idea of progress and practical good works as the exponent of the author's own position. The temptation is one that some critics have been unable to resist.

But Chekhov's intention was not to confirm an "elementary moral truth"; on the contrary, he rejected elementary truths in order to reveal the complexity of what to everyone else seemed simple and self-evident.

Ananyev's words are a kind of sermon, addressed not only to one listener but to young people as a whole. Alas, preaching the most beautiful truths may either have no effect or lead to consequences that are completely unforeseen by the preacher: on this sad rule of life Chekhov reflects in "No Comment" (1887) and "The Nervous Breakdown" (1888). The motif of impotence, of the practical futility of sermonizing, also makes itself distinctly heard in "Lights."

Ananyev sets out to prove to the student that he is "thinking in an unseemly fashion" (just as the old abbot does with his monks in "No Comment" and the student Vasilyev with his friends in "The Nervous Breakdown"). But the student listens without interest, grins, and, at the conclusion of what Ananyev regards as the instructive story of Kisochka, declares: "All that doesn't prove or explain anything. You need to be very naive to believe in human speech and logic, and to attach decisive importance to them. You can prove and disprove whatever you like with words."

From his story and his discovery, Ananyev draws what seem to him universally binding conclusions, and he sees the story as "an object lesson" for any young person. But this particular young person does not respond to the sermon in the expected way. The story and the conclusions drawn from it, Shtenberg says, do not apply to his life, which has its own specific problems that dictate a certain way of thinking.

So what the argument tells us, first, is that one set of facts does not lead to one set of generally significant conclusions. Perhaps, though, this is a consequence of the student's disagreeable personal qualities (there are several references to the expression on his face of "spiritual stagnation and mental inertia")? In that case the interpreter's task would obviously be simplified: the author's sympathies and antipathies could be apportioned in a traditionally clear-cut way. Some critics are inclined to base their interpretation of "Lights" on the difference in personal qualities between the characters.

"Balancing the pluses and minuses"[3] is a technique that Chekhov makes full use of in "Lights," the pluses and minuses being balanced differently, of course, in each of the characters; but

---

3. *Letters*, 3:19.

Chekhov does not make these differences the basis for a final assessment of the characters' positions.

There are evidently certain essential reasons why "you can prove whatever you like with words," or why the most instructive examples and precepts can have no influence on human actions. Shtenberg, we are told, is passing through the same stage of life, with its characteristic yardsticks and ways of thinking, as Ananyev previously did. So perhaps the point is this: that it is always the lot of different generations to have a different sensation of time and, in consequence, different moral criteria, different experiences, and a different kind of vitality, and that verbal persuasion of any sort is indeed powerless in the face of these natural obstacles. As in other works from the end of the 1880s, Chekhov here points to natural reasons for the existence of different truths, outlooks, and opinions.

But "Lights" is not only about the two protagonists' inability to agree. Perhaps the most interesting train of thought belongs to the third character: the narrator, who is present at the argument. It is he, after all, who eventually concludes that "you can't make anything out. . . ." The narrator, who is said to be a doctor and man of letters, does not adopt a neutral position in the argument; the impartiality of this third party is deceptive. While making the reader feel sympathetic toward Ananyev, he also sees the world at the beginning and end of the story in the same way as Ananyev's opponent, Shtenberg—from the point of view of eternity.

At the beginning, when describing his first impressions of the steppe at night, the narrator speaks of this "exceptional environment" that reminds him of "primeval chaos," while the lights shining in the night seem to be hinting at "some important secret." Immediately after this, when Ananyev is admiring the embankment, "which is costing millions," and speaks of the civilizing role of the railway, these ways of measuring achievement seem manifestly less significant. At the end of the story new factors come into play which the protagonists, as in later Chekhov arguments, ignore and lose sight of, whereas in the narrator's eyes they ought to be taken into account, linked together, and explained. "A great deal had been said that night, but I did not carry away with me the answer to a single question." All that remains in the narrator's memory are the lights— i.e., something eternal, Shtenberg's side of the argument—and the temporal, Ananyev-inspired image of Kisochka. Next morning both the student and the engineer are immersed in everyday affairs and have forgotten about the argument of the night before. But the reader is left to wonder what connection there can be between the story of Kisochka and, say, the dog Azorka or the peasant carting the boilers up and down the line. This is important and is referred to directly in the text. The narrator "glanced for the last time at the student and Ananyev, at the hysterical dog with the dull, drunken-looking eyes, at the laborers appearing and disappearing in the early morning mist, the embankment, the little horse stretching out its neck and thought: 'You can't make anything out in this world!' "

So that is what generates the narrator's final conclusion: the difficulty of finding any reasonable explanation of the link between a single phenomenon or finite fragment of life and the world's infinite variety.

"Lights" takes one last look at the world, and again it is seen from the viewpoint of eternity: "As I stood there thinking, the sunburnt plane, the huge sky, the dark strip of faraway oak forest and the hazy distance seemed to be saying to me: 'No, you can't understand anything in this world!' " The vast distant spaces evoked by this sentence are directly linked with the Shtenberg concept of eternity, and this looks like a further argument against accepting without qualification Ananyev's concept and system of proofs derived only from temporal standards.

Nor had Ananyev himself been all that consistent in the previous day's argument. Having philosophized to his heart's content, he then says that the lights remind him of human thoughts. "Each individual person's thoughts are scattered about randomly in just that way, they run along a single line toward a goal somewhere in the darkness, and without lighting anything up or making the night any brighter, they disappear somewhere—far beyond old age. . . ." This is already close to the final conclusion of the narrator, who thus gains support for his inferences from the fact that without noticing it, each of the protagonists whom he portrays may begin to reason like his opponent. This will be a constant feature of all the arguments among Chekhov's characters, right up to his last plays.

Finally, the narrator's summing-up conclusion, "you can't make anything out . . .", is further reinforced by the way in which the whole tale is literally permeated by a purely artistic play upon the many and diverse aspects of time. The most diverse measures of time appear equivalent in the tale, in close proximity, intersecting but not excluding one another. This approach comes straight from the author (not from a character and not from the narrator).

There are at least ten of these time levels in "Lights."

There is time understood as eternity, to be measured in thousands of years and swallowing up not only the individual creations of human hands but whole peoples (the Amalekites and Philistines referred to by Shtenberg).

There is time linked to the idea of progress, to be measured in terms of the lives and activities of individual people and individual generations (the outward manifestations of this aspect of time are "civilization," the railway that is being built, and the factories, schools, and hospitals referred to by Ananyev).

There is the time span of an individual human life (thus Ananyev was young at the time of his affair with Kisochka, and now, like Othello, he has already begun "to decline into the vale of years"; he in his turn has children who are growing up and getting older, etc.).

There is time in the sense of everydayness and routine (Ananyev, we are told, snores every night; the peasant carts his boilers up and down the line day after day without finding anyone to give them to; the student and the engineer, having spent the night philosophizing, are immersed next morning in the most humdrum concerns).

There is time as it defines a psychological process (Ananyev's intimacy with Kisochka, his flight, his troubled conscience, "I was already clearly aware that . . .", his two nights of anguish).

There is the time an event occupies (Kisochka cried, then

"about three-quarters of an hour later she became my lover," "Kisochka spent an hour and a half in my room and already felt quite at home," etc.).

There are also references to time signifying a historical period ("in those days, at the end of the '70s . . . and then at the beginning of the '80s . . ."), or a particular stage in a person's life ("I was in Petersburg before, now I'm here in the barracks, when autumn comes I'll go back to Petersburg, then down here again in the spring. . . . What sense there is in all this I don't know and no one else knows either"); and to time conceived of as that of a particular generation. . . .

Each of these levels of time is presented, moreover, with its own past, present, and future. Thus time-eternity signals the past through the destruction "of Old Testament peoples" and the future through the inscription on the cemetery gates: "For the hour is coming in the which . . ." Ananyev, who inclines toward a positive conception of time, "liked to eat and drink well and praise the past"; he describes his present way of life by saying: "Anyone with a wife and two children cannot afford to be idle. Feed and clothe them now, and save for their future"; while his whole cast of mind speaks of how he views the future: "I'm well fed, healthy, and content, and the time will come when you young people will be well fed, healthy, and content too." The frequency of these time combinations in "Lights" is remarkable.

In Chekhov's other works the aspect of time is nowhere near as essential as it is in "Lights," where it is subordinated to a mainly epistemological problem. What purpose is served by this elaborately contrived system whereby the author attempts to link everything in his narrative with the category of time?

Had we, the readers, wished to side with one of the protagonists, Ananyev, the narrator reminded us how much in the objective world does not coincide with his view of things; and the author, having constructed that kind of relationship between the characters and the narrator, then adds this extra factor which is external to the plot: the organization of time.

Seen against the almost limitless number of time variations, the story of Ananyev and Kisochka proves not to be universally binding at all but rather a highly individualized instance that has determined the lives of particular people and produced a particular way of thinking and behaving. But how does this isolated instance connect to the general, to the world with its infinite variety in time and space, its infinite variety of human destinies? The narrator-hero cannot see any links, while the author shows the immense difficulties that confront the human consciousness trying to find its bearings in the world.

The end aim of the author is not to proclaim, "you can't make anything out," but to establish the causes that might make a human consciousness reach such a conclusion. That is why it is so easy to mistake the narrator's final conclusion (which Chekhov goes out of his way to make seem well founded) for the sum total of the story. Chekhov's conclusion is not ontological, i.e., the world is chaos; it is epistemological: these are the circumstances in which a contemporary mind might conclude that the nature of the world is chaotic. The possibility of drawing a conclusion that is morally dangerous (Shtenberg), and the shaky or illusory character of conceivable counterarguments (Ananyev)—such anxieties underpin the thinking behind "Lights."

So there is no question of describing Chekhov's position in "Lights" as "vague"; it is carefully considered and given appropriate artistic expression.

Chekhov attached special importance to "Lights." In his letters he did not defend the story itself—he never rated his own work highly—but he did defend the right to adopt its particular authorial position. In his letter to Aleksei Suvorin of May 30, 1888, he defends an artist's right not to solve "such questions as God, pessimism, etc." but "only to record how and in what circumstances someone spoke or thought about God or pessimism." The elaboration of this idea he regards as self-evident: "My job is simply to be talented, that is, to know how to distinguish important evidence from unimportant, how to throw light on the characters and to speak with their voice." In other words, objectivity, in Chekhov's opinion, does not make it impossible for an author to be clear about his intentions and his criteria of selection, but directly presupposes it. An author may not know where the truth lies, but it is his job to know and point out where it does not lie, to distinguish truth from falsehood, what is relevant to the problem of truth from what is not relevant.

Should an artist in the course of his investigation of life—or more accurately, of the solutions and answers offered to life's problems—reach a negative conclusion, Chekhov looks upon this as positive knowledge of considerable social importance: "So if an artist who enjoys the crowd's confidence decides to come out and say that he understands nothing of what he sees, that in itself is a big contribution to the realm of thought and a big step forward."[4]

In Chekhov's work as a whole, "Lights" can be seen as an important point of departure for a whole series of works, though one he would later leave behind and even come to regard as unnecessary. What would remain constant, however, was Chekhov's interest in "knowledge in the realm of thought" and in man's efforts "to understand something of what he sees," "to make something out in this world." What would survive also was Chekhov's most frequent kind of generalization.

In Chekhov's world, assertions are in the first instance negations: negations of what is not true but appears, or makes itself out, to be true; negations of claims to possess knowledge of a universal truth, when all that the maker of such a claim possesses is at best his own "definite view of things." This is the first and most frequent Chekhov generalization.

In the stories written in the months immediately after "Lights" ("An Unpleasant Incident," "The Nervous Breakdown," "The Cobbler and the Devil," "A Dreary Story," "Thieves"), Chekhov would return time and again to attempts by the most varied people to understand something in this world. In every instance the attempts

4. *Letters*, 2:280–281.

prove unsuccessful: the heroes of all these works behave absurdly or abnormally from the point of view of "common sense."

But this is not simply a series of stories about ill-fated attempts "to make something out in this world," however loud that motif may sound for the moment. Even at this period we need not speak of Chekhov's pure "agnosticism." The very frequency with which he portrays characters who are struggling with a "problem" speaks of his conviction that such attempts are inevitable and universal. In Chekhov's world the urge "to make something out" appears as a permanent, ineradicable property of human nature. This, as we shall see, is another kind of Chekhov generalization.

But first we should say that the beginning of 1888 is also the time when Chekhov defines his basic interests as a writer, his basic preoccupations, not only artistically but in a theoretical, conceptual way.

Chekhov is known to have planned writing a sequel to "The Steppe" that would have followed the life of his young hero Yegorushka Knyazev after he came to St. Petersburg or Moscow, where he would "without fail come to a bad end." It is impossible, of course, to suppose what kinds of events and encounters Chekhov might have had in store for his hero, but we do know definitely what conception, what basic thought, Chekhov intended to make the foundation of this unwritten sequel: "Russian life crushes Russian man like a ton weight and quite obliterates him. . . . There is so much space that the ordinary little person *does not have the strength to find his bearings*" (letter to D. V. Grigorovich of February 5, 1888; italics added).[5]

It would be hard to overestimate the importance of this evidence for anyone interpreting Chekhov. Chekhov himself has indicated the point of view that would determine his selection of events in the works following "The Steppe," and the general conclusion to which he intended to lead his readers.

The hero's attempts "to find his bearings" in life, to "make

5. *Letters*, 2:190.

something out" in this world, the failure of these attempts, leading in the end to man being destroyed by life "as if by a ton weight"—to judge from these words, Chekhov was attracted by the epistemological aspects of the problem. Man's cognitive activity, his orientation in reality, his ideas about the world and his consequent behavior— these become the self-sufficient objects of Chekhov's analysis.

It has been convincingly shown that in Chekhov the surrounding world is always seen through the prism of a specific perceiving consciousness.[6] To show life first of all as someone's knowledge of life—this creative aim of Chekhov's was inseparably linked with another aim: to evaluate this knowledge according to the criteria of rightness, i.e., of the "norm"—how things ought to be—and of "real truth."

In the autumn of 1888 Chekhov expressed his well-known opinion on the tasks facing the artist: "You are right to demand that an artist should have a conscious attitude toward his work, but you are confusing two concepts: *solving a problem* and *posing a problem correctly*. Only the latter is obligatory for an artist" (letter to Suvorin of October 27, 1888; Chekhov's italics).[7] These words are often quoted, and they do indeed express very graphically the undogmatic nature of Chekhov's world. But it is sometimes overlooked that not solving problems does not by itself constitute the essential part of the creative approach being formulated. The emphasis in Chekhov's celebrated formula, as he himself underlined, falls on the *correctness* with which the problems are posed. To point to the undogmatic nature of Chekhov's world is not enough; this world is just as strongly oriented against skepticism and relativism.

It is not, then, for the author to assert his own previously formulated knowledge of life; it is part of his task to evaluate other people's knowledge, opinions, and "truths," and to investigate the signs

---

6. A. P. Chudakov, *Poetika Chekhova* (Moscow, 1971); translated by Edwina Jannie Cruise and Donald Dragt as *Chekhov's Poetics* (Ann Arbor, 1983).

7. *Letters*, 3:46.

and conditions of truth. Are the questions posed correctly? Is what people see as truth "real truth"? What prevents us from "finding our bearings," from making sense of life? These and similar questions will become central in Chekhov's world.

# 5

## Defining the Comic Element in Chekhov

as Chekhov's interest in an epistemological theme, in ways of "orienting" oneself in life, confined to what he called "matters intellectual," to problem pieces like "Lights" and to his earlier "stories of discovery"? To what extent did this sharpening of interest in the latter 1880s develop naturally from tendencies in his work?[1]

One may say that it had been a latent part of his artistic world from the very beginning. Chekhov's humor—the main element of his early works and still present in his very last—can be largely defined in terms of this interest.

In Chekhov's world a comic effect is most often the result of a simple confrontation or collision, a superimposition or juxtaposition, of incompatibles. But what exactly is colliding with what?

The answer is the same again: *different conceptions of the world.* These conceptions are both individual and collective; expressed in words, gestures, and behavior; rooted in the social hierarchy; reflected in systems of ideas, rules, opinions, and judgments, and in

1. An earlier translation of this chapter, by David Woodruff, was included in *Critical Essays on Anton Chekhov*, edited by Thomas Eekman (Boston, 1989), pp. 61–68.

the styles of speech used to convey thoughts and feelings; and culturally fixed in such phenomena as literary and rhetorical styles.

When incompatibles collide, a comic spark is struck; and in the densely populated, motley world of Chekhov the humorist, such collisions are inevitable.

What governs the behavior of Chekhov's comic heroes as they try to orient themselves in the life around them? First and foremost, life's legally sanctioned and generally accepted "regulators," its ready-made forms and conventional signs. Rank or title, ritual or ceremonial, general opinion or established custom, set styles of speech or a favorite theatrical or gastronomic repertoire, the canons of popular literature or the verdicts of the press—from this mass of available signs (broadly understood) which embody society's attempts at regulation, Chekhov's heroes derive the guidelines by which, either voluntarily or under duress, they order their lives. Each of Chekhov's hundreds of characters has his own system (correct or incorrect, well ordered or incoherent, conscious or automatic) of available signs: systems showing that he belongs to a particular social group based on class, age, profession, etc. And Chekhov has a wonderful feel for the multiplicity of these systems that are foisted on man by his position, and how he contrives to assimilate and adapt them.

In his early works Chekhov captures and records in all their colorful variety our different ways of perceiving the world and orienting ourselves within it. At first the author finds this variety and dissonance amusing. As time goes on, his attitude will change, but from start to finish his attention is focused on exactly the same range of phenomena.

"The Village. To Grandad." This address on a letter implies a system of orientation that contains only two geographical concepts: Moscow and the village where Grandad Konstantin Makarych lives ("Vanka").

But what is self-evident to nine-year-old Vanka Zhukov is absurd from the point of view of the post office employees. Their world is divided along different lines. Asked in the geography portion of his promotion exam to name the tributaries of the Ganges, a post office clerk flounders—"The Ganges, that's the river in India what flows into the ocean"—and finally becomes quite tongue-tied; there's nothing in post office regulations about the river Ganges! But asked about the town of Zhitomir, he fires back without hesitation: "Route 18, area 121!" ("The Civil Service Exam").

The dog Kashtanka divides the human race into masters and customers. Her master, too, has his own universe, with its fixed points and relative values: "You, Kashtanka, fall as far short of a man as a carpenter does of a cabinetmaker" ("Kashtanka").

The warm humor of Chekhov's stories about children ("Grisha," "Kids," "An Event," "Boys," "The Runaway") is based on the same idea of perceiving the world in unexpected ways:

> Mama looks like a doll, and the cat looks like Papa's fur coat, only the fur coat doesn't have eyes and a tail. . . . Papa is a most mysterious kind of person! Nanny and Mama are easy to understand: they are there to dress Grisha, to feed him and put him to bed, but what Papa is there for—Grisha has no idea. Then there is another mysterious person, and that is Auntie, who gave Grisha the drum. Sometimes she's there, sometimes she's not. Where does she disappear to? Grisha has looked several times under the bed, but she was never there. . . . ("Grisha")

Comedy arises when a person who follows one system of ideas is incapable of mastering any other. This happens to civil servant Merdyaev when his chief makes him read books and starts him off with *The Count of Monte Cristo*. However hard he tries, Merdyaev, whose whole life has been bounded by quite different ideas, is incapable of coping with what anyone else would find light reading. " 'I've started it four times,' he said, 'but I can't make a thing out. . . . All about some foreigners . . .' " ("Reading").

The opposite situation—when a person is operating more than one system of ideas and judgments—also provides Chekhov with a rich source of comedy.

"Do devils exist or don't they?"

"How shall I put it, my friend?" answered the orderly, shrugging one shoulder. "Scientifically speaking, of course, they don't, because that's a superstition, but looking at it simply, as you and I are doing now, then they do. . . ." ("Thieves")

Likewise in "The Chameleon": if it is running loose, the dog and its master will be subjected to the full rigors of the law: "I'll teach you to let dogs roam! It's time we took a closer look at these people who won't obey regulations! A good fat fine'll teach the rascal what I think of dogs and suchlike vagrant cattle!"; but if the dog is the general's, the strict upholder of regulations changes his spots straightaway and adopts a kindly, highly informal value system.

Many of Chekhov's works derive their humor from mixing up different sign systems. The outcome may be perfectly harmonious, as in the story of the civil service clerks who replace the cards and suits in a normal deck with photographs of their professional colleagues ("Vint"); or it may lead to the kind of dissonance provoked by retired Rear Admiral Revunov-Karaulov at a petit bourgeois wedding with his flow of navy terminology ("Wedding with a General").

Comedy also arises when a person is trying to display effortless mastery of a system that he has obviously understood only partly or not at all. This applies to all those situations where Chekhov's heroes "want to show off their education and talk about things other people can't understand," as in the case of chief railway guard Stychkin in "A Happy Ending": "I'm a member of the educated class, I'm in funds, but if you look at me from a point of view, who am I? I'm a loner, like some kind of a Catholic priest. That's why I'm extremely desirous of being united by Highman's bonds, that is, of entering into lawful matrimony with some worthy individual."

Irrelevant quotations, inappropriate scientific jargon or high-flown phrases, foreign words used incorrectly, proofs that fail to prove anything—right from his first "Letter to a Learned Neighbor" (1880), Chekhov the humorist was unsurpassed in his ability to notice and exploit the comic effect of such absurdities.

The characters in Chekhov's comic stories live in a strictly regulated world where every action must be slotted into a sign system: a table of ranks, a timetable, a set of rules, etc. For the little man who is the central character of the stories, this appears to be the world's unshakable foundation, and any breakdown of the system, be it the abolition of ranks or a spelling reform, is the equivalent of a personal disaster.

> "If I'm not a junior ensign any more, then who am I? A nobody? A nothing?" ("Abolished")

> "Grot [the grammarian] also proves the theory," the teacher was muttering, "that *vorota* ['gates'] is masculine, not neuter. . . . Well, he can think again on that one! I'd rather take early retirement than change my views on *vorota*." ("To Paris!")

Conversely, being able to attach oneself to a system of guidelines and general concepts is the equivalent of attaining happiness or a meaning in life. Olenka Plemyannikova, in "The Darling" (1899), shrivels up when she has no one whose opinions she can repeat, and blossoms when she can find her bearings in the world in line with the ideas of each of her successive loved ones: the theater proprietor, the timber merchant, the veterinarian, and the little schoolboy. It is this motif that links Chekhov's late masterpiece with his early comic stories.

Characters in early Chekhov are frequently nonplussed when they try to work out their response to a particular situation.

> "So where *do* I write him down? 'For repose' if he's dead, 'for health' if he's alive. . . . Don't you see my problem?"
> "Hmm. . . . Write him down on both lists, dear, they can sort it out up there. It won't matter to him either way, he's a useless good-for-nothing."

This attempt by sexton Otlukavin in "A Lengthy Business" to squeeze the unforeseen complexity of life into a sign system that recognizes only an either/or division ("for health" or "for repose") ends in failure. For the time being this theme is still comic, but later the heroes of "Neighbors," "Fear," "The Story of an Unknown Man," and *Three Sisters* will feel desperate about their attempts to make any sense of the world, i.e., to assign an event or phenomenon to any kind of reasonable category.

Time after time Chekhov derives a comic effect from situations where it is impossible to be sure of orienting oneself correctly in the hierarchical world of different ranks, titles, decorations, and positions, and from the misunderstandings that arise from this colorful social diversity and inequality ("Two Men in One," "Fat and Thin," "The Decoration," "The Mask," "At the Bathhouse," and many others). "Ranks and people": this constant comic theme in Chekhov can also be interpreted in the wider, more universal sense of orienting oneself in the surrounding world.

The frequent collisions in Chekhov's comic writing of phenomena from different literary and rhetorical genres have been superbly illustrated by V. N. Turbin.[2] Chekhov's attention to the interchangeability of genres, his constant intrusions "behind the scenes" of a genre, his heroes' attempts to conform to a certain genre, whether in a serious article or just a topical news item ("The First-class Passenger"), the depiction of the same event in two different genres (newspaper account and firsthand recollection, as in "Rapture"), the outrageous jumble of different genres in "The Complaints Book"—these are all particular cases or variants of those collisions and confrontations that are so numerous in Chekhov's comic stories.

So far we have been exploring the juxtaposition in Chekhov's comic work of sign systems, i.e., of *general* forms of assimilating the world and orienting oneself within it. But another source of the comic is the way in which different people become absorbed in their

2. V. N. Turbin, in *Problemy poetiki i istorii literatury* (Saransk, 1973), pp. 204–216.

own *individual* interests, behavior, and ways of thinking, how each person takes these individual preoccupations to extremes, and the incongruities and collisions that result.

Again, examples are to be found everywhere. In "The Impresario Under the Sofa" the impresario's main aim is to hide from the jealous rival pursuing him, whereas that of the actress is to exploit the piquancy of the situation to obtain a salary increase; hence their completely different interpretations of what is and is not moral.

The comedy in "Lost" is not simply that the friends lose their way in the dark and stumble into someone else's dacha, but that while the host is filled with pleasurable anticipation at the thought of seeing his wife, having something to eat and drink, and chatting until after midnight, his visitor desperately wants to sleep.

In exactly the same way in "A Drama," the anecdotal crime is committed only because the writer-hero is longing to escape, if only to the cellar, from the heat and having to make conversation, whereas his visitor is quite determined to read him the whole of her play.

In "The Siren" a biological specimen—a civil service gourmand capable of talking for hours about food—is contrasted with Milkin, the local philosopher, "at odds with his environment and seeking the purpose of life," who listens to the stories of preparing various dishes with a scowl of contempt on his face. Chekhov makes equal fun of both characters, preoccupied as they are with their different aspirations.

At first glance a gulf separates these humorous pieces from "The Duel," "The Black Monk," "Three Years," "My Life," and "Ionych," in which people talk at cross-purposes and each one has his own "definite view of things," which absorbs him completely. . . . Yet this theme of mutual incomprehension riveted the attention of Antosha Chekhonte (his early pen name) and the mature Chekhov alike. But what originally evoked laughter later acquires philosophical and at times tragic depth.

The simple juxtaposition of different sign systems or "views of things" in itself constitutes the richest source of the comic in Chekhov, but it is not specific to him. The type of comedy that is peculiar to Chekhov arises when rigidly formalized systems collide with something that has no name in language and that "music alone"—actual and unspoken—"seems capable of conveying" (the words applied to the parents' grief in "Enemies").

"The Village. To Grandad." is comic in itself. But the collision of illusion and a false idea with the semi-literate Vanka Zhukov's real pain and suffering is calculated to evoke a more complex response in the reader. In "Polinka," through the salesman's patter and flow of incomprehensible (and therefore funny) terms, we glimpse the love drama of two characters who are comic and at the same time evoke our sympathy: the salesman Nikolai Timofeyich and Polinka the milliner.

> "We have two kinds of lace, madam! Cotton and silk! Here, if you please, are the cotton ones—Oriental, British, Valenciennes, crochet, and torchon, and over here we have the silk ones—rococo, soutache, and cambric. . . . Do wipe your eyes, I beg you! Someone's coming."
>
> Seeing that her tears are still flowing, he continues even louder:
> "Spanish, rococo, soutache, and cambric. . . . Fil d'Ecosse stockings, cotton ones, silk ones. . . ." ("Polinka")

A very specific kind of sign system—the language of haberdashery—is superimposed on something quite different, beyond the external action and spoken words.

In "Yearning," Iona Potapov, the cabby who has recently buried his son, does not need simply to share his sorrow with someone; the only way, he feels, in which he can give full expression to his grief through words and tears is by using ritualized forms:

> It will soon be a week since his son died, and he hasn't talked about it properly to anyone yet. . . . He needs to talk about it sensibly, taking his time. . . . He must say how his son fell ill and suffered, what he said before his death, and how he died. . . . He must describe the funeral and the trip to the hospital to collect his son's clothes. Then there's his daughter Anisya still living in the village. He must say something about her, too. . . . There's so much for him to talk

about now! His listener ought to respond with sighs and groans and lamentations. . . . Better still would be to talk to the women. They're foolish, of course, but they start howling in two seconds.

In the unhurried life of the village this artless ritual, this traditionally established sequence of events, might still have been realized. But in the hustle and bustle of the capital, neither his gentlemen fares, nor the yard porter, nor his fellow cabbies have time to listen to Iona; they are too absorbed in their own affairs. Like future Chekhov heroes, Iona is incapable of correctly understanding the reasons for his suffering: "I haven't earned enough to buy oats," he thinks. "That's why I'm miserable. A man as really knows his job, as can feed himself and his horse proper . . . he never has to worry." In the end Iona does carry out the ritual, but in a highly ridiculous manner: his fellow participant is the little horse. But if the hero's false conceptions or absurd behavior strike an ironical note, this response is dissolved by the story's lyrical pathos.

The bitter humor of "Vanka" and "Yearning" is heard again more than ten years later in "At Christmas" (1900). A mother's unspoken longing for her faraway daughter, and the empty words of the self-intoxicated clerk, convinced that everything can be expressed in the language of military regulations; the tears of the daughter Yefimya, who has only to glance at the letter from the village to understand everything without words, and the well-ordered respectability of the consulting rooms and treatments in Doctor B. O. Moselweiser's hydropathic establishment where her husband works: in both cases real life—longing, weeping, inarticulate and unordered—is contrasted with the complacent self-assurance of established signs and those who uphold them.

This general principle, giving rise to his most comic and most tragic stories, this ability to treat the same situations either comically or sadly, ensures the profound inner unity of Chekhov's work throughout his career. Humor will never disappear, since both his humorous and "serious" works are written on essentially the same theme and devoted to the same range of phenomena.

In this chapter we have not dealt, of course, with the full range of Chekhov's humorous writing but only with the nature of the comic in Chekhov. It was in the humorous stories of 1884–1887 that he found himself as an artist. Their aim is no longer to make the reader laugh at all costs but to formulate in comic terms Chekhov's central underlying theme: how we orient ourselves in the world around us, our attempts to make sense of that world and to find truth. To make the point again: what underlies Chekhov's humor is not simply his powers of observation, his telling details and colorful language, but an overall *conception* which makes it essential that the philosopher Milkin appear alongside the gourmand, and Moselweiser alongside Yefimya. In exactly the same way in his "serious" pieces, Chekhov's conception reveals itself in the juxtaposition of the ardent conviction of the sermonizing Ananyev with the "mental inertia" of the skeptical Shtenberg, and in many similar confrontations in the later works.

Chekhov's world is inhabited by different people arguing irreconcilably and (for reasons natural and artificial, objective and subjective) holding different beliefs. What provided fertile soil for Chekhov's comic masterpieces in the latter 1880s was not simply, though, the difference between people, but epistemological problems: their self-absorption, mutual incomprehension, and the absence of reliable, satisfactory guidelines in life.

But the main fact of Chekhov's artistic development in those years was that he became deeply absorbed "in the realm of the serious." To the reader accustomed to the mask of the mocking Antosha Chekhonte, Chekhov might have answered in the words that Dr. Ovchinnikov, the hero of "An Unpleasant Incident," uses in a different context: "You can smile! You think these are all trifling details, but don't you see, there are so many of them they can build up into the whole of life, like a mountain out of grains of sand!"

When he spoke of becoming absorbed "in the realm of the serious," it was not only trifles growing into problems that Chekhov had in mind, but that the life of ordinary people consists only of such problems; and it is their life that is of overriding interest to him as a writer.

# 6

## Chekhov's "Irrelevant" Details: "An Unpleasant Incident" (1888)

The structure of "An Unpleasant Incident" is close to that of the stories of discovery, but by 1888 Chekhov had refined his technique. He does not simply make his hero start thinking (i.e., shift him out of a state of everyday mental inertia) but moves him on further.

The event that triggers the hero's conscious activity appears to be an everyday trifle: Ovchinnikov, a zemstvo doctor, loses his temper and strikes his medical orderly, who has turned up for work drunk. It sounds like the plot for another humorous episode from the life of country physicians, nothing more. But the story goes on to show how the "problem," which at first seemed simple, gradually becomes more complicated and tangled, and how the hero comes very gradually to perceive the impossibility of "solving" it, even though to begin with he feels (and the people surrounding him remain convinced to the end) that a great many standard, ready-made solutions are available.*

Some interpretations of "An Unpleasant Incident" reveal an approach that is typical of Chekhov criticism generally. It is as if the story had not been read through to the end. Some interim conclusion drawn by a character is presented as the author's final conclusion.

Thus, according to I. Gurvich, the essential meaning of the unpleasant incident is this: an average man, who represents the toiling masses, stages a legitimate revolt, which is resolved in a way that discriminates unfairly against the hardworking orderly; no reconciliation is possible between the orderly in his subordinate position and the doctor representing authority.[1]

Such direct ways of extracting socially significant elements from Chekhov's work are not simply methodologically dubious (the story is read "only so far"; a monologue that favors the interpreter's case is wrenched out of context) but also completely obscure the genuine social content of the work.

By 1888 Chekhov had already formulated his principles for treating social themes—in particular, for depicting the situation of the hardworking subordinate—in stories like "Vanka," "Yearning," "The Malefactor," "Enemies," and "Let Me Sleep."

Thus "Let Me Sleep," written a few months before "An Unpleasant Incident," operates on two distinct levels. On one level it describes a day in the life of the unfortunate Varka, a thirteen-year-old who is desperately overworked by her employers. Chekhov conveys very graphically the sense of physical exhaustion that this little slave experiences, her desire to throw everything up and snatch a few moments' sleep.

Taken on this level only, the story would excite sympathy for the hard worker and indignation against her "owners." Chekhov's readers understand and respond to the sufferings of Varka and of Vanka Zhukov, the yearning of Iona Potapov and the grief of Dr. Kirilov.

But it is the other level of the story that is specific to Chekhov. What interests him most is how these hardworking subordinates *understand* their situation and how they *behave* as a result. As always in Chekhov, they understand incorrectly and react absurdly, inap-

---

1. Gurvich, *Proza Chekhova*, p. 49.

propriately. What is peculiar to Chekhov in each of his peasants, workers, and hardworking intellectuals is the heavy burden of their working situation *plus* their inability to understand the reasons for this correctly and their inappropriate reaction.

The heroes of "Vanka" and "Yearning" are acutely distressed, but when they seek to pour out their feelings to someone, they do not know whom to address. Kirilov's suffering in "Enemies" is perfectly genuine, but his behavior, as Chekhov stresses at the conclusion of the story (one where the author's position has been much argued over) is "unjust" and "absurd": Kirilov's preoccupation with his grief "does not unite but divides" him and Abogin, who is preoccupied with his own unhappiness. Chekhov's late story "The New Dacha" (1899) expresses a similar outlook: the author's democratic sympathies are beyond dispute, and the misfortunes of the rich are not to be compared with those of the poor, but the peasants, though sympathetic to the author, do not possess true knowledge: they simply cannot understand "why it was they had failed to get on well" with the "quiet, good, and gentle" owners of the new dacha, and why "they had parted as enemies."

Throughout Chekhov's literary career the philosophical/epistemological view will be at the center of his treatment of the social theme. Social observations and epistemological problems are not opposed but are closely connected and interdependent: they become the form of each other's existence. Chekhov considers the social theme from the epistemological angle, while the problems of "orienting oneself in life" and attempting to understand it are inseparable from the hero's social situation. What provides the final touch in the picture of the onerous life led by the villagers of Obruchanov in "The New Dacha" is thus their failure to *understand* the nature and cause of what has happened in their lives:

> As they plod along, exhausted, they are thinking. . . .
> What kind of fog was it that had blotted out the most important thing and left nothing visible but damage to the crops, bridles, pincers, and all those little things that seemed so absurd on looking back? . . .

Not knowing how to answer these questions . . . they walk on in silence, heads bowed.

The social theme always acquires this added dimension in Chekhov, and it is impossible to understand how he differs from his predecessors and contemporaries in the treatment of social themes without taking it into account.

In "Let Me Sleep" we follow the main character's thought process:

> She understands everything, she recognizes everyone, but through her half-sleep there is one thing *that she simply cannot grasp*: the nature of the force that binds her hand and foot, that oppresses her and makes life a misery. . . . Worn out, she makes one last, supreme effort to concentrate her attention, looks up at the winking green patch, and, as she listens to the sound of crying, finds it, this enemy that is making life a misery.
>
> It is the baby. . . .
>
> *A false idea* takes possession of Varka. . . . To kill the baby, then sleep, sleep, sleep. . . . [italics added]

A false idea that leads to a false action. Here, as in "Enemies" a year earlier, Chekhov is still spelling out explicitly the hero's false idea or unjust reaction. Later these promptings by the author will cease, and the reader will be required to know how to pick up from a story's internal connections the indications of false ideas, judgments, and actions.

When Tolstoy touches on the problem of how a man of the people makes sense of life and his situation, the emphasis is exactly the opposite. In "The Power of Darkness," Tolstoy makes us feel that it is the tongue-tied Akim, and he alone, who understands and assesses everything correctly, and delivers the final verdict.

Reverence toward the people, seeking ways back to "the soil" and to peasant "truth and simplicity," learning from the people— everything characteristic of Tolstoy and the populist movement (broadly understood) in Russian literature was alien to Chekhov the writer. "Peasant blood flows in my veins and you cannot astonish me with peasant virtues"; "don't bring Gogol down to the people, bring the people up to him"; "we are all the people . . ."[2]—in these and other remarks Chekhov expresses a kind of democratic outlook that was new to Russian literature, a natural, instinctive feeling. And to express it he did not need to adopt the simple life, convert to new positions, or destroy something in himself.

Chekhov was well aware, of course, of the gulf separating the intelligentsia from the people ("My Life"); he knew better than most the burdens of the people's lives ("Peasants"); and he also understood the secrets of popular thought, wisdom, and culture ("In the Ravine"). Our point is different. A representative of the masses— whether peasant or intellectual—is not regarded by Chekhov as material for ethnographic study, nor as an object of worship or penitential confession, nor as the bearer of final truths, but first and foremost as a being drawn into the same process of cognition/ "orientation," and conforming to the same laws of this process, as anyone else. Chekhov concentrates his attention on investigating those general, all-embracing laws, equally distributed, that govern the processes of "orientation" and of the search for "real truth."

As in the case of "Enemies" or "Let Me Sleep" earlier, "An Unpleasant Incident" is an example of a purely Chekhovian treatment of a social theme. The social manifests itself in the epistemological: from start to finish we follow Dr. Ovchinnikov's thought processes. And Chekhov does not simply make Ovchinnikov realize that orderlies (like clerks, shop assistants, etc.) have no rights—though he does that too, of course. When the doctor is talking to the magistrate about the "average man's" situation and is prepared to shift all the blame from the orderly onto himself, the logic of the story shows that this too is an inconclusive and mistaken solution of the "problem," though it may contain part of the truth.

By this time Chekhov has enabled the reader to understand the root cause of the unpleasant incident. From the doctor's heated, confused complaints to the magistrate, it becomes clear that his irritation was not accidental but had been provoked by his own position

---

2. *Letters*, 5:283; 11:294; *Works*, 17:9.

of subordination to and dependence on the authorities. The doctor regards the attitude of the local authorities—the marshal of nobility, the chairman of the board, and the zemstvo—as one continuous insult. He is spied on as if he were "a nihilist"; he has been surrounded by their "lackeys and intriguers"; and "everyone reckons they're entitled to meddle in my affairs, tell me what to do and keep an eye on me." The accumulated irritation and anger has finally boiled over. "I can't take any more! . . . It won't be long, I assure you, before I shan't stop at bashing in people's faces, I'll start shooting at them! I'm made of flesh and blood, too, you know, not wires."

As the situation develops, the hero becomes completely entangled. He would like the conflict between himself and the orderly— who is also an oppressed subordinate—to be settled by a higher moral authority, with justice and due seriousness. But everything is decided ridiculously simply: the authorities come down solidly on his side against "that boorish creep." So he, a decent, conscientious, hardworking intellectual (Dr. Ovchinnikov sees forty-five patients a day in his surgery!), finds that he is a part of what he himself detests: brute force which oppresses the weak and those without rights. This "problem" is so complex and absurd that the hero cannot grasp it or work it out for himself.

At his disposal there would seem to be an extremely wide choice of standard, ready-made solutions and actions known to everyone, from fighting a duel and remonstrating with the orderly, to the district court and measures of administrative punishment. But the hero rightly feels that all these "general solutions" do not apply to the specific "problem" and are merely play-acting.

Once again the conflict is worked out in the same way: in Chekhov's world man is not simply subordinate, deprived of rights and unhappy; *he is not strong enough to understand* the laws governing life and human relationships. He understands and explains them only half-correctly or quite wrongly, and he reacts and behaves absurdly. Within the confines of the real world to which he has access, the hero can find no solutions to his problem; those solutions that are generally accepted and have long since been recognized turn out to be false.

"What a chaotic situation!" Mariya Vasilyevna, the school-mistress-heroine of Chekhov's late story "A Journey by Cart" (1897) exclaims indignantly, and like Dr. Ovchinnikov she enumerates in detail all the insults and burdens of the "hard, uninteresting life" that falls to the lot of an educated Russian working in the country-side. Chekhov is always honest and accurate in describing this side of life, and for many of his contemporaries the information he pro-vided was an eye-opener. But in 1897, as in 1888, what chiefly makes Chekhov's character unhappy is "not knowing why and for what reason" everything in life happens the way it does. "In effect the whole arrangement of life, and the complications of human rela-tionships, are so impossible to understand that when you start thinking about it, you're scared out of your wits and your heart sinks." These are Mariya Vasilyevna's thoughts, but the outlook is also that of Dr. Ovchinnikov at the end of "An Unpleasant Inci-dent."

From now on, epistemological dead ends and fiascoes of this kind will form almost the main subject of Chekhov's artistic explo-ration—bearing in mind that for him the chief characteristic of Russian life was, after all, that "the ordinary little person does not have the strength to find his bearings." In "An Unpleasant Incident" life forces "a little person" to play a role that he cannot understand, that is contrary to all logic and to his own nature. He is disturbed and tormented both by the falsity of this role and by the way in which other people refuse to see the falsity and incomprehensibility that have become plain to him. Man is compelled to play a role in life that is not his own and that he therefore cannot understand—right up to the characters in *The Cherry Orchard* remarking "who I am, what I'm for, no one knows," this type of nonunderstanding of life will be one of Chekhov's most constant situations.

Another highly important feature of Chekhov's world is revealed in "An Unpleasant Incident": the author offers no solution to a prob-lem that is beyond his hero's strength, but he does state the problem correctly. He indicates the complex totality of circumstances in life that needs to be reckoned with. Alongside the whole web of circumstances in which the hero is entangled, he shows another life, a world that knows absolutely nothing of all these problems and lives by certain laws of its own ("You had only to climb on the windowsill and bend over slightly to see the young grass growing a few feet away . . ."), and that somehow influences the emotional state of those posing and trying to solve their problems ("When on a quiet overcast morning he was driving to the magistrate's, he no longer felt ashamed, but irritated and disgusted"). Characters and readers usually fail to take this emotional dependence into account, as is confirmed by everyone's failure to notice the description of the first snow in "The Nervous Breakdown," written three months later.

Dostoevsky frequently points out how his hero's states depend on external phenomena, which he records at times with fullness and detail, to the point of describing the flame-colored feather in the hat of the street singer whom Raskolnikov stops to listen to, the signboard that he reads on his way to the Hay Market, even the grammatical mistake that he notices on the signboard. But in the final analysis all these phenomena are related in some way to the hero's idea and further the author's aims of refuting it.

In Chekhov, on the other hand, there is no apparent connection between the fullness and variety of life described and the problems that preoccupy the hero. Life follows its own laws of which the hero is ignorant, laws that are waiting to be explained, and explained in a way that would necessarily take into account both what people consider important (the "problems" that the characters are trying to solve) and what they fail to perceive or notice, and pass by.

Thus Dr. Ovchinnikov is racking his brains over problems that he (and others like him) cannot solve, while at the same time we read that

—the ducklings in the road are squabbling over "some piece of gut,"

—the young grass under his window is "rather beaten down and shiny" after the previous day's downpour,

—at the court he sees the clerk "in a barge-man's jacket with bulging pockets,"

—during his conversation with him the magistrate catches a

mosquito and, "screwing up his eyes intently, examined it from all sides before squashing it and throwing it into the slop-basin,"

—and the doctor himself, on taking his leave, "mechanically downed a glass of vodka with some radishes," etc., etc.

In any work by Chekhov we may find these details, apparently unconnected with plot or characterization, which give the impression of being accidental and chosen at random. But Chekhov attached cardinal importance to them, and their place and function in his work are an expression of his "conception of life."

The first critics (Mikhailovsky, Pertsov, Golovin, and others) pointed out that Chekhov's choice of details, events, and individual actions was governed by chance, and they censured him for this. But in recent years critics have singled out this particular feature of Chekhov's poetics for special attention. A. P. Chudakov, arguing that contemporary critics were right to note these characteristic new features of Chekhov's poetics but wrong in their assessment, has drawn attention to the distinguishing feature of the accidental in Chekhov's world: that it enjoys equal rights with the nonaccidental. Whereas in earlier literature, Chudakov writes, the accidental does no more than show what is typical, in Chekhov it is "strictly accidental, having an independent value in existence and an equal right with everything else to be embodied in art."[3]

The idea of Chekhov's fortuitous depiction of the world in all its random multiplicity is true only as a first approximation. What have to be studied are the principles, the mechanism of choice that creates the illusion of randomness and fortuitousness. Here it is worth making a literary comparison.

Chekhov's closest predecessor, and indeed teacher, in the art of creating a picture of the world that integrated the "accidental" and the "nonaccidental" was undoubtedly Tolstoy. Not the Tolstoy of *War and Peace* and *Anna Karenina* so much as the Tolstoy of the 1880s, who sought to subordinate art to the demands of preaching and yet remained an incomparable artist, an exceptionally keen ob-

3. Chudakov, *Poetika Chekhova*, p. 262.

server of life in its tiniest details. It is important to emphasize the similarity and difference here between him and Chekhov.

Tolstoy's Ivan Ilyich is dying, but he refuses to apply to himself the syllogism about Caius being mortal like all men. Caius is man in general, and the syllogism is true in relation to Caius; but surely, Ivan Ilyich thinks, he himself is and always was a being unlike all other men, surely no one else had ever experienced . . . and he recalls "the smell of that little striped leather ball," the touch of his mother's hand, his rebellion over the pasties, the distinctive taste of wrinkled raw French prunes "and how your mouth filled with saliva when you got as far as the stone," and much else besides. Details more accidental and individual than these would be hard to imagine! Their presence appears to be motivated solely by Tolstoy's urge to present life in its "randomness" and colorful variety. But the uncontrolled randomness and absence of an organizing idea in such pictures by Tolstoy (and by Chekhov too) are misleading.

Here and everywhere Tolstoy is seeking maximum individualization not for its own sake but to show how all this colorfulness, diversity, and apparent chaos in human life is subject in the final analysis to a higher authority and may be "right" or "not right," as he shows in relation to the life of Ivan Ilyich. However accidental the choice of details in Tolstoy may be in relation to other "important" and "necessary" elements in the work, these details are still in a continuous hidden relationship with the final truth that Tolstoy is expounding.

The "chance" impressions of Anna Karenina on her way to the station or of Konstantin Levin on his wedding morning; the irrelevant details to which Pozdnyshev, the hero of *The Kreutzer Sonata*, draws attention on the night of his fateful return home—Tolstoy's prose is not short of details that fail to fulfill any of the demands of plot or characterization. So the presence of "accidental" details alongside "nonaccidental" ones cannot in itself be regarded as an innovation by Chekhov or a distinguishing feature of his poetics—although, as we shall see, it is of essential importance in explaining his originality.

"Accidental" in relation to what? "Accidental" for what purpose? These questions are unavoidable if we wish to understand the originality of Chekhov's treatment of the "accidental" and the "nonaccidental" when compared with other writers.

Chudakov's insistence on the special quality of the empirical details in Chekhov's world is entirely justified and objectively valid. The critic isolates in Chekhov's work those specific details that cannot be explained away as individual manifestations of the essential and general.

If we return to the examples from "An Unpleasant Incident"—the squabbling ducklings, the clerk's "barge-man's jacket with the bulging pockets," the dead mosquito thrown into the slop-basin, etc.—it is certainly difficult to find any significant connection between these details and the requirements of plot and characterization. The Chekhov hero who wears down-at-heel shoes and smart neckties, the heroine who keeps dropping matches in the course of a conversation, another heroine in the habit of eating iced apples while reading magazines, and the hero who is always examining the palms of his hands during a conversation, etc., etc.—countless details like these must have their own special kind of link with the basic demands of plot and characterization. These links cannot be explained as the traditional links between the individual and the general, where the individual serves only to reveal and give shape to the general—as in Gogol's world, where every detail, for example, in Sobakevich's house bears witness to the character of its owner, or in Goncharov's world, where Oblomov's dressing gown is an individual manifestation of the general phenomenon of Oblomovism.

In Chekhov these details possess far greater autonomy in relation to the general. The traditional distinction between "general" and "individual" needs to be amplified when dealing with the details in Chekhov (and other writers). Chudakov does this by distinguishing between what he terms "individual-essential" details and "individual-accidental" details, which exist alongside and enjoy equal rights with the former.

Those who disagree with Chudakov refer to the "secret meaning," the special "intention," and the "symbolic potential" of the objects and minutiae in Chekhov's work, to the "regularity" and "necessity" of all the details in the world he is describing, and to the careful selection of apparently accidental details with the aim of creating "the illusion of life's randomness." Invariably these critics insist on going back to the distinction between general and individual. In that case there is no difference between Chekhov's approach and that of Gogol or Goncharov.

Trying to show, however, that behind every Chekhov detail there must always be a "secret meaning" often leads to very strained interpretations. The distinction on which Chudakov insists is essential.

Chekhov's purpose in introducing these autonomous details, actions, and events is part of the new thinking that he embodied in his work, i.e., his epistemological view of the world. When we are taken aback by Chekhov's "irrelevant details," this is because we are always witnessing the juxtaposition of two different visions of the world, two kinds of orientation.

One vision belongs to the self-absorbed hero, blinkered by his "definite view of things" and not noticing a great deal around him. The other is that of the author: an incomparably broader vision, seeking to take into account all the world's richness and complexity, not connected with any "special" problems, and polemically opposed to any attempts to make individual points of view absolute.

Every detail that is unconnected with the hero's character, his current problem or his outlook, sounds like an indication of the limitedness and incompleteness of that outlook. Where Chekhov is not writing about his problem-centered hero but "simply" reproducing life, the same polemical attitude and juxtaposition of different views of the world are present; only here the target is not the hero's outlook but that vision of the world which is currently accepted and sanctioned by literature or any other tradition.

Thus "The Steppe" is filled with these autonomous details. Chekhov's "super-objective" in that story was to show Russian writers "how much wealth and how many layers of beauty still remain untouched, and how much space there still is for a Russian artist."[4] To state the problem of life correctly, as Chekhov affirms by the whole composition of "The Steppe," one should include not only what occupies and absorbs us but also what we fail to notice, the whole of that huge, "austere and splendid" world that surrounds us.

In the stories of this period it is not only the beauty of nature—which in Chekhov always takes new and unexpected forms—that emerges as an important theme and rich source of details. There is also the beauty of free and fearless passion ("Agafya"), creativity (the unknown poet-monk in "Easter Night"), female beauty ("The Witch," "Beauties"), and the "subtle, barely detectable beauty of human grief that we are far from being able to understand and describe, and that music alone seems capable of conveying" ("Enemies"). The question of beauty's place in human consciousness and behavior remains constant for Chekhov. Most often it is wasted and dying (as in "The Witch" and "The Requiem"), to be persecuted and punished ("Agafya"), or it fails to attract anyone's attention ("Easter Night").

The obscure but inescapably pressing, passionately felt search for answers in Chekhov must include not only the most important things and the trifles of life, but also without fail beauty, that beauty to be glimpsed when you "climb on the windowsill and bend over slightly to see the young grass growing a few feet away. . . ."

In Chekhov's artistic system the "important thing"—that center around which subject matter, characterization, the organization of the world of objects and the world of ideas all gravitate—ought not to be thought of as a set of static units but as a dynamic process: the process of searching for truth, stating problems, and analyzing false conceptions. In his artistic world the specific character of details and of objects in empirical reality can only be understood in conjunction with the main task of searching for "real truth" and "stating the problem correctly."

Like Dostoevsky and Tolstoy, Chekhov saw before him a real

4. *Letters*, 2:173.

world in which many things appeared accidental, devoid of any "central focus"; but in contrast to his great predecessors, he rejected those unifying links that they saw or wished to see, each in his own fashion and often in defiance of the evidence. For Chekhov the links, solutions, and prescriptions that are generally acknowledged and shielded by the authority of intellectual giants like Tolstoy are meaningless, illusory and false. The falsity of written laws and statutes, the deceit of prescriptions for religious salvation, or the illusions shared by the greater part of the Russian intelligentsia—all found in Chekhov an implacable enemy.

But in rejecting every kind of "central focus" (and, in effect, all the various claims to possession of the truth known at his time) and logically renouncing any attempt to define "truth" or "the norm," Chekhov was not denying the existence of a "central focus" or of "truth" in general. If the inspiration of his work is to expose illusions and reject "false conceptions," this is inseparable from the inspiration to seek the unknown "real truth" and to "state the problems correctly." For Chekhov, stating the problem correctly means including a great many components (including the beauty no one notices!) that must be taken into account; it means pointing out the true complexity of any problem. In Chekhov's world, complexity is a synonym for truth.

# 7

# Excitement and Exhaustion: "The Nervous Breakdown" (1888)

Written in the same year as "An Unpleasant Incident," "The Nervous Breakdown" begins with a typical "story of discovery" situation: "it seemed . . . but it turned out that." Previously the student hero Vasilyev "knew about fallen women only by hearsay and from books," but after visiting the houses in S-ev Alley it became clear to him that his existing ideas "had nothing in common with what he was seeing now," and that "the situation was far worse than he could have imagined."

The collapse of his illusory ideas is the leitmotif of sections 1 to 4 of the story. Contrary to his expectations, Vasilyev does not find in the prostitutes of S-ev Alley any consciousness of sin or guilt, any hope of salvation or yearning to escape, but only apathy, indifference, and even contentment. The sources of the hero's previous illusion are also pointed out: books and gossip about fallen women, a story "read somewhere at some time" about a fallen woman saved by a pure, self-sacrificing young man, and the way in which "that world" was depicted on stage and in the comic journals. The illusion of Chekhov's hero is one that is shared by most people: it is a false idea prevailing in society. *The Island of Sakhalin* will later be written in the same spirit of exposing a common illusion.

Once again a story about a social phenomenon (in this case that of legalized prostitution) is treated by Chekhov as a story about a *false idea* of this phenomenon and how its true complexity is revealed.

It is wrong, therefore, to see "The Nervous Breakdown" as inspired only by the idea of exposing the curse of prostitution. The hero, Vasilyev, is in the grip of such feelings, but hero and author are directing their attention at different things. Chekhov is writing a story not simply about the curse of prostitution but about how someone confronting this phenomenon in the real world is unable to formulate a correct idea about it and to "solve the problem" correctly.

Tolstoy thought that the presentation of the hero's moral sufferings in "The Nervous Breakdown" was illogical: "the hero should have made use of the prostitute first and only felt anguish afterward."[1] But the whole point of Chekhov's story is that it is *not* about pangs of conscience, or seeing the light, or resurrection. Taking a subject already treated by Garshin, Maupassant, Tolstoy, and other writers, Chekhov concentrated on his own theme, based on different material.

No sooner does Vasilyev take a good look at what other people ignore and merely accept, than he feels himself to be helpless and incapable of "making anything out" or doing anything "in this alien world that he found incomprehensible." These words signal a family resemblance between "The Nervous Breakdown" and those stories in which "the little person does not have the strength to find his bearings" or "you can't make anything out in this world," and those about "false conceptions" and the "absurd" solution of problems—in other words, with the main line of Chekhov's prose, its philosophical, epistemological questioning.

What makes the world "alien" and "incomprehensible" to the hero? Chekhov once again analyzes the different kinds of illusions and incorrect solutions.

In "The Nervous Breakdown" it is the general, ready-made, and

1. See *Works*, 7:664.

universally recognized categories and judgments that prove to be worthless.

The unfortunate women of S-ev Alley should be saved: this general proposition is undeniable. The objects of this concern, however, are quite indifferent to efforts to get them to talk about their need for salvation; yet at the same time Vasilyev feels that "they are human beings, real human beings, they feel insulted, suffer, cry, and seek help just as human beings do everywhere."

"Is prostitution an evil or not?" "My dear chap, that goes without saying," is the answer Vasilyev gets. In theory everyone agrees, but not one of the men he knows refuses to visit the houses in S-ev Alley.

Vasilyev's general assessment of his friends—"slaveowners! butchers!" (in the first version of the story), "murderers!" in the final text—seems true. But the specific behavior of one of these friends, Yegor Rybnikov, who intervenes on behalf of the abused prostitute, looks more moral than that of Vasilyev himself, who "lost heart and felt like a frightened child," even though earlier he had experienced "an acute feeling of pity, and of rage against the offender."

Specific manifestations of evil, as of good, cannot be subsumed under the general, stereotyped categories with which the hero tries to operate. More than anything else, this makes the "problem" complicated and incomprehensible, forcing Vasilyev to alter his judgments—for example, his attitude toward his friends—and eventually to become more and more entangled in the problem's complexity.

In "The Nervous Breakdown," even more clearly than in "An Unpleasant Incident," the problem of becoming aware of the real world is linked with the problem of reacting to this awareness. Impotence in "finding one's bearings" in relation to the problem leads to impotence in the choice of action to resolve it.

What actions can save "all those women whom he saw today"? This is the question that Vasilyev—by nature an extremist "in the Garshin mold"[2]—tries to resolve.

2. On Vasilyev's resemblance to Garshin, see M. L. Semanova, "Rasskaz o cheloveke garshinskoi zakvaski" in *Chekhov i ego vremya* (Moscow, 1977).

To begin with, he divides all the ways he knows of trying to save fallen women into "three groups," and comes to the conclusion that all these means are "impossible." Then, continuing "to exercise his imagination," he "posed the question differently" and concludes that "the men must be saved." Then he feels he has found "the only way out": to preach morality. Eventually Vasilyev concludes that this is not the kind of life for a "timid insignificant person" like himself, and that to follow it genuinely would mean not only preaching but taking action.

So the circle is closed, and Vasilyev finds himself back at his original question: what actions can save the women? Chekhov has described how his hero's thought moves round the closed circle, scrupulously tracing his swings of thought, inconsistency, and changes of position—thereby continuing an experiment he had begun in "An Unpleasant Incident" and even earlier in *Ivanov*.

On this occasion the hero's inability to make any sense of the problem facing him is shown to be the reason for his acute spiritual anguish, nervous breakdown, and near suicide. He is taken from a state of ecstasy and inspiration, "when the problem seemed to be solved," to one of weariness, despair at his impotence, awareness of his insignificance, and finally of indescribable pain. In "The Nervous Breakdown," Chekhov gives his own medical and literary account of why a man of the Garshin type might commit suicide. His hero nearly throws himself off the bridge—"not out of loathing for life, not for the sake of killing himself, but to hurt himself so much that one pain would distract from the other."

Vasilyev the law student, Ananyev the engineer, Shtenberg the apprentice, Ovchinnikov the doctor, and Ivanov the landowner—all these heroes of 1888 belong to the type of person that interested Chekhov most throughout his writing career. He best described his heroes and his relation to them as author in a letter in which he tried to explain to Suvorin, and through him the director and actors of the Alexandrinsky Theater, the meaning of his play *Ivanov*.

What Chekhov emphasized above all (and what the theater people, the critics, the public, and the actors playing the parts of Dr.

Lvov, Sarra, and Sasha found most difficult to grasp) was that he had not created his characters as objects of praise or censure, as positive or negative examples, or as "villains" or "great men." It was a matter of principle for Chekhov that his heroes not be the embodiment of "preconceived ideas" but "the result of observing and studying life."[3] From this it follows that the hero's actions and utterances are only symptoms of the interaction between his nature and his situation, not manifestations of the author's ideas of how things ought or ought not to be.

It is important to emphasize this once again, since in many interpretations of "The Nervous Breakdown" Vasilyev is presented almost as Chekhov's ideal of moral perfection and one of his "positive heroes." It goes without saying that Vasilyev is more attractive to Chekhov than those who ignore the "accursed questions"; like Ivanov, he has a nature that is "excitable, ardent, easily carried away by enthusiasms, honest and upright." And there can be no doubt that Chekhov applied to his own case the "observation and study" from which these characters resulted, and put a good deal of himself into them. But introducing some of the author's own personality traits into a character's image does not in Chekhov's world signify an intention to make that character the mouthpiece of the author's own ideas.

Ivanov and Vasilyev do not, of course, repeat each other. Vasilyev has a quality that places him above Ivanov (who is simply "a good man"), namely, his unusual sensitivity to the pain of other people. But taken as a whole he represents the same kind of average person. And the transition from "excitement" to "exhaustion," which in *Ivanov* spans a lifetime, has a different time span in "The Nervous Breakdown," where it covers only a few days.

Another point needs to be emphasized. Chekhov directs his attack with merciless accuracy both at the general delusions and illusions of society, and equally at the weaknesses of the "good man's"

3. *Letters*, 3:116.

noble but short-lived outburst of "protest," which is incapable of making the slightest impression on evil and ends in tears for the protester. Nothing could be more mistaken in the interpretation of Chekhov than giving the author credit for his sympathy toward characters like Vasilyev and Ivanov (undoubted though such sympathy is), or reducing the meaning of the work to a contrast between the hero's virtues (which are also obvious) and the shortcomings or vices of the other characters. To interpret the author's intentions in "The Nervous Breakdown" in that way is to ignore the story's main strength and to identify only the first link in the author's profound chain of thought. Chekhov does not approach characters of the Vasilyev type—who will recur frequently in his work, right up to the last stories and plays—with a feeling of tenderhearted warmth and sympathy but in a spirit of sober, tough-minded inquiry.

"The Nervous Breakdown" showed how different were the aims being pursued by Chekhov and Garshin in their treatment of the social evil of prostitution. Garshin's stories ("Nadezhda Niko-layevna," "An Incident," "Night") contain a cry of disgust, an acute sense of empathy with the victim, and a hope of agitating one's contemporaries with graphic descriptions of the evil—everything, in other words, that Chekhov attributed to Vasilyev. In Chekhov there is an analysis both of the evil itself and of the outburst of protest, or "excitement," which is followed by "exhaustion." This not only shows Chekhov's self-confidence but also does justice to Garshin at a higher level: a story which is essentially about the weaknesses of Garshin's approach to the manifestations of evil, succeeds at the same time in sounding a note of panegyric to what Chekhov saw as best and most noble in people "of the Garshin mold."

Chekhov made a distinction, of course, between what he himself once called "a good commonplace"[4] and what may be called a bad one. But he considered it his duty as a writer to show up the inconsistencies of the good as well as the bad commonplaces. It was his

4. *Letters*, 2:280.

unwillingness to share and proclaim the good commonplaces, and indeed his constant downgrading and exposure of the inner weaknesses of commonplaces widely accepted by young people and the intelligentsia, that the majority of his contemporaries found most incomprehensible and unforgivable. It was no accident that the critics—the preachers of good commonplaces like Mikhailovsky, Skabichevsky, and Protopopov—felt that Chekhov was alien to them.

As in "Lights" and "An Unpleasant Incident," so in "The Nervous Breakdown" Chekhov offers no solution of a problem which has proved insoluble in the real world; he limits his task to showing how the hero struggles with the problem and is defeated, and the extent to which well-known, generally accepted solutions are inadmissible. But it would be wrong to conclude that the point of "The Nervous Breakdown" is simply to show the failure of yet another attempt at finding one's bearings.

"You can't make anything out in this world": that conclusion might also be drawn from Vasilyev's unsuccessful attempt to "make sense of the situation" and "solve the problem." But it is no less important to the author to say that the problem itself remains, and to ignore it is the equivalent of blindness. The need to seek an answer is indicated by the entire composition of the story: not only the pictures of what Vasilyev sees in S-ev Alley and his reflections on them, but also the description of something that no one notices ("How can the snow fall on this street!").

One further point: however obvious the inability and failure of people of the Vasilyev type to "solve the problem," such attempts to "make something out" will continue: the age-old yearning of good, honest people to challenge evil is ineradicable, even though their strength is not equal to the task and their attempts are doomed to failure.

In his letter to Grigorovich about the intended sequel to "The Steppe," Chekhov described the biosocial disharmony which in his opinion determined the fate of Russian man. In the same letter he mentioned as distinctive features of his characters "a passionate thirst for life and truth" and "restless analysis."[5] This abiding sense of the unceasing quest for truth, passed on from one work to the next, distinguishes Chekhov's sobriety and skepticism from agnosticism, which in principle denies the possibility of discovering the truth.

We have talked about the "epistemological" basis of Chekhov's work and how it is linked with his primary interest in "knowledge in the realm of thought," with efforts to "orient oneself" and "make something out in this world." So far the material we have analyzed has been limited to Chekhov's works from the latter 1880s. But even that is enough to show that we are not dealing simply with a separate theme or problem relating to a narrow range of works.

Many distinctive features of the content and form of Chekhov's work converge, as it were, in the epistemological theme. This is true, for instance, of the individual situations in which Chekhov most often places his characters: the situation of discovery, of mutual incomprehension, of the argument that does not reach a conclusion and the sermon that fails to persuade, etc. Individual devices, like the organization of time in "Lights," are subordinated to it. Without taking this theme into account, it is impossible to interpret correctly how Chekhov organizes the details in his work, and the relationship between the general and the particular.

Chekhov's treatment of the social theme also acquires, as we have seen, a special epistemological dimension. And the cognitive function of his work is linked in the first instance to his concentration on problems of orienting oneself in the world and perceiving it correctly. The aesthetic effect of Chekhov's work is also determined to a considerable extent by his special understanding that one of his tasks as a writer is to take issue with wrong ideas about the relationship between truth and beauty—and this constitutes another variety of the argument about knowing the truth.

Briefly, a considerable amount of Chekhov's artistic world is

5. *Letters*, 2:190.

built around this axis. We are dealing with a special way of seeing and depicting the real world. And it is one that leads to special assertions and generalizing conclusions that are exclusive to Chekhov. Without understanding them, a correct interpretation of his work is inconceivable.

# 8

# A Play About Nonunderstanding:
## *Ivanov* (1887)

The main theme of Chekhov's 1888 stories had already been heard in the autumn of 1887 in his first play to be presented on stage, *Ivanov*.

Chekhov's contemporaries understood the play as the story of a clash between two figures, Ivanov and Lvov, representing different social tendencies in the late 1880s, and gave contrasting and sometimes directly opposed assessments of the author's intentions. This kind of critical approach to *Ivanov* persisted until recently. Most stage interpreters of the play see the opposition between the hero and his hostile environment as the basic source of dramatic conflict. John Tulloch, while rightly pointing out Chekhov's interest in the ideas of the Russian psychiatrist I. P. Merzheyevsky, reduces the aim of the play to the depiction of "the social psychology of the neurasthenic."[1]

Where do we find the criteria for understanding the play correctly? What was the author's ultimate aim in writing a text that has been so differently interpreted? The text of *Ivanov*, if carefully studied, may suggest such criteria. Of considerable importance, too, are

---

1. John Tulloch, *Chekhov: A Structuralist Study* (London, 1980), pp. 6–9.

*75*

the author's own explanations of the play's meaning, which we can draw upon here for the first and last time in Chekhov.

Chekhov made changes to the text on several occasions, turning what was a comedy in its first version into a drama in its final version. But whatever new shades of meaning may have been introduced by each new edition, one should obviously pay most attention to those elements that were present at the outset and remained unchanged (or were strengthened) in subsequent reworkings.

The most important constant element was the portrayal of the central character as a basically ordinary, average individual.

As a comedy, *Ivanov* stood out sharply from the preceding generation of Russian comedies, most notably the plays of Ostrovsky. The prime mover of the action in Ostrovsky is the difference between the characters in their class, financial, and family situations.

Not so in *Ivanov*. Here the author places at the center of the play a character whose universality he wishes to emphasize. Ivanov is a landowner, "a local government official responsible for peasant affairs"; his social status is realistically indicated. The estate has been ruined, its owner is in debt, and he has appealed for extended credit to the money-grubbing Zyuzyushka. But these are not the circumstances that provide the source, or at least the basic source, of drama or comedy in *Ivanov*.

During the course of the play, Lebedev goes behind his wife's back and offers Ivanov money, perhaps assuring Ivanov's marriage to Lebedev's daughter Sasha. A traditional happy ending is indicated, but Ivanov irritably brushes aside Lebedev's offer. So Chekhov is not seeing "a landowner's ruin" as an essential part of what is going on.

In playing down or removing the class explanations of what is happening to Ivanov, Chekhov highlights the average qualities that he shares with many others like him. After completing the comedy, Chekhov wrote to Suvorin that in Ivanov he had taken "an ordinary sinful mortal" and defined him in ways that underlined how prevalent his type was: "a member of the Russian intelligentsia," "a university man," and, even more broadly, "a Russian" and "a man."[2]

2. *Letters*, 3:109–115.

Chekhov insists that he is not an apologist, a glorifier, or an un-masker, and that he wishes only to investigate what is happening to the type of person most prevalent among his contemporaries, embracing people of different classes and situations.

What exactly *is* happening in the play to this hero in whom features of the "average man" predominate? What constitutes an event in *Ivanov*?

As mentioned above, events connected with lack of money or the ruin of the estate are merely accompaniments to other events that seem incomparably more important to the hero. The same can be said of the family/love relationship between Ivanov, his wife Sarra (Anna Petrovna), and the young Sasha. "It would seem to be a traditional love triangle," Z. S. Paperny comments. "But Ivanov, having lost interest in Sarra, is inwardly indifferent to Sasha too."[3] The sufferings of the central character have nothing at all to do with love; he sees his unsuccessful marriage as one in a long series of other mistakes. Finally, the action of the play might be said to boil down to the spreading of slander, to which an honorable man (albeit with certain weaknesses) eventually falls victim. In interpretations of this kind, *Ivanov* looks like a variation on Griboyedov's *Woe from Wit*, and Ivanov like a variation on its hero, Chatsky.

There is indeed plenty of rumor and gossip surrounding Ivanov in the course of the play. But unlike Chatsky, the chief protagonist of *Ivanov* is not a hero expressing many of his author's thoughts but an average man whom the author treats with consistent irony. And slander in *Ivanov* is not there to motivate the intrigue but to provide further evidence of the unreliability of the judgments that are passed on individuals. The slander that originates in Zyuzyushka's drawing room is one variation among the wider range of judgments on Ivanov.

The discovery of a husband's infidelity, a wife's death, slander, a wedding that never took place, and the death of the bridegroom—these are not the events and dramatic situations in *Ivanov*. All this

3. Z. S. Paperny, *"Vopreki vsem pravilam . . .": P'esy i vodevili Chekhova* (Moscow, 1982), p. 34.

represents the outline of the play's external action. Of basic importance is what is happening in the realm of the heroes' consciousness. And the basic events of the play (prior to its denouement) remained the same in every version. These are the events and situations that are familiar to us from Chekhov's prose: making a discovery, trying to work something out, failing to understand.

One can say in general terms that *Ivanov* is a play about *nonunderstanding*. Its main character's comments and speeches contain a whole system of echoes that repeat the motif of nonunderstanding very logically and persistently. Ivanov talks about it to Lvov at the very start of the play: "I'm not capable of understanding myself. I don't understand other people or myself . . . even I don't understand what's going on inside me. . . . Maybe you can understand me. . . ." To his wife he says: "I feel such boredom! Don't ask me what's causing it. I don't know myself." Later on he will talk about his inability to understand to Lebedev, to Sasha, and again to Lvov.

What is it that Ivanov is trying to work out? It is the change that has overtaken him during the past year. "I've become so irritable and quick-tempered, so harsh and petty-minded, that I can't recognize myself. . . . I've cracked up completely . . . nothing like this has ever happened to me before," and so on. He is referring to some event that predates the start of the play.

Here it is worth noting a comparison that critics have often made between *Ivanov* and Shakespeare's *Hamlet*. Ivanov has been called "the Russian Hamlet," though this is invariably qualified by the comment that Chekhov's character does not attain the same level of significance as Shakespeare's hero. Critics have also been embarrassed by Ivanov's clearly stated unwillingness to see any similarity between himself and Hamlet.

But Chekhov, one might argue, was taking his example not from a heroic type but from a principle of construction in this, his favorite Shakespearean tragedy. Having an event take place offstage, and making the action consist only of conversations about that event—something often regarded as a dramatic innovation by Chekhov—has an ancient pedigree.

The event in *Hamlet*—a king's murder, the loss of a father—has taken place before the play begins and is presented in the form of narration. What the dramatist shows on stage is the never-ending succession in the hero's mind of questions, reflections, moral shocks, and dramatic struggles that the event has generated. External events merely help to unfold before the spectator or reader the complicated and gripping struggle taking place in his consciousness. Hamlet himself regards his conscience, his consciousness, as the source of all his torments. It is this and only this that gives dramatic interest to all the external action and episodes in Shakespeare's tragedy.

Chekhov too made use of this principle of dramatic construction, but without any idea of giving his hero the dimensions of a Hamlet. Shakespeare's hero is an individual of exceptional moral nobility and worth, who embodies great ideas. Brilliance of thought, depth of feeling, and irresistible charm place Hamlet among the ranks of the chosen few. Ivanov, on the other hand, is "an average man," though Hamlet's words—that he is too complicated an instrument to be played upon—are also applied to him. But as Chekhov describes him, Ivanov is the "most ordinary person," simply "a good man," "not remarkable in any way," of "an honest and upright nature" but with "an unstable mind" and a proneness to "nervous instability and exhaustion."[4] Chekhov uses a dramatic construction going back to *Hamlet* in order to analyze the consciousness of his "average man."

What happens to Ivanov might happen to anyone (or at least to a significant majority). For that reason the dramatist is convinced that it should be of special interest to contemporary audiences. Ivanov's fate should make the audience reflect on a basic and extremely common situation of the time.

The event that determined the hero's fate is invisible but fully defined. Chekhov was writing in the play (and in his stories) about a person's transition from one state of viewing the world to another.

4. *Letters*, 3:109–113.

Something was discovered, something appeared in a new light, yesterday's beliefs vanished, and with them went self-confidence. What comes next? A new belief, a new enthusiasm? Or is there no longer the strength and desire for that?

Explaining these two stages in his hero's life to Suvorin, Chekhov refers to them by the medical terms "excitement" and "exhaustion." But this use of medical terminology merely confirms the reflections on contemporary man that had entered Chekhov's work much earlier. In "On the Road" (1886) he had described a man whose life consisted of "an uninterrupted succession of beliefs and enthusiasms" and who was never "carried away for long" by any one thing.[5] Likharev's fate, and how he relates to people around him and to life as a whole, were presented as a retrospective summary. In *Ivanov*, Chekhov took a much closer look: two stages in the fate of such a person—but the most characteristic ones—are examined. In an uninterrupted "Likharev" chain, an "Ivanov" break is bound to happen.

The first stage is the prehistory of Ivanov. To find his bearings in life and his course of behavior, the hero has chosen certain ready-made forms and general ideas that he is convinced are right. He "wages war on evil and applauds the good," he is ready to transform everything around him: social and civic affairs, the domestic economy, education, personal relations. He throws himself into all this with enthusiasm, he is carried away and carries other people (especially women) away with him, he jokes and puns, making up ridiculous stories, turning somersaults in the hay, laughing, etc. The way in which Ivanov has behaved "unlike other people," living and believing unlike other people—that too is a very familiar form of behavior, a "commonplace," as it were, in reverse.

That was in the past, the very recent past, a year or so ago. The second stage, which Chekhov regards as inevitable and extremely common, is when his method of orientation and behavior comes to seem false to the hero. He renounces it and is "ready to deny" everything he was asserting the day before—an extremely common

5. *Works* 5:468, 470.

situation in Chekhov. Ivanov falls out of love with his wife, gets into difficulties with the estate that he has been energetically reforming, and tires himself out with his own reforms and undertakings. He becomes "a grumbler."

Even before the action begins, therefore, the hero has undergone this major change in his perception of life and his relation to it. The change has occurred without him or the people around him being aware of it, and has determined his subsequent fate.

Chekhov has deliberately set himself a very difficult artistic task. For how can you depict or act out an unseen event? How can you attract the spectator's attention to it, how can you avoid obscuring it by what is happening at the level of external action? Chekhov, we know, was counting on a very talented performer in the main role: he must be "a flexible, energetic actor," who "can be gentle one moment and furious the next," and he must be able to deliver one speech "as if he were singing and another in a fierce tone."[6] In any case, in playing "Ivanov today," an actor is somehow obliged to indicate "Ivanov yesterday," letting the spectator feel that only yesterday everyone viewed this grumbler and whiner as the "cheerful, laughing, radiant" Ivanov.

That he was counting on his audience to recognize in *Ivanov* the most widespread phenomenon of the time and a situation that was highly typical of "our youth," Chekhov made clear in the same letter to Suvorin:

> Take the present day. . . . Socialism is one of the types of excitement. Where is it now? In Tikhomirov's letter to the Tsar. The socialists have got married and are running down the zemstvo. Where is liberalism? Even Mikhailovsky says that all the pieces on the board are muddled up these days. And how much are all those passionate Russian enthusiasms worth? We're tired of the war [against Turkey], tired to the point of irony by the Bulgarian question, tired of Zucchi [an Italian ballerina], tired of operetta.[7]

6. *Letters* 3:131–132.
7. *Letters* 3:111–112, 368.

Chekhov seeks to embrace within a single overall concept the most varied changes of conviction and mood, ranging from the defection of a former populist terrorist, Tikhomirov; the loss of nerve on the part of recent ideological idols like Mikhailovsky; and the cooling of society's interest in yesterday's burning political issues, to changing fashions and enthusiasms in the world of art.

This approach means that Ivanov is not confined within the limits of any one ideological tendency of his time: Chekhov insists on considering the nature of mass "excitements" and "exhaustions" as a whole, seeing it as his artistic task to consider the most general foundations of these changes. To do so, he moves down several rungs in comparison with his ideological predecessors in Russian literature: to considering how the most commonplace, ordinary consciousness works, and to observing its characteristic traps, mistakes, and deceptions.

Ivanov, as we have seen, does not understand what has happened to him and what has caused his present depression. But at the same time he tries to draw broad general conclusions and to offer advice to a member of the next generation. This happens in his famous speech in Act I, when he is persuading Lvov not to fall into the same errors as himself: "Make your life as conventional as possible. . . . Find your niche and do the little job that God has ordained for you."

In this speech Chekhov makes us very much aware of the obvious defects in Ivanov's thinking: how he veers from one behavioral stereotype to another (living unlike other people, living like everyone else; demolishing everything, accepting everything) and how he attempts to justify himself. False conclusions, false explanations—and a good measure of irony on the author's part in depicting them. Chekhov was not proposing a new idea, he was proposing a new method of shedding light on *any* idea in literature.

The theme of Ivanov's nonunderstanding of what is happening to him is developed in the course of the play. Life, after all, "goes on regardless," it is constantly "making legitimate demands on him," and he is "having to resolve problems."[8] Sasha's declaration of love catches him unawares, and Ivanov's first response is the same: "But why, why! Heavens above, I don't understand anything. . . ."As the climax of Act III approaches, this note sounds more and more insistently, accompanying the whole of Ivanov's speech like a refrain: "I don't understand. . . . What's the matter with me? . . . I don't understand, I don't understand, I don't understand." To Lvov, a man who "understands" everything, Ivanov replies: "Think for a moment, my clever friend: you reckon there could be nothing simpler than understanding me, don't you?" Then follows a variation on the Hamlet theme: "No, doctor, we each have too many wheels, screws, and valves to be able to judge each other on first impressions or on two or three outward signs. I don't understand you, you don't understand me, and we don't understand ourselves." The same note runs through Ivanov's conversations with Lebedev and Sasha.

From time to time the main character's complaints at not understanding are echoed by those of other characters. (In the later plays these repetitions and the equal distribution of the basic theme among the characters will be one of Chekhov's major techniques.) In Act I, Anna Petrovna says to her husband: "I don't understand you. . . . Why have you changed?"; and to Lvov: "How do you understand this depression of Nikolai's?" Lebedev admits that his Sasha "can't understand her own father! . . . She can't understand!"—and after his conversation with her he says: "I don't understand a thing. Either I've gone daft in my old age, or you've all grown very clever and I'm the only one who can't understand anything, however hard I try."

But running along parallel with the "I don't understand" motif, which is repeated so frequently and insistently, is another motif in the play: "I understand!" The confused and uncomprehending hero is assessed and judged by the people around him. Each person claims to understand Ivanov, and in passing judgment each has his

8. *Letters*, 3:111.

own system of ideas, his "personal view of things." Chekhov reveals a whole spectrum of different kinds of nonunderstanding and unfair judgments.

From the viewpoint of "a normal person," says Borkin, Ivanov's steward, Ivanov is "a psychopath, a crybaby." To Borkin everything is simple: he exemplifies a busy, active life, but this simple, businesslike approach conceals a monstrous vulgarization of life's goals and motives. Nor do Zyuzyushka and her circle find any difficulty in understanding Ivanov. Fully convinced that they have understood him correctly, each of them speaks of Ivanov's base calculations in marrying Anna Petrovna ("he strikes me as an adventurer") and on the eve of his marriage to Sasha ("He came a cropper with the Jewess . . . and now he's got his eyes on Zyuzyushka's moneybags"). Lebedev reports to Ivanov on the way this slander spreads: "You're said to be a murderer, a bloodsucker, a robber, and a traitor."

The obvious antagonism between Ivanov and his environment gives rise to the widespread interpretation of him as another variation of the "superfluous man."

But in Chekhov's play the hero's relationship to his environment is not the same as in works about "superfluous men." In the classic examples of such works by Pushkin, Herzen, and Turgenev, an alien environment does not accommodate the hero and often "consumes" him. But the environment did not stand in the way of Ivanov when he entered enthusiastically into activities on his estate and in the district. It was he who changed and ceased to understand himself. The people around him do not understand him, either. But in Chekhov's play the nonunderstanding of the hero by a vulgar environment is only one kind of false interpretation among others, including those for which he himself and others at odds with their environment are responsible. In *Ivanov* the theme of antagonism between the hero and his environment is subordinated to the "epistemological" theme of nonunderstanding.

"You've been consumed by your environment, my friend!" Lebedev says to Ivanov.

"That's stupid, Pasha, stupid and out of date."

"Yes, it is stupid. I can see that myself now."

Chekhov's aims in *Ivanov* are of quite a different order. In works about the "superfluous man," judgment is passed on the hero—by the author, by other heroes, and especially by the heroines. However much the various verdicts may disagree, in their totality they provide a compound formulation of the hero.

Not so in Chekhov's play! Verdicts are likewise passed on Ivanov from all quarters. But what interests the author is not trying to find among these discordant verdicts the one true one, or a sum of truths (as had been the case in his own play *Platonov*). More important to him is to show that the judgments are relative and conditional, however much the hero might deserve them, that a human being cannot be reduced to a formula, and that a conclusive judgment is impossible.

The nonunderstanding of Ivanov by figures like Zyuzyushka is traditional: this is not what moves the action. The hero's fate is determined by the false understanding of him by people who are as hostile to their uncultured environment as he is: Anna Petrovna, Sasha, and Lvov.

Anna Petrovna was capable of appreciating Ivanov as he was yesterday, the "excited" Ivanov. The whole of his subsequent transformation she refuses to understand or accept. But on seeing her husband with Sasha, she comes to the most simplified and inescapable conclusion. With the hatred of a deceived wife who had once gladly accepted her own mistaken view of Ivanov, Anna Petrovna repeats: "Now I understand you. . . . Now everything's understandable. . . . Now I remember and understand everything."

Tired of hearing all the slanders against Ivanov, Sasha is convinced that she alone understands him properly: "Nikolai Alekseyevich, I understand you. It is loneliness that is making you unhappy. You need someone around you whom you could love and who would understand you." Needless to say, she considers that person to be herself. Ivanov becomes the object of her "rescue operation." As Chekhov writes, "she doesn't love Ivanov, she loves her mission."[9]

These two types of women—one who can love only a strong hero, and the other only a weak one—are united in the play by a concealed common feature. Each sees not the real Ivanov, who is changeable and contradictory, but her own one-sided picture of him. False understanding, the absolute conviction that they are right, and the refusal to accept any other point of view lead to fatal consequences. A. P. Skaftymov's opinion that Ivanov causes evil without evil intention does not go far enough:[10] Chekhov shows that Anna Petrovna and Sasha bear as much responsibility for the misfortunes that befall them as does Ivanov himself. True, meeting Ivanov ends in misfortune for them both. But at the same time he is himself a victim of their false understanding, and the source of their misfortunes is to be found in their own false pictures of him.

Dr. Lvov brushes aside the suggestion that Ivanov cannot be understood: "Oh, don't talk to me about your Nikolai, I understand him perfectly." From the standpoint of the "thinking person" and "honest man" that he considers himself to be, he judges Ivanov, who offends his "truth." A "Tartuffe" and a "scoundrel": this is his irrevocable, unconditional verdict. "Now we understand each other perfectly," he says, on catching sight of Sasha coming in to see Ivanov.

These three, then, do not understand Ivanov. From Chekhov's point of view there is a very important distinction: unlike the minor figures surrounding Zyuzyushka, all three have their own definite positive principle, their "truth." All of them, as Ivanov says about Sasha, show "the stubbornness of an honest nature"—and "honest" is the key word. And all fail to understand Ivanov precisely because of their virtues and superior qualities: in spite of them, they do not understand (or they misunderstand) him; they confuse an already confused character even more, and each in his or her own way pushes him toward suicide. The actors, Chekhov emphasized, must

9. *Letters*, 3:114.
10. A. P. Skaftymov, *Nravstvennye iskaniya . . .* , pp. 438–440.

not play these roles as caricatures but should bring out the sense of inner conviction, the sincerity and seriousness that lead objectively to the destruction of an individual.

So this theme of understanding and nonunderstanding can be seen to embrace every character in every edition of the play. Chekhov took as material for the dramatic action what was happening in the realm of consciousness, of passing judgments and forming opinions. This was the real originality of the play (though Chekhov, as we saw, was following a distinguished historical precedent).

This approach to the depiction of characters had far-reaching consequences for Chekhov's own style of drama: at the base of his play is not only a clearly defined problem but the methods for its artistic development.

Originally *Ivanov* was called a comedy. To define this more accurately, it was a comedy of misunderstandings, of illogicalities. The inability to link cause and effect; absurd remarks arising from incorrect thought processes; ridiculous behavior as a result of drawing wrong conclusions—illogicalities of this kind often become objects of derision in life and in art. This aspect of the comic predominates in Chekhov's play.

A dispute between the "I don't understand" and "I understand" motifs runs right through the play; the characters are forever "understanding" inappropriately; completely opposite points of view collide with each other, mutually exclusive judgments are offered by the same character. The illogicalities may be obvious or hidden, transparent or opaque.

The illogical stupidities that are revealed by the judgments of local society and its slanders against Ivanov are relegated to the fringes of the play. Chekhov pays greatest attention to developing a more subtle form of illogicality: the unfounded confidence in understanding things correctly that results from "the stubbornness of an honest nature." Anna Petrovna, Sasha, and Lvov all possess that "invincible faith in oneself" that Hegel regarded as the chief quality of a comic character.

In Chekhov's play, therefore, the comic basically takes the form of making fun, openly and covertly, of mistakes, blunders, and un-founded pretensions "in the realm of thought."

In revising the play, Chekhov strengthened the image of Ivanov. In the first version Lvov makes his unjust accusation and Ivanov, who is ready to start living by a new "truth," dies of a heart attack. In the final version Ivanov receives the insult "coldly": he himself is fully aware by then of everything that Lvov can say about him. At the end of the play the author forces the hero to make a new discovery, to arrive at a realization of his (and not only of his) situation.

Ivanov comes to understand how alien to life his condition is. No one can be blamed for the breakdown that occurred after he had taken on a burden, during the period of "excitement," that was beyond his strength. But to go on living in a state of "exhaustion," grumbling and poisoning his life and the lives of those around him, or to accept the modest truth of "small deeds"—this his conscience and pride will not allow (and conscientiousness had been introduced into Ivanov's character from the very beginning as one of its chief components). Not feeling the strength to continue life, Ivanov finds the strength to quit it: "this is the old Ivanov speaking."

In the final version the image of Ivanov is magnified because the scale of the questions he began asking has been magnified. Not only "What is happening to me?" but the fundamental question: "Who am I, what am I living for, what do I want?" Ivanov is now attempting to find his bearings not in his personal life but in life as a whole; he wants "real truth." His link with his times and his generation also becomes closer. The additions made to his speech in 1896 place Ivanov's experience in a wider context: "And tell me, how could it have been otherwise? There are so few of us, after all, and there's so much to be done! So much!"[11] Alongside the ironic treatment of how the hero switches from one stereotype and misconception to another, there is now an awareness of the tragic situation of an individual and his generation who have collapsed beneath the weight of problems that were objectively too strong for them.

11. *Works*, 12:74.

The conclusion, the denouement, expresses the author's assessment of the situation. It is noteworthy that in searching for a resolution of the "Ivanov situation," Chekhov invariably starts from the criterion of the value of human life. Preserving human life is the measure of everything in Chekhov, as his conclusions remind us— from Ivanov's suicide to Firs's "They forgot about me" in his final play, *The Cherry Orchard*. Chekhov's humanism revealed itself in his purely artistic searchings.

Thus *Ivanov* is Chekhov's response to a situation that was suggested directly by the era of the 1880s: mass disillusionment with past enthusiasms and a correspondingly hasty conversion to new ones; the collapse of authorities and doctrines; unpreparedness for practical steps to carry out accepted programs, etc. By analyzing the most commonplace and mass forms of consciousness, Chekhov is trying to capture in dramatic form the most general errors and mistakes "in the realm of thought." To say that in *Ivanov* the author intended to support or discredit a specific trend in the social thought of his time would be to play down both the socio-historical and the universal note in the play.

Chekhov was studying the consciousness of an epoch, moving from its individual manifestations to broad generalizations. Portraying the characters at a certain time in society provides a specific framework for the manifestations of this consciousness. But the "Ivanov situation" is not confined within the boundaries of Chekhov's epoch only.

To the reflections, searchings, and illusions of an "average man" of his time, Chekhov attached an important universal meaning. He transferred attention to the average man not because he was in favor of becoming reconciled to the trivial everyday world (the accusation made by his critics) but in order to study how the most general questions of human consciousness may be interpreted in the broadest possible context.

*Ivanov* developed in many ways from earlier stories in which Chekhov had placed his characters in similar situations: the situation of discovery, making the transition from "it seemed" to "it turned out that" ("The Hired Pianist," "The Chorus Girl," "A Nightmare," "An Unpleasant Incident," etc.); the situation in which characters do not understand each other ("Enemies," "Good People"); the situation of the dispute that leads nowhere and the sermon that fails to persuade ("No Comment" and later "Lights"), and of changing moods and convictions ("On the Road"). At the close of the 1880s they are all concentrated in the "Ivanov situation."

But many things were tried in the play for the first time. The discovery in *Ivanov* of the "epistemological" type of hero, dramatic event, conflict, and genre was to have far-reaching consequences for the whole of Chekhov's approach to playwriting.

## 9

# Chekhov's Debt to Medicine:
# The Zakharin School

In the latter 1880s another fundamental characteristic of Chekhov's view of the world, his approach to life's raw material, begins to make its appearance.

As "Lights," "An Unpleasant Incident," and "The Nervous Breakdown" had shown, it is not an event in itself but our knowledge of it that becomes a subject for analysis in its own right. Man in Chekhov's world is the comprehending self, the self orienting in reality.

But noting the simple fact of Chekhov's loyalty to his epistemological theme, to examining failures of comprehension and "false conceptions," does not go far enough. The various kinds of delusions he examines tend toward a clear center, clustering around one basic form of delusion.

Time and again Chekhov comes back to the theme of *false generalizations* and *stereotyped solutions*. In his logically relentless undermining of illusions having to do with "knowledge in the realm of thought," he was primarily concerned to point to the unsoundness of "commonplaces" and generalized solutions, constantly bringing them into conflict with specific "instances," with individual, isolated events.

This applied to "Lights": trying to derive a universal moral from a highly individual human event was unjustified. It applied to "An Unpleasant Incident": the hero found himself in a situation where conventional solutions were "ridiculous." It applied to "The Nervous Breakdown," where generalized ideas prove bankrupt: the stereotyped formulas offered by medicine are as powerless to relieve a particular individual's "tears and despair" as the formulas advanced in books, journals, and the theater are to save fallen women.

The doctor in the last chapter of "The Nervous Breakdown" is portrayed by Chekhov almost as sarcastically as the "celebrated doctor" whom Tolstoy portrays in Chapter 4 of *The Death of Ivan Ilyich*. Tolstoy is nauseated by the celebrated doctor's certainty that "we know beyond a doubt how to arrange everything in exactly the same way for everyone"—that certainty to be found among doctors and lawyers that general solutions may be applied to any individual instance.

But Tolstoy, while pointing out the pretentious claims of doctors and magistrates to universal solutions, always offers in exchange moral and religious solutions of his own that are just as universally binding. While rejecting generalization in particular instances, he does not reject the principle of generalization itself but vigorously affirms it. Denying what is generally accepted, Tolstoy affirms what is universally binding.

Chekhov says that you cannot apply any of the well-known general solutions to the questions that confront his heroes. He denies both generally accepted and universally binding solutions—the principle of generalization as such. General categories are contradicted by specific instances; generally accepted standpoints turn out to be false; no one truth will satisfy everyone—these are the conclusions to be drawn from "Lights," "An Unpleasant Incident," and "The Nervous Breakdown."

Chekhov's conscious and enduring preoccupation with the problem of the general and the individual is primarily a reflection of the lessons he learned within the walls of Moscow University from his professor in the medical faculty, G. A. Zakharin, and his scientific approach.

It is generally accepted that Chekhov owed to medicine such features of his writing as scientifically based materialism, objectivity, and keenness of observation, and that he was better qualified than anyone before him in Russian literature to highlight the symptoms of an illness and its course. (Apropos of "The Nervous Breakdown" he wrote proudly in a letter: "I described spiritual anguish correctly, according to all the rules of psychiatric science.")[1]

But it was not only this general medical experience that formed part of Chekhov's equipment as a writer. Zakharin taught his students how to apply the scientific method they had acquired not only in their medical practice but "in every other field of practical activity in the real world."[2] It was the methodology of the Zakharin school, the ability "to think medically," that was significant for Chekhov. Zakharin's ideas, assimilated and reinterpreted, became one of his main principles of artistic construction.

The Zakharin school of medicine was an attempt to overcome the defects of therapeutic science in the second half of the nineteenth century, defects both in the theory of illness and diagnosis and in practical methods of examining and treating patients. L. V. Popov, a well-known clinician and contemporary of Chekhov, analyzing current medical knowledge, noted "how much ballast had built up over the centuries of sub-scientific data obtained by very imperfect methods of research," and pointed out that in the latest nomenclature of diseases all kinds of different underlying principles were "mixed up and confused," with the result that the very "classifications and terminology of diseases frequently do not correspond to the actual state of affairs."[3]

The average doctor responded to this situation either with growing skepticism ("They think I'm a doctor," Chebutykin admits in *Three Sisters*, "that I can treat all kinds of diseases, when really I don't know the first thing about it") or with stereotyped methods of treatment "based on ready-made textbook symptoms."[4] Chekhov

1. *Letters*, 3:68.
2. G. A. Zakharin, *Klinicheskiye lektsii*, no. 1 (Moscow, 1889), p. 10.
3. L. V. Popov, *Klinicheskiye lektsii*, no. 2 (St. Petersburg, 1896), p. 41.
4. M. M. Volkov, *Klinicheskiye etyudy* no. 1 (St. Petersburg, 1904), pp. 3–4.

describes an example of the latter in the final chapter of "The Nervous Breakdown." The psychiatrist to whom Vasilyev is taken by his friends frames his questions to the patient in such a way as to make the case fit one of the general diagnostic categories that he knows about. He asks the questions "that diligent doctors usually ask"; with regard to the evil of prostitution that is making his patient suffer, he talks "as if he'd long ago settled all those questions for himself." His self-confidence in prescribing treatment is matched only by its inappropriateness to the specific situation: "on one prescription there was potassium bromide and on the other morphine. . . . All this Vasilyev had been prescribed before!"

To counteract both medical skepticism and stereotyped methods of treatment, Zakharin proposed his own method, which, according to one medical historian, "led to a sharp rise in the standards of clinical medicine at that time and was subsequently adopted throughout Russia."[5]

Basic to Zakharin's teaching was the rigorous individualization of each case of disease and the uncompromising rejection of stereotypes in treatment. There were no illnesses "in general," there were specific sick people: to this basic proposition Zakharin attached special importance. Do not treat the *illness* as if it were identical for everyone, he declared, treat the *patient* with all his individual peculiarities. The clinical picture must be defined precisely, i.e., "very specifically, with all its distinctive features and usually its complications (simple cases of a disease are seen far less frequently than complicated ones)."[6] "To avoid falling into routine diagnosis," he taught, "a doctor must indicate all the peculiarities of the cases he encounters—he must individualize."[7]

In furthering individual therapy, i.e, treating the person, not the illness, Zakharin developed his own scientifically based method of questioning and examining the patient in a way that would define his individual peculiarities very accurately and allow for the diagno-

5. A. G. Lushnikov, *Klinika vnutrennikh boleznei v SSSR* (Moscow, 1972), p. 150.
6. G. A. Zakharin, *Klinicheskiye lektsii*, no. 2, (Moscow, 1889), p. 5.
7. G. A. Zakharin, op. cit., no. 1, p. 10.

sis of diseases without clearly marked external symptoms. Paying special attention to how patients perceive their own condition became another important principle of the Zakharin school of medicine. Emphasis was placed on "the most detailed study of patients, on turning the questioning of them into a highly skilled art."[8]

Chekhov, who placed Zakharin on a level in medicine with Tolstoy in literature,[9] acquired from his teacher this "method," this ability "to think medically,"[10]and worked to develop it further. He is known to have intended at one time to deliver a course of university lectures designed "to draw his audience as deeply as possible into the world of the patient's subjective feelings,"[11] i.e., to juxtapose objective data about an illness with the subjective anamnesis.

But these scientific principles also had a powerful influence on the formation of Chekhov's writing methods. The principle of individualizing each separate event became one of his basic artistic principles.

Chekhov describes on more than one occasion how the scientific method may be applied to the most complex human phenomena. Especially important in this respect are two stories, one written at the beginning of his creative life, "A Story Without an Ending" (1886), and one at the end, "About Love" (1898).

"A Story Without an Ending" is about an attempted suicide. Its hero, Vasilyev (the same name as the hero of "The Nervous Breakdown") tries to shoot himself and misses. Later he has a conversation by chance with a stranger, who is a doctor and writer. They touch upon a problem directly related to literature: how to explain and describe in a story or novel an event like an attempted suicide, avoiding stereotypes and "commonplaces," and conveying the event with complete authenticity.

At first glance the explanation seems obvious: the poor man shot

8. G. A. Zakharin, op. cit., 2nd ed., no. 4 (Moscow, 1894), p. 206.

9. *Letters*, 4:362.

10. *Letters*, 3:37.

11. G. I. Rossolimo, "Vospominaniya o Chekhove" in *Chekhov v vospominaniyakh sovremennikov* (Moscow, 1954), p. 589.

himself because his beloved wife had just died. But Vasilyev himself rejects this explanation as too general and superficial.

"Any moment now," he says, "you'll start asking me what causes prompted me to suicide! . . . I admit, I don't understand it myself. . . . There are standard newspaper clichés like 'hopeless love' or 'desperate poverty,' but *the reasons are unknown.* . . . Man can never understand the psychological subtleties of suicide! How can you talk of causes? Today a cause makes me grab my revolver, tomorrow that very same cause doesn't seem worth a kopeck." Later, speaking of the only acceptable route to understanding, he says: "Everything probably depends on *the state of the individual at a given time.* . . . Take me, for example. Half an hour ago I passionately desired death, but now, with the candle burning and you sitting beside me, I'm not even thinking of my final hour. Try explaining that change! Have I become richer? Has my wife come back from the dead? Has this light or the presence of a stranger had an effect on me? . . . And it doesn't say much for the heroes of your novels if a trifle like a candle can turn the whole drama upside down! . . . Half an hour ago I tried to shoot myself, now I'm striking attitudes. . . . Try explaining that if you can!" [italics added].

The argument used by Zakharin to persuade his students of the individualization method is extended here to cover the diagnoses of any human phenomena that literature undertakes to explain.

Here too we have an illustration of how the main event (suicide) and "a trifle" (the candle) are artistically related. The candle is not simply "an incidental detail." Chekhov is individualizing as fully as possible a phenomenon that can only be understood and explained by taking into account the totality of accompanying processes and phenomena. The principle of individualization is closely connected with his main theme of seeking answers, trying to understand, orienting oneself in the real world.

The heroes of Chekhov's late story, "About Love," also talk about the impossibility of containing human psychology within overgeneral, self-evident schemes, and how complex and unique each event in life is.

"What makes people fall in love?" said Alyokhin.

"Why couldn't Pelageya have fallen for someone more suited to her mentally and physically? If personal happiness is important in love, why did it have to be that ugly mug Nikanor, as everyone round here calls him? *No one knows, and you can interpret the subject how you like.* So far only one incontrovertible truth has been said about love, 'this is a great mystery'—everything else said and written about it doesn't solve anything but simply poses questions that still have to be answered. *The explanation that would seem to fit one case doesn't fit a dozen others.* The best we can do, in my opinion, is *to explain each case separately*, without trying to generalize. We must *treat each individual case in isolation*, as the doctors say."[12] [italics added]

Chekhov shows in these stories how individualization is appropriate whenever you need to explain the causes leading up to a particular event in life, or to convey it in the most complex, authentic form. These were problems he addressed and sought to resolve in his writing. The scientific viewpoint became one of the main formative ideas behind his writing.

There are no illnesses "in general," there are specific sick people. In studying life, do not approach it with preconceived and supposedly universal ideas; look at the actual person and you are bound to find something in his life that is not explained by these theories and renders them far from universal. As the stories of 1888 show, these are Chekhov's starting points in transferring individualization from medicine to literature. The stories and tales of the latter 1880s became a school of their own for Chekhov, a course in individualization.

In denying the existence of illnesses "in general" and proposing that each case be treated in isolation, what Zakharin succeeded in doing, of course, was to combat the diseases themselves, and with

---

12. "To learn how to individualize each case of disease that presents itself . . . is the best way of becoming a genuine, fully scientific doctor," L. V. Popov wrote in 1896 (*Klinicheskiye lektsii*, no. 2, p. 23).

huge success. Chekhov too was posing and seeking to resolve problems that the whole of classical Russian literature had posed and tried to resolve before him. But in his method of resolving those problems, in "individualizing each case," Chekhov is unique.

Without studying Chekhov's highly original method of individualization you cannot properly understand the significance of his work, for he applies the principle to ideas, to individual psychology, and to the description of events.

A final point: Chekhov's epistemological approach to portraying human beings and phenomena, and his principle of "individualizing each separate case," did not, of course, originate only in his medical training. There were other reasons, social and literary, that conditioned Chekhov's special interest in the problem of man's "orientation" in the world, and his specific answer to the problems of the general and particular.

But before considering them, let us examine one more work from the end of the 1880s, the tale "A Dreary Story," at the center of which lies this very problem of the "general idea" and its relation to human existence.

# The Problem of the "General Idea": "A Dreary Story" (1889)

In "A Dreary Story," as in *Ivanov*, Chekhov treats a situation in which the hero has passed from one stage in life to another, and is trying to grasp what has happened to him and why his life has changed for the worse. Its hero, Nikolai Stepanovich, is a far more significant figure than Ivanov (who is simply "a good man"), and his long career as a celebrated scientist has brought many benefits to science and to society. But what interests Chekhov in both cases is the same: how a person perceives the situation in which he finds himself, the correlation between the true and the false in that perception, and how the hero and his situation are perceived by the people around him.

Like Ivanov, Nikolai Stepanovich is prepared to deny the previous meaning of his life and to dismiss as valueless what earlier seemed important to him. Only the specific form of the reevaluation differs. In the case of Nikolai Stepanovich, his epistemological reflections lead him to the conclusion that his life and activity have always been missing a "general idea."

In the overall structure of the tale, this notion of the "general idea" is only one of the stages in the hero's reflections and attitude toward life. To begin with, he is in the grip of what he calls "Arakcheyev" (malevolent) thoughts (Chapters 1–4). Then the presentiment that death is near fills him with sudden dread (Chapter 5, the "sparrow night"). This leads straight to the next stage, that of complete indifference (start of Chapter 6). Finally, at the very end of his memoir, the hero "noted in himself" the absence of a "general idea."

Each successive stage must overcome the one before. In a Chekhov character, as we know, this kind of struggle will go on as long as the character remains alive. As in "The Nervous Breakdown," by following the course of the hero's thoughts and juxtaposing each new conclusion with its predecessor in the chain, Chekhov enables us to see that each stage is transitional and not absolute.

So one should never lose sight of the fact that in "A Dreary Story" the conclusion about the "general idea" takes its place alongside a series of other mental states through which the narrator-hero passes. But the overwhelming majority of critical interpretations of this story have always concentrated on this last link in what is in principle a continuing chain. From the start, critics of the most varied kinds have looked upon the old professor's words about the need for a "general idea" as the author's own conclusion.

Approached in this way, "A Dreary Story" is seen as a variation on the theme of Tolstoy's *The Death of Ivan Ilyich*. "God" is that "general idea" whose absence from his life is belatedly mourned by Tolstoy's hero once his eyes have been opened. The tale is an undisguised and passionate appeal by the author to the millions of people like Ivan Ilyich to fill their lives with "God," "the light," and "love" before it is too late.

Like Tolstoy, Chekhov depicts a man who is appalled by the realization that his life contains no conscious unifying principle. But whereas Tolstoy generalizes and regards his conclusions as binding on everyone, Chekhov individualizes the problem of the "general idea." As in "Lights," the author's aim is not to endorse the conclusion that his narrator reaches but to examine the circumstances that force a man of contemporary awareness to arrive at a conclusion of that kind.

How is the problem of the "general idea" examined in "A Dreary Story"?

The tale is told in the first person, leaving no room for authorial commentary. Where the author parts company from his hero is revealed on those occasions when the latter contradicts either himself, objective logic, or the facts that we learn from his story. Such inconsistency ("evasiveness")[1] is indeed to be found in Nikolai Stepanovich's judgments.

Thus Chekhov shows that the professor himself is well aware that "commonplaces" are worthless in science, literature, and criticism, and that general stereotyped methods of treatment are equally useless in medicine. He frequently rejects generalizations that do not apply to a concrete situation, and can be said to reject "general ideas" quite explicitly. (The whole context of the story makes it clear in what sense the concept of a "general idea" is being understood: as a conviction, faith, or scheme of knowledge that is held *in common* with other people and shared with them, and that remains *constant* throughout the different stages of a person's life.)

So, when at the very end of his memoir the hero says that only a "general idea" can save one from despair and give meaning to a human life, this looks like an inconsistency, an "evasion," a fear of acknowledging in his own case a stern truth with which as a scientist he is perfectly familiar.

Here, for example, is Nikolai Stepanovich reflecting that no "general idea" can really be of any help to Katya in her hopeless position: "It is easy to say 'work,' 'give everything you own to the poor,' or 'know thyself,' and because these things are so easy to say, I don't know how to answer her." These beautiful "general ideas" will no doubt save someone and fill someone's life with meaning, but to this particular person (Katya's individuality has been fully defined by the time of this episode) they are completely inapplicable. Nikolai Stepanovich considers it an objective law that general solutions do not apply to individual cases:

My colleagues the therapists, when they're giving practical instruction, advise their students to "treat each individual case in isola-

1. "These reflections," Chekhov wrote to his editor Pleshcheyev, "characterize my hero, his mood and his evasiveness" (*Letters*, 3:252).

tion." You need only follow this advice to realize that the remedies recommended in the textbooks as the best and as standard practice turn out to be completely unsuitable in individual cases. The same is true of psychological illnesses.

Here we recognize the individualizing approach that was championed by Chekhov's idol, Zakharin, in medicine and by Chekhov himself in literature.

To individualize is to see in each separate case a unique phenomenon to which generalizations do not apply. This is perfectly clear to Nikolai Stepanovich in relation to Katya. But in relation to himself?

Or take another example. In Chapter 3 the professor is listening to attacks by Mikhail Fyodorovich (his colleague from the literature faculty) and Katya on "the younger generation." He is irritated by their talk, for "the charges were unfounded and based on such worn-out old commonplaces and bugbears as degeneracy, lack of ideals, or glorifying the past." (The choice of examples here may well be deliberate, since these were just the sort of charges leveled against contemporary literature and against Chekhov as its most typical representative by the populist critic Mikhailovsky, who contrasted the spiritual impoverishment of the "children" with the "general ideas" of the "fathers.")

Nikolai Stepanovich has his own reasons for being dissatisfied with modern youth, but he thinks you need to bring specific charges against them, without recourse to "a fog of commonplaces," beginning with those that obviously do not fit into any general categories (students smoke and drink too much, they marry late, etc.) and going on to more substantial ones: failing to help fellow students who are starving, being ignorant of foreign languages, not speaking good Russian, being ill-informed, preferring to remain in junior positions until the age of forty without showing any independence and initiative, etc. While listing specific symptoms of what is wrong with the present generation of students, Nikolai Stepanovich regards it as a mistake to make sweeping generalizations—for example, to extend these symptoms to all future generations or to see them as indications of irreversible student degeneracy.

Nikolai Stepanovich's portrait of the present generation of students is a model of individualization, in contrast to the "commonplaces," the stereotype, in the picture given by Mikhail Fyodorovich and Katya.

From these and other examples throughout the tale we can see that Chekhov's professor handles the individualizing approach very confidently, applying it to a variety of phenomena in life, and consciously contrasting it with the kind of approach that deals in "commonplaces." Only on that one occasion, when he ought to have applied the approach to himself and realized that a "general idea" was no solution for him either, did he fail to be consistent and in his search for salvation resort to the thought of a "general idea."

The hero's hope of salvation through a "general idea" is therefore at odds with his whole intellectual makeup. Not only that. From it stems the old scientist's false assessment of his path through life.

The past in "A Dreary Story" throws light on everything in the present; the hero's thoughts and judgments of today are corrected by his life of yesterday. Nikolai Stepanovich perceives the past as something alien: his fame, he thinks, has let him down. In other words, in solving the problems of life and death confronting him in his final months, neither fame, nor reputation, nor achievements are of any help. But for the reader, this psychological alienation of an old man from his "name" and past life does not cancel out the significance of that life or the "name" it has created. At one point Nikolai Stepanovich remarks: "These last months of my life, waiting for death, seem to me far longer than the rest of my life put together." In the same way, we realize, the significance of the thoughts arising during these months has become unnaturally inflated in his mind in comparison with the significance of his life as a whole— "that talented artistic composition."

This man, clearly, is very far from having lived his life in vain; some of his judgments may be wrong, but his scientific achievements are of indisputable value. And as Chekhov shows, so long as this remarkable individual and outstanding scientist was able to lead a fully active life and engage in useful creative work, he saw no need for any special "general idea." His whole life was evidently governed by the consciousness of serving humanity and progress through science.

Only when confronted by death, by the illness that brought him down from the creative scientific heights to a more prosaic level, at which the dozens of threads linking talent to the ordinary world were laid bare, did he feel in need of some kind of redeeming suprapersonal dogma. The "general idea" that he would now like to possess must be able to justify his past life and reconcile him to death while enabling him to act as spiritual adviser to ordinary people like Liza and Katya who are making a mess of their lives.

Nikolai Stepanovich does not appear to see that he has already tested two kinds of "general ideas"—an "Arakcheyev" (malevolent) attitude and indifference, both of which he comes to reject, thereby earning the reader's sympathy. From our knowledge of him, let us try to think of any other "general ideas" that might have served his purpose.

As we have seen, Nikolai Stepanovich wastes no time on precepts like "work," "know thyself," or "give everything you own to the poor": their unacceptability is self-evident. Both populism and the teachings of Tolstoy are alien to him, as they were to Chekhov. Nor could Nikolai Stepanovich have been satisfied by, say, the Stoic philosophy of Marcus Aurelius (his favorite author and Chekhov's too): "Know thyself is a splendid and useful piece of advice; the only trouble is, the ancients never thought of showing us how to put it into practice."

Also alien to him is the doctrine of Christian resignation arrived at by his older contemporary, the celebrated surgeon N. I. Pirogov, whose memoirs had been published in 1884. Any "general idea" to be acquired at the cost of surrendering oneself to a force hostile to science is out of the question for Nikolai Stepanovich. The "god of a living man" referred to by the hero of "A Dreary Story" is completely different from the God of *The Death of Ivan Ilyich.*

Nikolai Stepanovich describes himself as a man who is "more interested in what happens to the bone marrow than in the final goal of creation." But that strictly scientific optimism on which, for example, the works of another remarkable contemporary scientist, I. I. Mechnikov, were based, and which was shared by the hero of "A Dreary Story," could not rise above "all external influences"—the sufferings, grief, and doubts of a living person.

That exhausts the range of "general ideas" that were available and known to Chekhov and his hero.

No "general idea," therefore—if by that term we understand a philosophy or faith that equips one with a single program of behavior for use in every situation in life, and answering one's higher intellectual and moral requirements—could have satisfied the professor as Chekhov portrays him. In "A Dreary Story" the craving for a "general idea" expresses the psychological need of someone who is sick and suffering, and who finds that the problems of life that suddenly overtake him are more than he can cope with. There are Chekhov stories about overcoming illusion, and stories about submitting to it ("The Boredom of Life," for example). "A Dreary Story" is about the impossibility of a man of Nikolai Stepanovich's type being satisfied by any illusion.

To prove that in "A Dreary Story" Chekhov was expressing his own as well as his hero's longing for a "general idea," critics sometimes quote from one of his letters: "My story . . . ends with something that has been known for a long time, namely, that an intelligent life without a definite worldview is no life at all, but a burden and a nightmare."[2] But this letter refers not to "A Dreary Story" but to some unknown work, perhaps unfinished for the very reason that Chekhov could not prove something that had "been known for a long time." "A Dreary Story" embodies a far more tragic ideological and artistic conception: subjectively, for a particular individual, life without a definite worldview is "a burden and a nightmare," and at the same time it is impossible for a person of that kind to settle for any "general idea." The sense of "a burden and a

2. *Letters*, 3:80.

nightmare" is thereby intensified. What we see is not something that has "been known for a long time" but the genuine complexity of the problem.

Some critics not only took the hero's opinion about a "general idea" to be central to the story but also pointed out what "general idea" Chekhov had in mind. "A Dreary Story" was seen as a hidden call to "active struggle," "a protest against the attitude of indifference to social evil," merely camouflaged to outwit the censors. According to this approach, Chekhov was contrasting "educated society" and the image of a "man of the people" . . . Nikolai the university porter! From what has already been said, however, it should be clear that it was not Chekhov's intention in "A Dreary Story" to endorse the need for a "general idea."

Chekhov's tale is not written *in defense* of the "general idea"; but does that mean it *denies the importance* of the "general idea"? Certainly not. Chekhov's position cannot be reduced to one of skepticism and relativism. What the tale rejects are not "general ideas" in themselves but the tendency to make them absolute and to overgeneralize.

The reader sees that Nikolai Stepanovich is struggling with contradictions and problems that are not imaginary but very real: his whole life has been spent in the lecture hall teaching, but he does not know how to teach those who live alongside him; all his glorious past cannot relieve the pain of the present or halt the approach of death. Indifference to everyday matters has helped him devote his whole life to scientific work, but because of it he has failed as a father to see that his daughter became a complete stranger to him. And (who can deny it?) a "general idea" does indeed help its possessor to live confidently and die peacefully, in the knowledge of having fulfilled one's duty.

The critic M. M. Smirnov, analyzing where Chekhov and his hero diverge in "A Dreary Story," comes to the entirely valid conclusion that the professor's thought about lacking a "general idea" is "merely symptomatic of someone undergoing a crisis, no more, no less; it is not, of course, a literal expression of the story's idea."[3] But in putting the emphasis on the ways in which Chekhov shows up "the unsoundness of Nikolai Stepanovich's thinking," Smirnov ignores the other side of the author's position in "A Dreary Story": Chekhov's genuine involvement in the problems that his hero is trying to solve—an involvement which makes us feel that this tale is Chekhov's confession, the confession of a generation. The hero may be mistaken in his conclusion, but the importance of the problem is not thereby reduced: this applied to "An Unpleasant Incident," "The Nervous Breakdown," and *Ivanov*. "A Dreary Story" likewise incorporates two elements: the impossibility of being satisfied by any conceivable "general ideas," and the craving for "real truth," for an unknown "general idea."

Important and close to him though the problem was, Chekhov does not come out in favor of any "general idea" but leaves the question emphatically open: there is no dogma or faith that could attract the author and his hero, and it is more correct, Chekhov believes, to depict the "vicious circle" in which the hero found himself (see his letter to Suvorin of October 17, 1889).[4] The author sees it as his artistic task to describe as authentically as possible the circumstances giving rise to and accompanying the opinions uttered by his hero. In other words, he individualizes—attempts, that is, to pose the question of the "general idea" correctly.

"A Dreary Story" describes a phenomenon no less socially significant and painful than that in "The Nervous Breakdown," and one that was especially characteristic of its time. Three similar scenes from the tale show how all-pervasive the phenomenon was.

1. Nikolai Stepanovich is complaining to Katya (Chapter 3): "But I'm spoiling the finale. I'm drowning, I run round to you for help, and all you can say is: go ahead, drown, that's how it ought to be."

3. M. M. Smirnov, "Geroi i avtor v 'Skuchnoi istorii'" in *V tvorcheskoi laboratorii Chekhova* (Moscow, 1974), p. 219.
4. *Letters*, 3:265–267.

2. On the "sparrow night," Liza is imploring her father to help her ("I don't know what's wrong with me. . . . I feel terrible!") But he is "feeling terrible" himself that night and thinks:

> But what can I do? Nothing at all. The girl is deeply troubled by something, but I've no idea what, and all I can do is mumble: "There now, there. . . . It'll pass. . . . Try to sleep."

3. In the hotel room at Kharkov, Katya is making her last appeal for help to Nikolai Stepanovich: "I can't go on living like this! I can't! For God's sake, tell me quickly, straightaway: what am I to do? Tell me." To which the reply is: "Honestly, Katya, I've no idea. . . . Would you like some lunch?"

Not one of these people has a "general idea," no one can point out the right path to anyone else. Their plight is similar, says Chekhov. That was why he called his story a "dreary" one.

But is Chekhov not guilty here of betraying the principle of individualization, since he is writing about such an all-pervasive phenomenon? Is this not a stereotyped diagnosis, the same for everyone? No, here too one should see individualization, not generalization.

The unacceptability of existing "general ideas" which have been discredited by corrosive criticism: this is how the question relates to people of Nikolai Stepanovich's type and stature. "Even Mikhailovsky says that all the pieces on the board are muddled up these days," as Chekhov had remarked ironically in his letter about *Ivanov*.[5]

But the question of the "general idea" is quite different in relation to other characters. Pyotr Ignatyevich, for example, the "plodding old carthorse," does possess a "general idea" and is perfectly happy with it: he "knows the purpose of life and is a complete stranger to the doubts and disillusions that make more talented heads turn grey." Very different again is the way in which the "general idea" applies to Katya and Liza, where it depends on their indi-

---

5. *Letters*, 3:111.

vidual natures. In demanding instructions about what to do from Nikolai Stepanovich "quickly, straightaway," Katya is hoping for a miracle. She and Liza, finding themselves in the most complicated situation of their lives, need a strong authority in whom they are prepared to have blind faith. The saving deception of a "general idea" might have delayed the outcome of their personal dramas. They throw themselves on Nikolai Stepanovich, but he has no one to turn to. He finds himself in a crisis situation six months before his death—they do so at the start of their lives.

This is the "individualization of each separate case" as applied to literature.

Let us return to the comparison between "A Dreary Story" and *The Death of Ivan Ilyich.* In creating a story about the need for a "general idea," Tolstoy started from the conviction that in the "absence of God" the life of *each* person was "not right"; for *each* person's life to make sense, it must contain God. Chekhov is showing that in the life of a *given* person, the question of the "general idea" arose in certain *given* circumstances; in other circumstances, for other people, the question would have arisen and been resolved quite differently.

What distinguishes the two works is not simply that Chekhov offers different ideological answers to the kinds of problem that Tolstoy raises. He also offers new principles for seeing the real world and its problems.

Chekhov sees in each person not a vehicle for confirming this or that ideology or dogma, but an individual world whose contradictions always require their own unique resolution. The opposite of the Tolstoyan generalization is the Chekhovian idiograph, the individualization of each separate case.

This method presupposed that life is too complex to be contained within any solution that claims to be universally applicable. It also enabled Chekhov to depict the natural laws of real life that were inaccessible by any other route.

# I I

# Judging Other People:
# "The Duel" (1891)

At the end of the 1880s, Chekhov was not only having to defend his original new principles against those who wanted
him to adopt well-tried traditional ways of raising and discussing problems (see his letters apropos of "Mire," "Lights," and
"Thieves"); he was also having to overcome his own doubts. In his
letters of 1887–1889 he frequently wonders whether he is right to
offer his readers a picture of "life as it really is" without at the same
time giving them a stock of concrete ideas that might have some
practical application. It was only through contact with the real
world that he succeeded in overcoming these doubts. His creative
convictions were to be confirmed and strengthened by his visit in
1890 to Sakhalin.

In his book *The Island of Sakhalin*, and in other Sakhalin works,
the principles that had become established in Chekhov by the end
of the 1880s were extended still further. The book on Sakhalin ex-
posed not only the horrors of penal servitude but the lies about it,
disseminated both by official propaganda and also by superficial
"denunciatory" literature. Once again Chekhov is interested not
only in phenomena but in how people judge those phenomena; he is

interested in exposing general illusions and general stereotyped solutions to problems, whether these are handed down by the authorities or are used voluntarily and deliberately by society as a means of assuaging its conscience.

General indifference and a refusal to see what the hero saw as a blatant problem had, after all, been one of the main reasons for the suffering of the student Vasilyev in "The Nervous Breakdown." The evil that had taken root in Moscow's S-ev Alley and the evil of Sakhalin are not only related ontologically; in both instances society had a "false idea" about them. *The Island of Sakhalin*, like "The Nervous Breakdown," showed that "the situation was far worse than could have been imagined." Exposing the general—and for that reason simplified—ideas about the penal island was to be the main inspiration behind Chekhov's book and the whole of his visit.

It seemed to "educated society" that all the blame for Sakhalin could be put on "red-nosed prison governors," but it turned out that "the governors are not the guilty ones, we all are."[1] Society had grown used to evil and indifferent to it, reassuring itself with "general" answers. Not even protest was of much value.

The problem of protest made its first appearance in Chekhov's work after Sakhalin. Pavel Ivanych, the hero of the first post-Sakhalin story, "Gusev" (1890), refers to himself as "protest incarnate." For many critics, what he says is equivalent to Chekhov's own protest: the author, they claim, intended to use Pavel Ivanych as the "mouthpiece" for his denunciation, and this is confirmed by the hero's sincerity and the indisputable justice of almost all his attacks and accusations.

It would certainly seem logical to suppose that after visiting Sakhalin, Chekhov would write a work of denunciation in which he glorified the protester. But the logic of that kind of critical assumption is flatly contradicted by the logic of the story itself. On his way back from Sakhalin, Chekhov wrote a story showing that while

1. *Letters*, 4:32.

protest is justified, the "ardent protester" is a narrow, unintelligent man who deals in general categories of "denunciation" and is essentially indifferent to the actual individuals alongside him.

On Sakhalin, Chekhov witnessed the terrifying extent of the evil prevailing in the world; but what he also realized was how carefully thought out and responsible any word of protest against that evil must be. In *The Island of Sakhalin* he mocked the emptiness and futility of denunciation for denunciation's sake, and expressed himself even more definitely in that sense in "Gusev."[2]

Chekhov's long story "The Duel" (1891) is also a response to Sakhalin, though neither its events nor its setting or characters would seem to have anything in common with the island. But a careful reading shows that it has a "criminal," it has laws and standards that he infringes, and it has a "prosecuting counsel." The basic conflict in "The Duel," the argument between the two antagonists, Layevsky and von Koren, is built around the problem of judging human behavior correctly, and in particular of judging the unlawful life of a weak person. It was on Sakhalin that Chekhov saw how claims to reform humanity might lead to disasters for specific people, and how the categorical and unconditional application of such universal concepts as "the law," "crime," "sentence," etc. to individual lives might result in the multiplication of evil instead of its destruction.

In the argument, Chekhov brings into conflict two people of obviously unequal worth. Layevsky is weak-willed and hysterical, and has built his life on a perpetual lie. The young zoologist von Koren, a man of clear mind and cold will, is an adherent of Social Darwinism and the ideas of Herbert Spencer ("I'm a zoologist or sociologist, which is one and the same thing"). He "prosecutes" Layevsky in the name of moral law, believing that society should be protected

---

2. See V. B. Kataev, "Avtor v 'Ostrove Sakhalin' i rasskaze 'Gusev' " in *V tvorcheskoi laboratorii Chekhova* (Moscow, 1974), pp. 232–252.

against the corrupting influence of people like him, and that in the interests of humankind the "sickly, scrofulous tribe" of Layevskys should be exterminated.

If we look beyond Chekhov's artistic world to his memoirs and letters, there can be no doubt that Chekhov had people like Layevsky in mind when he spoke of the "rascally spirit to be found in your petty, hopelessly incorrigible brand of average Russian intellectual."[3] There can also be no doubt that in his basic features von Koren belongs to that group of "heroic individuals" like Przhevalsky, Livingstone, Stanley, and Miklukho-Maklai, to whom Chekhov dedicated his famous journalistic article.[4] But in Chekhov's *artistic* world these two human types were differently related.

Having apparently blackened Layevsky's character, Chekhov nevertheless at the end makes him undergo a great change as a result of various shocks, and begin leading a new life. Von Koren, on the other hand, is not shown performing the heroic deed of which he is undoubtedly capable: he is simply given the chance to admit his mistake and sadly to acknowledge that life is absurd and incomprehensible. The critic A. Gornfel'd saw the disparity between the assessments of these two contemporary types in life and in art as one of the riddles in Chekhov. To solve it he had to attribute to Chekhov a special sympathy for people who are "weak and helpless" but "conscientious and trying to make sense of their lives"[5]—in other words, he was still seeing Layevsky as Chekhov's representative of the "norm," the way things ought to be.

There is indeed a difference between how Layevsky and von Koren are depicted, but it is of a "technical" nature and concerns the distribution in the story of "points of view."

Throughout "The Duel" only the "defendants," Layevsky and Nadezhda Fyodorovna, are granted the right to constant infor-

---

3. *Letters*, 3:212–213.
4. *Works*, 16:236–237.
5. A. Gornfel'd, *Chekhovskiye finaly.* *"Krasnaya nov'"* (Moscow, 1939), no. 8–9, pp. 289–300.

mation about the motives for their actions, and about their own self-assessments, self-justifications, and self-accusations. Von Koren acquires the right only in Chapter 21, the concluding chapter.

Previously von Koren has played the role throughout of prosecuting counsel, and the whole of the narration has consisted of evidence, addressed in the first instance to people like himself, and in the end disproving what has seemed to him an absolute and universal truth—or, more accurately, convincing him of the conclusion that he eventually comes to ("no one knows the real truth"). Once having reached that conclusion, which the author sees as the only acceptable position, he acquires the right to be depicted like "anyone else," i.e., from within, with the same doubts, warmth, sadness, etc. that "anyone else" has.

For Chekhov, the arrangement of "points of view" in the narration, like the plot and its denouement, are primarily arguments within the debate, a debate to which he attached cardinal importance. Why does he conclude the debate between his characters in the way that he does?

The conclusions of Tolstoy and Dostoevsky bring the hero to a state of resurrection in which the light of truth—final, supra-personal, eternal, capable of moving generations and millions—is revealed to him. The scales fall from his eyes, and the past is seen to have been a delusion; he arrives inevitably at the truth as a result of particular determining factors in his character.

Chekhov does not regard the change that has happened to his hero as a transition from darkness to light, from ignorance of the truth to its acquisition. There is no apotheosis of the "new" Layevsky; in the conclusion he cuts a very pitiful figure. It is simply that this man has begun to lead a new way of life, having managed to reject the stereotypes on which his previous life had been built, and having run up against a mass of new problems. In Chekhov's endings there is no revelation and no enlightenment, only a discovery; no resurrection and no regeneration, only a change.

Such an ending is not intended, of course, to defend the previous Layevsky and his way of life. The story's essential conflict is not to be found in the contrasting of Layevsky's personal qualities with those of von Koren. Chekhov's verdict is not concerned with judging the characters or contrasting Layevsky's "truth" with von Koren's "truth." The characters are taken as life presents them; Chekhov accepts as given a world inhabited by these different people arguing irreconcilably. How can different people, different truths, different "general ideas," coexist in this world? On what basis can a person be judged fairly? These are the questions that Chekhov is addressing.

Is it possible, on the basis of a feeling of hatred or any "general theory" (in this case, Social Darwinism), to condemn a person, however much he might deserve it? Chekhov answered this question in the negative by affirming at the end that it is possible for anyone to change and begin a new life. Von Koren's system of ideas, though logically well-ordered and based on the latest conclusions of science, turns out to be narrower than life, which is always full of surprises.

On this deeper epistemological level, the link between "The Duel" and Chekhov's Sakhalin reflections becomes clear. The law—the theory establishing universal norms of human behavior and punishing those who deviate from them—is right in its own way, and one must live in accordance with it. But when the logical application of laws and decrees (those juridical and administrative general regulators) comes into conflict with the concrete reality of human existence, the consequences may be inhumane in the extreme—of that Chekhov had become totally convinced on Sakhalin.

The moral law that von Koren embodies is good, like every ideal conception of human life, but not everyone can be as irreproachable as the law. Layevsky is weak, like all those who break the law, but does this mean that the weak little people who burden the earth should be physically exterminated, as the Social Darwinist quick-temperedly suggests?

If his other works from the late 1880s and early 1890s are about individual examples of "false conceptions"—typical instances of illusions, mistakes, and baseless claims to possession of the truth—in "The Duel" Chekhov summarized his findings. The story is an original epistemological encyclopedia: a collection, above all, of the most varied kinds of ignorance of the "real truth" and also of the reasons why it is unusually difficult to acquire.

Can the judgments that human beings pass on each other be just and final? In "The Duel" it is not only von Koren and Layevsky who judge each other. All the major and even the minor characters embody certain opinions and convictions; they all pass certain judgments. The story considers these judgments for themselves, in relation to their origins, and in juxtaposition with one another and the real world.

Thus commentators have noted how the same character in "The Duel" is seen from many points of view. As in the case of Ivanov, Chekhov gives us glimpses of Layevsky through the eyes of different people. The judgments passed by the good-natured Samoilenko ("he's no different from anyone else. He has his weaknesses, of course, but . . ."), von Koren ("I regard Layevsky as a scoundrel"), Nadezhda Fyodorovna ("he's honest and committed, but he's a bore, biting his nails and annoying me with his whims and fancies"), Maria Konstantinovna ("a splendid young man"), the deacon ("Layevsky may be odd, crazy, and dissolute, but after all, he doesn't steal, spit loudly on the floor or scold his wife . . . and that's enough, surely, to make one feel charitable toward him?"), and by Layevsky himself ("I'm futile and despicable, a fallen man! . . . If only you knew, my friend, how eagerly, how passionately I long for a new start") turn out to be different and at times conflicting. While revealing something about Layevsky, each of these judgments reveals far more about the person judging. Conditioned by the personality of the judger, each judgment appears relative. The opposite case, in which a character expresses the same opinion about very different people (for example, Maria Konstantinovna or Samoilenko), likewise shows how relative and conditioned by their holder's personality such opinions are. In neither case does any of the judgers know the "real truth" about the person.

The judgments made at the same time about the same phenomenon by different people are also infinitely contradictory and conditional. Von Koren admires the green rays of the sunrise, but to Layevsky they are "superfluous and unnecessary"; Nadezhda Fyodorovna's dresses seem "pretty" to her, but Maria Konstantinovna finds them "ghastly"; Samoilenko cannot imagine "a more splendid region than the Caucasus," whereas Layevsky reviles it; he and Samoilenko hold completely different views on what constitutes family happiness, etc., etc.

Each person has his own "idea"/conviction, i.e., stereotype, by which he judges the most varied phenomena in life, and each "conviction" is built on its own logic, or more accurately, nonlogic: Samoilenko "seldom met any Germans and had not read a single German book, but he was of the opinion that the Germans were responsible for all the evils in politics and science"; Kirilin: "I'm a decent man"; Maria Konstantinovna: "Women are always the guilty ones"; Nadezhda Fyodorovna: "I don't see how anyone can be serious about studying bugs and insects when there's so much suffering among the people." Layevsky's stereotypes are the literary characters with whom he is constantly comparing himself: "superfluous men," Hamlet, and even Anna Karenina. Von Koren's stereotype is his conviction that "exact knowledge," "the logic of facts," "our knowledge and common sense" are suitable criteria for making infallible judgments on people and phenomena. In some instances Chekhov provides detailed evidence of the relative, nonabsolute character of these stereotypes, but in others a simple juxtaposition of these discordant "truths" is sufficient.

These persons even believe in the same thing "in their own way." Von Koren says to the deacon of Christ's teaching: "Just think of the different ways in which even that is understood!"—and as if to confirm that idea, replies to him immediately after: "No, I'm a believer, but I believe in my own way, of course, not yours."

At the end of the story Chekhov makes the former opponents shake hands and say: "no one knows the real truth." But the principle of individualization—the absence of general solutions—is not violated, for each of them understands something different by the same words.

In Layevsky's mouth they mean that a person cannot pass final judgment even on himself (he had reckoned earlier that for him the road to a new life would always be blocked by "a mountain of lies").

In von Koren's mouth the phrase is not simply an acknowledgment that "another person's soul is a mystery." Acknowledging that he was wrong about Layevsky means acknowledging that he did not know what criterion to judge people by (he had said earlier that "people must be judged by their actions"). Although he remains loyal to his conviction that socially harmful personalities should be isolated from humankind, now he will surely have to wait a long time before he finds anyone to whom he can apply the principle with a clear conscience.

In "The Duel" special attention is paid to those characteristics of human thinking, psychology, and memory that contribute to the formation of our convictions, judgments, and decisions. That our judgments are subjectively conditioned and inconclusive is determined also by the fact that judgments and the feelings generated by them may change significantly over time. The "it seemed . . . but it turned out that" situation is characteristic of Layevsky's attitude to his flight from Petersburg with Nadezhda Fyodorovna, their attitude to the Caucasus, Nadezhda Fyodorovna's attitude to Kirilin, and von Koren's to Layevsky.

Negative judgments are the most relative, since, as Chekhov shows, people as a rule already know everything bad about themselves. Layevsky frequently engages in self-reproach in "The Duel" and reads the story of his life "with revulsion." Von Koren's accusations thus lose much of their point, since they do not tell Layevsky anything new about himself but once again reveal more about the person passing judgment. Chekhov achieves the same effect by making Nadezhda Fyodorovna constantly accuse herself. This technique is the author's way of indicating the genuine complexity of the problem: to accuse is easy, just as it is easy to know a mistake when you see one; what is far more difficult is to find fully reliable ways of guaranteeing against mistakes in life.

One could go on listing the epistemological observations and sketches with which "The Duel" is crammed, but enough has been said to show how all-embracing they are. The final words, that "no one knows the real truth," acquire a wider implication that goes far beyond the limits of the actual plot.

In reaching beyond the limits of time and space by the end of the narration, and in its final reflections on "people searching for truth," the conclusion of "The Duel" makes us think about the whole contemporary human condition and at the same time reveals a precise positive implication: all the current passions, squabbles, and tragedies are as nothing compared with the time when "real truth" will be recognized and justice will reign in human relations; and, of course, no one contemporary theory, no one type of thinking, no one social institution can claim to be entitled to pass a fair and conclusive judgment on human life.

## I 2

------

# Making the Individual Individual

It was not only the ending of "The Duel" that contained Chekhov's answer to those who felt entitled to give clear-cut, irreversible answers to the problem of how to judge a person's life. Each individual human existence is unique and inimitable: that is Chekhov's basic argument. The principle of "treating each individual case in isolation" was to become the basic principle of his approach to psychology.

That psychological individuality takes the form in Chekhov of a highly ramified system of circumstances that give rise to each separate inner state in the hero, who is engaged in "orienting" himself in life, solving a "problem," choosing a course of action, or rejecting a system of ideas.

If we look at the actual technique of individualization, we find that every psychological process affecting the formation of the hero's judgments and general outlook is individual and unique for Chekhov, since it occurs in circumstances that cannot be repeated. What he is trying to do as a psychologist is to show how complex moods and inner states depend on a variety of external influences, and how a person may shift from one state to another as a result of each change in the surrounding situation.

Thus, in Chapters 15 and 17 of "The Duel," Chekhov records with medical precision the changes in Layevsky's mood in the hours before the duel. After receiving the challenge, Layevsky is over-whelmed and stifled by one feeling: an almost pathological hatred for his opponent ("He imagined himself knocking von Koren to the ground and trampling on him"). Some time passes; Layevsky dines and plays cards, has yet to take in the significance of what has happened, and thinks unconcernedly about the absurdity of duels in general. Another stage follows: "But after sunset, when it grew dark, he was overcome by anxiety. . . ." Layevsky gradually begins to feel scared ("He wanted to go to bed quickly, lie still, and prepare his thoughts for the night"). Soon after, he experiences the shock of seeing Nadezhda Fyodorovna in the arms of police officer Kirilin. The effect is like a stunning blow ("His hatred of von Koren and his anxiety—everything was wiped away"). In this new state Layevsky is so devastated that it takes him a long time to recover his senses ("On his way home he swung his right arm awkwardly and kept staring at the ground, trying to walk where it was even"). While the storm rages outside, he prepares himself for death and recalls his child-hood; his mood now is one of tenderness, forgiveness, and self-reproach. "By the time the storm had passed, he was sitting by the open window, thinking calmly of what lay ahead of him." In the morning he listens to the quiet conversation of the seconds and the snorting of the horses, and these sounds in the early morning dampness "filled Layevsky with gloom, like an evil foreboding." Looking at the sleeping Nadezhda Fyodorovna and then listening to her incoherent words, he "realized that this unhappy, immoral woman was the only person in his life who was near and dear to him, and could not be replaced. By the time he went out and took his seat in the carriage, he wanted to come home alive."

Chekhov plots the course of Layevsky's spiritual crisis by regis-tering the smallest nuances of his state of mind. The details of his surroundings and the various portents are there not to provide a background, or as a means of creating an "illusion of plausibility." They play a part in the hero's most vital decision-making; his state of mind, his mood, and consequently his actions depend on them al-most entirely.

In many stories from the 1890s and 1900s, Chekhov's basic aim is to show in more and more novel ways this interaction between his characters' states of mind and their surroundings, i.e., to individualize the process. Thus Ivashin, the landowner in "Neighbors," whose sister has run off to live with their neighbor Vlasich, is tormented by doubts about what attitude to adopt and what action to take. For the most chance reasons (the rain, his neighbor's outward appearance, how the house is furnished, his sister's smile), Ivashin's mood and his attitude toward what has happened oscillate violently between rage, introspection, fear, decisiveness, confusion, magnanimity, etc. The smallest changes in their surroundings may affect the state of Chekhov's characters. That is why, in describing their inner life, he may bring in details that would seem to be accidental and unconnected with their moods and trains of thought.

A. P. Chudakov has described the impression of "randomness" that is created when Chekhov depicts the causes of his characters' psychological states, actions, and opinions: "an accidental cause exists alongside a main cause and together with it—independently and on equal terms."[1] "The Duel" offers many examples of this proximity of "meaningful" and "nonmeaningful" causes. What is the decisive factor in the shift from the "old" Layevsky to the "new"? Compared to the heroes of Dostoevsky and Tolstoy, the "ceiling of motivation" for this change is considerably lower. Instead of Raskolnikov's apocalyptic visions, Mitya Karamazov's "dream of a sobbing child," or the purgatory of Nekhlyudov's troubled conscience, in Chekhov there is a dinner party with lively conversation, the onset of darkness, Layevsky witnessing Nadezhda Fyodorovna's fall, a deluge, the storm dying away, voices outside the window, a surge of tenderness toward someone close—and there you have your hero all ready to begin a new life. Chekhov describes nine or ten of these separate states, and the "unimportant" stimuli and causes (rain, dinner, darkness, voices outside the window) play as much a part in the shift as the "important" ones (Nadezhda Fyodorovna's fall, her re-

1. A. P. Chudakov, *Poetika Chekhova*, pp. 190, 199.

pentance). In "A Story Without an Ending," as we saw, the light of the candle likewise seemed to the would-be suicide just as important a factor as poverty and the death of his wife.

Fortuitousness? Rejecting the idea of a scale of importance? This does not go far enough. We need to explain the principle behind Chekhov's choice of psychological causes and the circumstances underlying mental events, and how it distinguishes his world from the artistic systems of his closest predecessors and contemporaries.

Treating each individual case in isolation, the basic principle of Chekhov's psychology, does not assert simply that in explaining the causes of suicide a candle is as important as poverty and the death of the hero's wife. The author of "A Story Without an Ending" is eager to say that the genuine causes of an event are unknown (and ought to be explained), since each mental event is far more complicated than any attempt to explain it in accordance with well-known general theories. The author of "The Duel" is eager to emphasize that the genuine criteria for judging a human life are unknown (and ought to be discovered), since a person's mental life follows specific paths that are uniquely unpredictable. In both cases the "accidental" (or singular) is introduced as a way of individualizing a specific happening, i.e., not "fortuitously" but with a definite aim in mind. Chekhov is demonstrating that each separate life is unique, and that to deduce general norms and criteria from separate isolated instances is invalid. This continues the line begun in "Lights" and later confirmed by Sakhalin.

Chekhov was not the first writer to combine the significant and the insignificant in human motivation.

Tolstoy the literary artist saw in every event a complex intertwining of many heterogeneous causes, and knew better than anyone how to introduce a chance external detail into descriptions of mental processes, building these details up to create "the atmosphere of an event." But Tolstoy has his own way of "regulating" everything in his artistic world. V. Ya. Lakshin puts it well when he writes: "Each particular impression, be it only the strip of birch trees lit up by the sun that Bolkonsky sees through the broken wall of the barn, acts as a stimulus to elucidating life's meaning, while a general view of life casts a new light on any little detail."[2]

In the world of Dostoevsky and Tolstoy (for all the contrast between them as psychologists), the unity of the person is a complex, contradictory unity of the hero's inner world, which is evolving toward some final goal: seeing the light, becoming one with God and with the spirit of truth and simplicity, or finally seeing through a world of lies and unbelief. How significant and how interesting the reader finds these heroes depends on the significance of the inner obstacles and contradictions they must overcome on their way to the final truth.

Thus the vivid individuality of Tolstoy's and Dostoevsky's heroes is directly conditioned by what the two writers are trying to achieve and by the basic course of the action.

If Tolstoy conceived of his characters on a "moral-psychological" plane, Chekhov conceived of his on an epistemological plane. The unity of the person in Chekhov's world is first and foremost the unity of the hero as a cognitive subject. While sacrificing the wealth of possibilities open to the writer who is willing to combine a variety of determining factors or to show the clash of conflicting passions within a character, Chekhov was able to achieve an unusual degree of concentration on those processes that have no significant outcome and yield only individual, not general, solutions—the kind of processes in which we are all involved.

It is in Chekhov that "the individual" first appears as individual in the proper sense of the word. Individualization does not mean creating vivid individual personalities or "types"; "the individual" is not simply the one that stands out by being different from all the others in a series. It is a special "self-regulating" system with its own world and self-consciousness, unique links with surrounding reality, and distinctive variations on general problems that do not lend themselves to general and universal solutions.

2. V. Ya. Lakshin, *Tolstoi i Chekhov*, 2nd ed. (Moscow, 1975), p. 248.

The individualization of mental processes acquires particular significance when one considers the close relationship that Chekhov establishes between a person's philosophy and the life going on endlessly around him.

Chekhov's "Notebook No. 1" (pp. 106–107), contains the following plot. The hero describes how he "was once an anarchist." He was expelled from school and thrown out by his father; "he had to go to work for a landowner as a junior steward; got annoyed with the rich, well-fed, fat people; the landowner was planting cherries, A.A. was helping him and suddenly felt a strong urge to chop off those fleshy white fingers, as if by accident; closing his eyes, he brought the spade down with all his strength, but missed. Then he went away, the forest, quiet open fields, rain, he wanted somewhere warm so he went along to his auntie's, she gave him tea and *boubliks* [ring-shaped bread rolls], and his anarchism disappeared. . . ."

As with other Chekhov characters, the hero's "convictions" are shaky, and this is no accident. But consider the indications that in Chekhov's view are necessary and sufficient to explain an essential change in a person's outlook: the forest, quiet open fields, rain, auntie's tea, and *boubliks*—and that's the end of anarchism. With such an approach Chekhov would find the idea of two identical anarchists inconceivable, just as any conviction, mood, or way of thinking is unique and cannot be reduced to general categories like "anarchism." Any variety of orientation acquires its own individual coloring.

"Treating each individual case in isolation," alongside his dominant interest in problems of "orientation," thus became another determining principle of Chekhov's work.

His individualizing method (not to be confused with creating vivid individual personalities) resulted in generalizations of considerable importance. It is not only negative conclusions—such as "you can't make anything out in this world" or "no one knows the real truth"—that must be taken into account when speaking of Chekhov's general conclusions. His method of artistic thinking and the approach he adopted also have a positive cognitive and aesthetic significance.

Just as in medicine and teaching, by studying the conditions, properties, and possibilities of the individual, and working practically with each person on his own, you achieve higher standards of treatment and education, so Chekhov's individualization—paying careful attention to the unique individual—opened up new possibilities for the study of humankind in literature. Chekhov's method showed that the solution of complex general social problems and conflicts was to be effected through individuals, through individual human beings of unique complexity.

It is important to note that these two principles—the epistemological and the individualizing—are closely connected and represent a system of coordinates on which Chekhov's world is built. This does not, of course, exclude the possibility of isolating other coordinates or of considering Chekhov's work from a different perspective. But if you accept the starting point chosen here, it is impossible to divorce Chekhov's study of orientation from his attempt "to explain each case in isolation."

In the Zakharin school of medicine, the "practice and method of individualizing" is inseparable from questioning the patient and taking into account how the person perceives his own condition. Chekhov's individualization is at its most original when he is considering the forms that our convictions, judgments, and decisions take. It is primarily a new principle for studying human beings, their ways of thinking, their views and opinions—their various kinds of orientation in the world.

Taking account of these coordinates of Chekhov's world is of direct practical importance in interpreting his work.

## 13

# Expressing One's Idea: "A Woman's Kingdom" (1894)

C hekhov differs from his predecessors in that he does not offer different answers to the same questions; he asks quite different questions and asks them in a different way. His interest in what he called "knowlege in the realm of thought," "orientation" and the search for "real truth," and his special way of throwing light on these problems by seeking "to explain each case in isolation"—all this is the product of a distinctive vision of life, humanity, and the traditional problems of being and thinking.

The real world assumes an unusual character in Chekhov: the "indisputable" appears problematic, the "categorical" is no more than hypothetical, and the "unconditionally true" needs to be substantiated.

Clearly, very many of the usual standards do not apply in this "strange world." It makes its own correlations between major and minor, the changing and unchanging, the soluble and the insoluble. The chapters that follow will deal with these practical problems of Chekhov interpretation.

Let us consider at this point another recurrent Chekhov concept. From the latter 1880s, when the main features of his artistic world became firmly established, he often referred to the concept of "the specialized." Commenting favorably on the work of his contemporaries, Korolenko and Shcheglov, Chekhov had only one criticism: "But—*Allah Kerim*—why do they both specialize so much? Korolenko refuses to be parted from his convicts, and Shcheglov feeds his readers on nothing but army officers."[1] Describing his own (then still unfinished) "The Steppe," Chekhov said: "It seems to me to be . . . too specialized. The modern reader finds this kind of subject—the steppe with its natural scenes and its characters—specialized and of little significance."[2] Of his more general understanding of the role of literature, he wrote:

> When I'm having discussions with fellow writers, I always insist on one point: that it's not an artist's job to solve highly specialized problems. It's no good if an artist tackles something he doesn't understand. We have specialists to deal with specialized problems, and it's their job to pass judgment on the peasant commune, the fate of capitalism, or the evils of drink, on boots or female complaints. . . . Whereas an artist should judge only what he understands; his sphere is every bit as restricted as that of any other specialist. I shall never stop insisting on this point.[3]

When the role of literature is discussed in Chekhov's fiction, his characters employ the same concept, as this passage from his unfinished story "The Letter" illustrates:

> How sad and upsetting it was that even good, clever people looked upon every event in such a specialized, preconceived, and self-centered kind of way. Take Travnikov. He was tormented by the specialized problem of God and the purpose of life; the arts could not solve this problem or explain what would happen after death, so Travnikov regarded them as prejudices and reduced them to the level of mere entertainment.[4]

1. *Letters*, 2:191.
2. *Letters*, 2:178.
3. *Letters*, 3:45.
4. *Works*, 7:515.

Compare the conversation about the aims of literature in "Three Years."

The insistence with which Chekhov returns to the problem of "the specialized" shows that it was a major concept in his aesthetic awareness. To make sense of the laws governing his artistic world, it is important to note this category and distinguish it from its opposites.

Chekhov can be said to differentiate between constants and variables; he defines what is of essential importance, and what is particular and insoluble. It is Chekhov's conviction that the writer ought consciously to avoid "the specialized" if he understands the essence of what he is doing correctly, and the possibilities and results that are within his reach. If the job of the specialist is to solve "specialized problems," the writer should know how to seek out the general truth that embraces different "specialized" phenomena, the overarching truth that makes the latter into particular instances.

What constitutes a "specialized problem" for Chekhov often turns out to be one that was central and all-defining for his predecessors. It is a measure of just how untraditional the relationship between constants and variables is in Chekhov that even "the problem of God and the purpose of life" turns out to be a particular, "specialized" problem!

So the interpreter's task is to find in each work that relationship between the essentially important and the "specialized" which corresponds to Chekhov's vision of the world. This makes it possible to mark out the area in which Chekhov made his own unique contribution and in which his generalizations are concentrated.

The logic of the author's artistic thought may be shown especially by those elements of content and poetics that are most persistent and make themselves felt in a number of works. Here the criterion of repetition comes into play. Parallel analysis of several works[5] makes it possible to discover what Chekhov himself re-

5. M. P. Gromov, for example, argues in favor of this approach to Chekhov. See "Povestvovaniye Chekhova kak khudozhestvennaya sistema" in *Sovremennye problemy literaturovedeniya i yazykoznaniya* (Moscow, 1974), pp. 307–315.

garded as central or particular, permanent or variable, essential or minor, in the artistic world he was creating.

Recent works of criticism have concentrated on analyzing Chekhov's *narrative structure* (the text minus direct speech). But it is equally important in interpreting Chekhov to clarify the relationship between the author and *a character's direct speech* as contained in monologues and dialogues. The characters' thoughts and utterances are, after all, the first source of information about how they have chosen to orient themselves in the world.

In the stories from the 1890s, Chekhov often portrays a situation in which a character (usually the one of most interest to him) expresses a thought in the form of an absolute assertion. Circumstances then change, and the opinion becomes "detached" from the character who expressed it. The assertion is perceived by the character in a new light, and its significance becomes relative.

This is what happens, for example, in the mind of Anna Akimovna Glagoleva, the heroine of "A Woman's Kingdom" (1894)—a capitalist and millionairess who feels ill at ease amidst the alien wealth and authority she has inherited. Here is what she says over dinner to the vulgar, cynical lawyer Lysevich:

> "Don't you realize what a huge enterprise I've got on my hands, that I'm responsible to God for two thousand workers? There are people who go deaf or blind in my employment. I'm terrified by all this, terrified! It makes me suffer, but you . . . you just smile!" Anna Akimovna banged her fist on the table. "To go on living in the way I'm doing now, or to marry the same kind of idle, useless person as myself—that would be quite criminal. I can't go on living like this," she said heatedly, "I can't!"

Anna Akimovna, as we see, is fully convinced of her own words. She is formulating a definite idea: that if a capitalist is morally sensitive and tormented by pangs of conscience over the sufferings of her exploited workers, she ought not to go on living in the way laid down for her by her class, but should fly in the face of its demands and traditions.

It is easy enough to imagine a writer deciding to make this subject-limited idea—"talented, clever, and noble" as it undoubtedly is[6]—central to his work, and concentrating his efforts on its artistic realization. The idea would be put forward as the author's wholehearted conviction and within the work would acquire the status of an "absolute truth." The author would be at pains to express his idea—either via the hero, or using his own authorial voice, or in the form of a natural conclusion—and to reinforce it by means of the work's whole structure.

But in Chekhov we find a fundamentally different kind of artistic thinking and vision of the world. He is at pains not simply to express this or that opinion in a story, but to show how relative and conditional the opinion is, and how it depends on circumstances—in other words, to "individualize" it. Why the opinion is relative, and what the circumstances are—these questions interest him most of all.

This is how Chekhov comments on his heroine's speech: "Anna Akimovna was glad to have spoken her mind, and cheered up. She felt pleased that she had spoken so well and had such honest, beautiful thoughts, and she was convinced that if, for example, Pimenov [a mechanic in her factory] fell in love with her, she would marry him with pleasure."

Here is another semi-ironic comment by the author on his heroine, at a moment when the opinion she had expressed still has the force of an absolute conviction for her:

> He [Lysevich] drew her attention to various subtleties and emphasized the felicitous expressions and profound thoughts [in Maupassant's novel], but all she saw was life, life, life, as if she herself were a character taking part in the story; her spirits were rising, she, too, kept laughing out loud and throwing up her hands, and she thought that to go on living like this was impossible, there was no need to lead an ugly life if you could lead a beautiful one; she recalled her words and thoughts over dinner and was proud of them, and when

6. This is the phrase that the professor in "A Dreary Story" uses in his reflections on contemporary literature (*Works*, 7:292).

Pimenov suddenly appeared in her imagination, she felt cheerful and wanted him to fall in love with her.

In works about Chekhov an individual thought is often taken out of context, for example: "To go on living like this was impossible, there was no need to lead an ugly life if you could lead a beautiful one." Critics present this thought as if it were the author's own, and see in it an expression of the whole point of the story; they forget that it is expressed by a character whose "spirits were rising," who "felt cheerful" and wanted someone to fall in love with her. The real point of this kind of subject-limited ("specialized") idea becomes apparent, however, only within the story's general structure.

After portraying the circumstances in which his heroine's opinion first appeared, Chekhov goes on to describe how in a different situation and influenced by new factors, her attitude begins to become more detached (in the evening Anna Akimovna talked about marriage with her relations, hangers-on, employees, and servants, and after that she felt lonely). The halo of absolute conviction that had surrounded her opinion begins to fade, and sober relativity takes its place:

> The feeling of festive excitement was already passing, and in an attempt to keep it up, Anna Akimovna sat down again at the piano and began quietly playing one of the new waltzes, then she remembered how clever and honest her thoughts and words had been at dinner that day. She looked round at the dark windows and the pictures on the walls, at the dim light coming from the reception room, and suddenly for no reason she burst into tears, and felt annoyed that she was so lonely and had no one to talk to or consult. To recover her spirits, she tried to picture Pimenov to herself, but this time nothing happened.

Chekhov goes on to describe another stage in the "life" of an idea that had originally been formulated as an absolute assertion. In a new period and in the light of a new reality, Anna Akimovna becomes completely detached from the words spoken earlier. The mood that gave rise to them has passed and cannot, it seems, be experienced again, and for the heroine this means that the same thoughts cannot be experienced again either.

> Only now, for the first time all day [after the footman had laughed at Pimenov], did she see clearly that everything she had thought and said about Pimenov, and about marrying an ordinary worker, was nothing but foolish pigheadedness. In an effort to persuade herself of the contrary and overcome her feeling of disgust, she tried to recall the words she had said at dinner, but could no longer remember them properly; shame at her thoughts and behavior, the fear that she might have said something indiscreet, and disgust at her weakness, all made her feel deeply distressed.

Such is the ultimate fate in the heroine's mind of the thought she had first expressed so heatedly as her conviction.

The author reveals himself in the semi-ironic tone of some of his comments, but chiefly in his objective depiction of how a person gradually becomes detached from her own words, and of the transition from attaching absolute to attaching relative significance to them. The linked stages in this process form the compositional core of "A Woman's Kingdom": all the events prepare for or contribute to the appearance of the heroine's all-important conviction or else prepare for her final attitude toward it.

Chekhov, of course, had his own definite attitude toward his heroine's idea (as directly understood). But the aim of the story, its inspiration, Chekhov's reason for writing, cannot be reduced to saying that Chekhov is asserting or rejecting the need for capitalists to break with the matrimonial traditions of their class. Chekhov wants to show that by saying "To go on living like this is impossible," a person has so far done very little.

Much more important and interesting than the words spoken by someone in a state of heightened emotion are the relations that the person has with life around them after the words have been spoken. Almost always it turns out that the person is so incapable of doing anything truly bold and unusual, so powerless when confronted by the stagnant vulgarity of the established order, that the original surge of feeling very quickly fades and the person readily seeks a pretext for repudiating it.

Chekhov is not saying: yes, it would be good to do this or that, or it would be good to be like this. He is saying how difficult it is to be human. Though aware of what she should be like, his heroine is too weak to fly in the face of life. This reveals the sober wisdom of the humanist who is under no delusions that the problems of human existence can be solved easily; it shows what Gorky called "the skepticism of a man who knows the value of words and the value of daydreams."[7]

The feature outlined above is characteristic of Chekhov's works in the 1890s. His love story "Three Years" (1895) contains the same linked sequence of opinion, intermediate state, and detachment. Here is Laptev's conversation with Yuliya Sergeyevna, with whom he is hopelessly in love:

> "I'm not a person who could be disturbed," she replied, pausing on the staircase, "because I never do anything anyway. Every day's a holiday for me, from morning till night."
>
> "To me that makes no sense," he said, going up to her. "I grew up in an environment where everyone worked every day, men and women without exception."
>
> "But what if there's nothing to do?" she asked.
>
> "One should arrange one's life in such a way that work is essential. Without work there cannot be a pure and joyful life."

Laptev says all this in a state of "sweet exaltation" connected with his hopes. Then follows his sudden declaration of love, proposal of marriage, and rejection.

> Laptev realized what this meant, and his mood at once changed abruptly, as if a light inside him had suddenly gone out. Feeling shame and the humiliation of someone who has been scorned, who

---

7. A. M. Gorky, in *Chekhov v vospominaniyakh sovremennikov* (Moscow, 1960), p. 494.

is disliked, offensive, and perhaps repulsive, a man from whom people run away, he walked out of the house. . . .

Everything he had just said struck him as abominably stupid. Why had he lied about growing up in an environment where everyone worked without exception? Why had he spoken in that sermonizing tone about a pure, joyful life? It wasn't clever or interesting, it was false—false in the Moscow style. But then little by little a mood of indifference came over him . . . he must give up all hopes of personal happiness and live without desires or hopes, neither dreaming nor expecting anything.

Once again the hero thinks and speaks "well, honestly, and beautifully," and once again the author uses the narrative structure to underline the relative, nonabsolute character of the idea the hero expresses. Opinions of this kind in Chekhov do not have the stamp of the author's approval (or rejection); they belong to the realm of the "specialized."

The point of Chekhov's work, of his artistic structures and "couplings," cannot be reduced to saying that he wanted to substantiate and express such judgments as "to go on living like this is impossible," "there's no need to lead an ugly life if you can lead a beautiful one," or "one should arrange one's life in such a way that work is essential; without work there cannot be a pure and joyful life." The inspiration behind Chekhov's work goes far beyond the expression of such ideas and is to be found on an altogether different plane.

Chekhov's poetic system requires different methods of analysis from those which can be applied to traditional works that put forward definite, subject-limited ("specialized") ideas.

In discussing this feature of Chekhov it would be wrong to describe it in a purely negative light, as a refusal to attach absolute significance to "specialized" ideas or opinions. It has a particular characteristic which may outwardly remind us of traditional approaches but at the same time enables us to see far more clearly what makes Chekhov original and unusual.

This is the distinctive way in which Chekhov's characters are made to formulate their ideas stylistically. An opinion that Chekhov wants to show as ultimately unfounded and relative is formulated by him as an absolute, well-ordered, finished, and internally consistent assertion.

This is true of the opinions of Anna Akimovna and Laptev quoted above. At the moment when they express their opinions, these characters—who are ordinary people—become ideologues, publicists, and tribunes. They cast their assertions into elegant, aphoristic, seemingly unique forms. These opinions often differ markedly from how they usually formulate ideas, and because they are cast in the form of generalized aphorisms, they can be taken out of context and retain the strength of a finished judgment.

These external stylistic indications are usually sufficient for the reader of traditional works to attribute such opinions to the author, who wanted in that way to signal the assertions to which he felt sympathetic. This regular feature of traditional literature has been described by M. M. Bakhtin: "Authorial approval finds objective expression in a special emphasis, a special placing of thoughts in the work as a whole, in the actual verbal style in which the opinions are formulated, and in a whole variety of other ways of presenting a thought as significant and author-approved."[8]

In Chekhov we find the exact opposite: in formulating the characters' opinions (opinions that will later be discredited by the very person who expressed them), he employs methods that are used by other writers solely to express ideas of which they themselves approve. If traditional criteria for recognizing approved ideas are applied, it is easy to take as a straight declaration what is actually an imitation or stylization.

---

8. M. Bakhtin, *Problemy poetiki Dostoyevskogo*, 2nd ed. (Moscow, 1963), p. 105.

## 14

# "These Thoughts Are Not My Own"

There is another typical device that Chekhov uses regularly when presenting his characters' views and opinions, and it is one that may puzzle the critic who imagines that Chekhov can be approached with the traditional criteria for uncovering an author's attitudes. This is the assignment of obviously "right" opinions (in substance and spirit) to the "wrong" heroes.

Chekhov's heroes very often speak in phrases that might have been taken from the pages of the most enlightened journalism and literature, and that by rights ought to bear witness to the progressive and noble qualities of the speaker's convictions. But these phrases are given to characters whose personalities and behavior are clearly intended to be unsympathetic.

In Chekhov's humorous works this is one of the most frequent instances of juxtaposing incompatibles, of a character taking over an inappropriate sign system; and this, as we have seen, is one of the basic sources of the comic in Chekhov.

". . . retired collegiate registrar Lakhmatov was sitting at his desk, and as he knocked back his sixteenth glass, was musing on the theme of liberty, equality, and fraternity" ("What a Drunk Man Said to a Sober Devil," 1886).

" 'We must always move ahead . . . each one of us ought to move ahead. . . . And you too are moving ahead. . . .'

'Where am I moving to now, for example?' the dark-haired man replied with a smirk.

'. . . Well, how about the refreshment bar . . .' " ("A Proud Man," 1884).

" 'No smoking!' the conductor shouted at him.

'. . . That's an infringement of individual liberties! I won't allow anyone to infringe my individual liberties! I'm a free man! . . .' he said, throwing away the cigarette. '. . . They're stifling me!' " ("Two Men in One," 1883).

"All around us there is theft and embezzlement. . . . And the suffering! The innocent victims!" declaims provincial secretary Ottyagayev in "Hard to Find a Title for This One" (1883).

"Life has become intolerable!" exclaims "office spokesman" Dezdemonov in "The Spokesman, or How Dezdemonov Came to Lose 25 Rubles" (1883).

In the work of Chekhov the humorist, characters like Ivan Kapitonych from "Two Men in One" ("That's an infringement of my individual liberties!", "They're suffocating me!" etc.) are the objects of mockery and satire no less than characters like Sergeant Prishibeyev in the story of that name (1885)—"Where's it written down that the lower classes can do what they like?"—or Ochumelov, the hero of "The Chameleon" (1884), switching from one "vocabulary" to another.

In his later work too, Chekhov is quite willing to resort to this device. Of course, when he assigns noble and progressive ideas and phrases to Dezdemonov and his like—and later to such characters as Lvov in *Ivanov*, Lysevich in "A Woman's Kingdom," and Serebryakov in *Uncle Vanya*—this cannot be taken to mean that Chekhov wishes somehow to discredit the ideas themselves. But to credit Chekhov when his characters utter phrases like "Forward!" or "Life has become intolerable!" would be equally unjustifiable. Yet some critics regard the simple presence of such pronouncements in Chekhov's characters as almost the only decisive proof of the social significance of his work. In many studies of Chekhov the characters' opinions are identified with the ideas of the author, thereby distorting the meaning of Chekhov's work; and it is not uncommon to find studies in which the whole of Chekhov's development as a writer is based upon the evolution of his characters' pronouncements.

"All these 'thoughts and reflections,'" Chekhov wrote to his publisher A. F. Marx on October 23, 1902, "are not my own but my heroes', and if a character in one of my stories or plays says that one should kill or steal, that certainly doesn't give Mr. Ettinger the right to present me as the advocate of theft or murder."[1]

But it is not obviously inadmissible statements of that kind but his characters' "right," "noble," and "progressive" thoughts and pronouncements that are so frequently attributed to Chekhov. That these thoughts are Chekhov's own is regarded as too obvious to require further argument, even though the critic might reject other specific cases of identification.

Thus S. N. Bulgakov objected to those who "merge the author and his characters" and are "not averse" to attributing Ivanov's thoughts "to Chekhov himself." But in the same breath he declared without any foundation that in "The House with a Mezzanine," Chekhov was speaking "through the artist," "through Masha" in *Three Sisters*, Sonya in *Uncle Vanya*, Trofimov in *The Cherry Orchard*, and so on.[2] That Chekhov was speaking through someone was not in doubt; the only question was through whom.

In discussing typical mistakes made by Chekhov's critics and commentators, A. B. Derman placed at the top of the list "attributing to the author the thoughts of a fictional character."[3] But when it came to analyzing specific works like "A Dreary Story," "The Story

---

1. *Letters*, 11:64, 382. A Mr. Ettinger had asked Marx to publish a volume of aphorisms he had compiled based on "the thoughts and reflections of Anton Pavlovich Chekhov." Before turning him down, Marx consulted Chekhov, who dismissed the whole idea as "completely childish."

2. S. N. Bulgakov, *Chekhov kak myslitel'* (Kiev, 1905), pp. 8, 14, 19.

3. A. B. Derman, *Tvorcheskii portret Chekhova* (Moscow, 1927), p. 317.

of an Unknown Man," and "Gooseberries," Derman made use of exactly the same technique.

The temptation is hard to resist! Ilya Ehrenburg, for example, did not even bother to qualify statements of this kind. "Take the story 'A Case History,'" he writes. "Anton Pavlovich, or in this case Doctor Korolyov, says that . . ."[4]

It might be objected that when the phrase "Life has become intolerable!" is proclaimed by the unprincipled Dezdemonov, that is one thing, but when the same phrase is uttered by the noble Ivan Ivanovich Chimsha-Gimalaisky in "Gooseberries," that is very different; and that Anna Akimovna Glagoleva's "right" judgments in "A Woman's Kingdom" are quite different from those of Lysevich. It is indeed true that in Chekhov both positive and negative characters—those being laughed at and those being taken seriously—can utter phrases that have the same absolute value out of context. The difference, however, is this: that in the speeches of characters like Anna Akimovna, Kostya Kochevoi ("Three Years"), and Petya Trofimov (*The Cherry Orchard*), Chekhov is emphasizing very strongly the passionate sense of conviction with which these phrases are uttered, the way in which the noble resounding phrase is inseparable from its speaker's philosophical and stylistic profile. The phrase does not cease to be a phrase, an object of imitation and stylization by the author, but at the same time it introduces another nuance into the hero's characterization.

This is further evidence of the special nature of Chekhov's aims as a writer. It is not the absolute, out-of-context content of the phrases that is important; it is what changes them into the relative, conditioned opinion of a given character. However attractive and striking a character's phrase may appear, in Chekhov's world it cannot be taken as a basis for establishing the author's position.

There is another special difficulty in interpreting Chekhov. It is not only that the "right" phrases are uttered by obviously "wrong" characters; the opinions of "negative" or insufficiently "positive"

4. Ilya Ehrenburg, *Perechityvaya Chekhova*, pp. 9–10.

Chekhov characters often coincide with opinions expressed in the author's own letters and notebooks!

But it is easy to see why Chekhov's characters say things that co-incide with passages from his letters or with his opinions as known from memoirs. It is part of his constant aim as a writer to show the individual foundation for every point of view expressed, the "truth" of each protagonist in an argument (and in that way to highlight the relativity of their opinions).

In any debate Chekhov assigns the same degree of internal logic, stylistic elegance, and aphoristic conciseness to the opinions of all the protagonists: to von Koren, Layevsky, and the deacon in "The Duel," to Ragin and Gromov ("Ward No. 6"), to Kochevoi, Yartsev, and Laptev ("Three Years"), to Poloznev and Blagovo ("My Life"), and to Vershinin and Tuzenbach (*The Cherry Orchard*). The author knows their limitations, but his characters and their opinions are not to be caricatured; these opinions should be sufficiently serious and sincere to be seen as the plausible viewpoints of intelligent indi-viduals.

Chekhov approached the task of formulating these viewpoints with the greatest seriousness. Only one course was open to him: to give his characters the kinds of ideas and opinions that might have been expressed in private conversation by Chekhov himself and the most interesting of his friends.

Naturally enough, both Chekhov and the people he associated with were touched and affected by the whole range of problems that were current in their epoch: general and particular problems, large-scale, epoch-making problems, and the kinds of problems that ceased long ago to be of any interest to anyone. Like it or not, each person, even if he understands that every problem is transitory, must seek out his own place in the real world of his time and address the problems of his epoch, knowing that a different epoch with dif-ferent problems will come to take its place. In common with his contemporaries, Chekhov had a network of opinions on the prob-lems of his epoch—opinions that were historically, socially, and in-dividually conditioned.

But to Chekhov, equipped with that higher "conception of life" that guided him in his writings, it was clear that these "special" ideas of his, like the ideas of Tolstoy, Suvorin, Pleshcheyev, and his other contemporaries and companions, were inevitably limited and conditioned. For this reason he assigned his own and other people's "subject-limited" ideas to characters in whom he wished to emphasize one-sidedness, intolerance of other opinions, and the urge to make their own convictions into absolutes.

Chekhov calculated that behind this chaos of assertions, arguments, and conflicting views—well founded and limited in equal degrees—the reader would see the guiding idea of the author, who was always concerned to show that life is more complicated than any one individual's understanding of it.

In the literature on Chekhov, various explanations of this particular feature of his work have become established over the years. Here are two of these critical legends.

According to the first, Chekhov would have liked to affirm this or that idea "through his characters" but could not find the kind of people in life to whom he could naturally attribute, say, the spirit of protest or the hope of a new life. For this reason, though Chekhov may make a particular character act as the mouthpiece of his ideas, he also gives that character features that indicate his or her weakness.

In this interpretation, the author's task is thought of as searching for a character to whom he can transfer his own "protesting" or optimistic pronouncements; but since there is no one who fully matches his requirements, he must make do with images of a "protester" or optimist with some defect (see, for example, many interpretations of characters like Pavel Ivanych in "Gusev" or Gromov in "Ward No. 6").

This idea that Chekhov "would have liked to but couldn't" inevitably leads the critic to say that Chekhov was only half successful in creating these images and that he failed to carry through his intentions.

According to the second critical legend, Chekhov would have liked to affirm certain "positive" truths but felt hesitant about proclaiming them "point-blank" or "at the top of his voice," and so he assigned them to characters who could not be seen as wholly "positive."

Referring to Chekhov's insistent demands that the opinions, say, of the hero of "A Dreary Story" should not be ascribed to the author, Ilya Ehrenburg considered that these objections related to "Chekhov's spiritual shyness and reserve" and could obviously be ignored in interpretation, for Chekhov, "like all writers, frequently put his own thoughts into the mouths of his characters."[5]

This idea of a "shy" Chekhov who felt compelled to dissociate himself outwardly from what he secretly wanted to affirm through his writings, has a long history. Perhaps the first time it occurs is in Pleshcheyev's letter to Chekhov about "The Name-Day Party," where he writes: "Forgive me, Anton Pavlovich, but are you not also holding something back for fear of being thought a liberal?" "I've never hidden anything," Chekhov replied.[6]

Different interpreters, as we see, put this notorious diffidence of Chekhov's down to different causes: tactical (his unwillingness to attach himself to any one "party"), biographical (his innate "shyness" or "reserve"), or artistic (rejecting the style of other writers). But the image of Chekhov that emerges from all these variations is rather odd: of an author who, out of a peculiar sense of delicacy, gave his "message" to people of doubtful qualities without stopping to think that this might distort and discredit the "message" in the eyes of readers. One could hardly imagine a stranger and more incomprehensible way for a writer to communicate with his audience.

What needs to be clearly recognized is that in his writings Chekhov said what he genuinely had to say and wanted to say, straight out, at the top of his voice. This straightforwardness had nothing in common with cheap tendentiousness, and there was no

---

5. Op. cit., p. 54.
6. *Letters*, 3:18, 324.

need for Chekhov to use intermediaries as the vehicle for the idea to be expressed. But the idea was not one that could be contained within this or that subject-limited maxim; Chekhov's new "message" was his "conception of the world," as Gorky put it. And he spoke his truth about life to the reader not "through his characters" but through the artistic composition of his works. The most important task for the interpreter of Chekhov is to understand the rich meaning of the actual forms of Chekhov's artistic thinking and their objective social significance.

## 15

# "Equal Distribution" in Conflicts: "Ward No. 6" (1892), "The Black Monk" (1894)

Closely connected with the question of the "specialized" and the general, and with the character of Chekhov's generalizations, is the nature of conflict in his work.

Chekhov's heroes, as we have seen, stand in a special relationship to the outside world. For Chekhov, human beings are not simply objects acted upon by certain social or natural forces; they are themselves always active cognitive subjects. Epistemological aspects are vitally important to an understanding of conflicts in Chekhov.

In the stories of confrontation between two characters, the commonest form of antagonism is mutual misunderstanding. Failure to understand the other person comes about because each person is absorbed with his own "problem," his own "truth," or his own "false conception." This enables Chekhov to see what there is *in common* between people, where others would see only irreconcilability and opposition.

Chekhov's new approach to conflict had already become evident in stories like "Enemies" and "The Malefactor" (1887), where the author concentrates on showing how very different people can be viewed in the same light, and how misunderstanding (unintentional and deliberate at the same time) is displayed by both sides.

This aspect of his approach—pointing out the similarity between opposing characters, what it is that unites them and makes them equal—was to become the distinguishing mark of conflicts in Chekhov from the end of the 1880s.

In "The Name-Day Party" (1888) self-deceit and falsehood are shown to be the source of emotional and physical suffering. But the story is not about the falsity of one person only, the heroine's husband, Pavel Dmitrich; Olga Mikhailovna, the heroine, to whom Chekhov is sympathetic, also lies constantly. The husband poses and shows off out of vanity and from habit, whereas the wife does so to maintain a conventional facade (of being a hospitable society hostess, when she should be doing far more thinking about their future "little person") and likewise from habit. She is continually recording the manifestations of his falsity while the narrator does the same to her in no less systematic a fashion. The husband may be more guilty in his falsity toward Olga Mikhailovna, but it is the falsity of both the "big people" that is responsible in equal measure for the disaster of the "little person" who never materializes. Once again the elements of conflict are shared equally.

This feature of conflict in Chekhov will appear on several further occasions, most notably in stories where the antagonists would seem to be traditionally contrasted: "The Duel," "Ward No. 6," and "The Black Monk."

Layevksy and von Koren, the heroes of "The Duel," would appear to occupy opposite positions on everything. Some interpretations of the story are built on the contrast between these two antagonists, with the preference usually being given to Layevsky, since von Koren advocates such inhuman methods for improving the human race. But what this interpretation fails to take into account is that here too, by pointing to the hidden similarity between the two heroes, Chekhov is equalizing their delusions and refusing to show a preference to either of them.

Thus at the very beginning of the story Layevsky is described as experiencing "intense hatred" for Nadezhda Fyodorovna. This same Layevsky, who can be presented as the object of von Koren's unjust hatred, "understood why lovers sometimes murder their mistresses. He wouldn't do that himself, of course, but if he chanced to be sitting now on a jury, he would acquit such a murderer." Later on, Layevsky pictures the agonizing punishment he would inflict on his opponent:

> He imagined himself knocking von Koren to the ground and trampling on him. . . . He could shoot him in the arm or leg and wound him, then make fun of him, and after that leave him to be swallowed up with his dumb suffering in a crowd of nonentities like himself, just as an insect that has lost a leg crawls off into the grass.

M. L. Semanova has rightly commented that in Chekhov's story the duel takes place between everyone and everyone else.[1] Layevsky is no less inhuman in his thoughts than von Koren is in words (and to some extent the former's cruelty is more refined than that of his Social Darwinist opponent). It is no accident, of course, that Chekhov draws attention to this, since these and other aspects of the hidden similarity between the heroes' outlooks provide further illustration of the idea that "no one knows the real truth." That each of them at the last moment succeeds in rising above his self-absorption and looking humanely at his neighbor only clarifies Chekhov's notion that people have more in common than they imagine.

Ilya Ehrenburg distributed the author's sympathies and antipathies between the heroes of "The Duel" along these lines: "Layevsky behaves badly but he has a heart; under the influence of life's cruel lessons he forces himself to become different. Von Koren is carried away by science and progress, but he is heartless."[2] But that can best be described as a pre-Chekhovian technique of characterization: a hero whose philosophy or journey through life will in the final account receive the author's blessing, is at the same time as-

1. M. L. Semanova, *Povest' A. P. Chekhova "Duel' "* (Leningrad, 1971), p. 3.
2. Ilya Ehrenburg, *Perechityvaya Chekhova*, p. 66.

signed certain delusions, weaknesses, and mistakes that he must constantly overcome. It is how Tolstoy, for example, builds the personalities and progress through life of his favorite characters in *War and Peace*.

Chekhov's work, on the other hand, is governed by generalizations of a radically different nature. Both of his antagonists are right, both are wrong, but it is not any of the positions they defend that is false—it is how each makes his "personal view of things" absolute, the absorption of each in his own point of view, their claims to possession of the truth, and their deafness and intolerance toward those around them. (The way in which the story is constructed as a proof addressed specifically to von Koren is something else again: that is shown by the distribution of points of view within the narrative.)

In "Ward No. 6" Chekhov shows two different characters and temperaments, two philosophies of life and ways of behaving, and two attitudes toward evil in the world. Dr. Ragin's outlook is passive: he hopes to get through life without intervening in anything or preventing anything from happening, and he soothes himself with a philosophy derived from his reading of Marcus Aurelius, Schopenhauer, and Merezhkovsky. Gromov, his patient, differs from him in his active temperament, refusal to accept evil, ardent sense of protest, and hope for revenge, if only from beyond the grave. Gromov's speeches of protest appear far more attractive and justified than Ragin's arguments. Chekhov brings these two antagonistic principles into direct conflict and makes the collapse of Ragin's philosophy his main theme.

All this is an essential part of the author's position, but most interpretations of "Ward No. 6" are content to stop there. Yet the opposition between Ragin and Gromov is valid only up to a point, beyond which it is their similarity and common fate that are striking. Compare the following, italics added:

Gromov: "*He read a great deal.* . . . This reading must have been one of his morbid habits, since he pounced on everything that came his way, even last year's newspapers and calendars, with the same degree of rapacity."

Ragin: "*He reads a great deal* and always with much pleasure . . . three of the six rooms in his apartment are piled high with books and old magazines. . . . He does not read rapidly and jerkily, as Ivan Dmitrich [Gromov] used to do, but slowly and with penetration."

Gromov: "But against that he suffered a considerable *loss of interest* in the outside world, especially in books. . . ."

Ragin: "Reading *no longer occupied his attention closely* and he found it tiring. . . ."

Gromov: "Ivan Dmitrich . . . stopped reasoning altogether and *gave himself up* entirely to despair and *terror.*"

Ragin: " 'One might as well *give in*, because no human efforts are going to save one now.' . . . 'So this is it, the real world!' thought Andrei Yefimych [Ragin] and felt *terrified.*"

Gromov: ". . . he asks for only one reward—*solitary* confinement."

Ragin: "Genuine happiness is impossible without *solitude.*"

Gromov: "Ivan Dmitrich gave a loud shriek. He must have been *hit,* too."

Ragin: "Nikita *thumped* him twice in the back."

Before being incarcerated in Ward No. 6, Ragin speaks of the "vicious circle" in which he has been trapped. How Gromov came to be confined in Ward No. 6 is a similar story of going round in "a vicious circle from which there is no escape." Both heroes are broken and crushed by the coarseness of life and its prevailing vulgarity, by violence and injustice. Both are powerless in the unequal contest, and Ragin is fully justified at the end of the story when he puts himself and Gromov on an equal footing: "We're weak, we're just rubbish. . . . And that goes for you, too, my friend."

The only weapons they both have against a hostile world are words and hopes for the future:

"Just wait for that time in the distant future when hospitals and madhouses will cease to exist—there'll be no barred windows or hospital smocks then. That time is coming sooner or later, rest assured."

Ivan Dmitrich gave a mocking smile.

"You're joking," he said, screwing up his eyes. "Gentlemen like you and your assistant Nikita couldn't care less about the future—but better times *are* coming, you can be sure of that, sir!"

A passion for philosophizing on common themes and for provoking an argument even when there are no grounds for one (they both, as we see, pin their hopes on the future, though they express themselves differently), increases the common ground between them, though they themselves do not see this. Gromov in particular denies it categorically.

They both use hopes for the future as a means of consoling themselves for their inability to effect the slightest change in the real world: "Well, there it is. . . . We'll have *our* turn in the next world," says Gromov. "My ghost will come back here and terrify these vermin." Apropos of such hopes Ragin sagely observes: "It's a good thing that you believe. With a belief like that you could be walled in and still lead a cheerful life." But a similar comment could apply equally well to Ragin's own philosophy.

The same end awaits them both. Gromov's prediction—"some peasants will come along and drag one's dead body by the arms and legs into a cellar"—comes literally true in the case of Ragin: "Some peasants arrived, got hold of his body by the arms and legs, and carried him off to the chapel."

These persistent reminders of the similarity between the characters (who tend to attach absolute significance to the differences between them) are tinged with a sad irony. They represent the most essential part of Chekhov's position in one of his saddest and darkest stories. For the objective conclusion to be drawn from this story of two characters who come to the same end by completely different routes (and here the principle of individualization is consistently adhered to) is this: whoever each of them may be, and whatever philosophical principles each may be guided by, if they try to stand out only slightly from the prevailing vulgarity, they will inevitably be driven to prison, penal servitude, or the madhouse, and thrown onto Nikita's fists.

It was Chekhov's intention to make his readers experience the physical sensation of being surrounded by forces that are hostile to the natural aspirations of human beings, who are created "from warm blood and nerves." These intentions were grasped by the most sensitive of the early readers of "Ward No. 6"—a story that was written at the time of Chekhov's gloomiest reflections in the post-Sakhalin years.

"The Black Monk" (1894) long ago acquired the reputation of being an "enigmatic" story. No other work by Chekhov has so divided the critics, who offer diametrically opposed interpretations of the author's sympathies and antipathies.

For those who consider that Chekhov is "unmasking" Kovrin, with his master's degree in psychology, and singing the praises of Pesotsky, the horticulturist, the point of the story is to be found in the contrast between "an unreal philosophy" and "real practical work," between false "decadent-romantic theories and the genuine beauty of the real world," and in debunking "the idea of unjustified greatness" held by Kovrin, "a renegade from life." Their opponents see Kovrin as "a sufferer of genius," they speak of "the beauty of Kovrin's dream of service to humanity," and they claim that through Kovrin, Chekhov was able to express "the search for the higher aims of life," whereas he used Pesotsky to condemn "narrow utilitarianism" and "poverty of interests"—for them the point of the story is to be found in the clash between "high aims and ideals" and "the world of vulgarity and narrow-mindedness."

The controversy does not die; more and more articles appear, and the two schools of thought acquire fresh adherents. But it's an ill wind. . . . In the search for new arguments both the "Kovrinites" and the "Pesotskyists" are finding out in more and more detail how Chekhov's text reflects the literary and ideological life of the period, and how "The Black Monk" is connected with Russian and world literature and philosophical thought: how the fantastic and symbolic elements in the story, for example, are related to the literature of symbolism; how its subject matter compares with the Faust legend[3] and with other works of Russian literature that develop a similar theme; and the parallels between the speeches of Kovrin's phantom—the black monk—and the ideas of Merezhkovsky, Minsky, Schopenhauer, and Nietzsche. The origin of the hero's ideas and the forms of his hallucinations can be clearly demonstrated in this way.

But the most sophisticated commentaries, and what would seem to be the clearest demonstration of the correspondence between the text of "The Black Monk" and external sources, do not take us one step closer to understanding its real point. For the attempt to discover in Chekhov a solution to the subject-limited, "specialized" problems that preoccupy his characters, and a justification of the "specialized" positions they adopt, is ill-conceived.

"The Black Monk" is the story of how the lives of Kovrin and his friends (and later relations), the Pesotskys, are shattered. At the end of the story, Kovrin reflects on the similarity in their fates, on the havoc that has been wrought "within a couple of years in his life and the lives of those near him."

Each side accuses the other of responsibility for this havoc. Kovrin says to Tanya and Pesotsky when they are trying to cure him:

"I was going mad, I had megalomania, but I was bright and cheerful, happy even, I was interesting and original. Now I've become more staid and responsible, but I'm just like everyone else—I'm a mediocrity, my life's boring. . . . Oh, how cruelly you treated me! I was seeing hallucinations, but what harm did that do anyone?"

Tanya's accusations are directed against Kovrin:

"My father has just died. I can thank you for that, since you killed him. Our garden is going to ruin, there are strangers in charge of it

---

3. Thomas Winner, *Chekhov and His Prose* (New York, 1966), pp. 116, 119.

now—so poor father's worst nightmare has come to pass. I can thank you for that, too. I hate you from the bottom of my heart and hope you die soon. Oh, how I'm suffering!"

Mutual accusations between self-absorbed characters (and there is a clear opposition in the story between two different conceptions of life) are nothing new in Chekhov. Most interpretations of "The Black Monk" start out with the intention of finding evidence to show that the author was sympathetic to one side or the other, to this or that life program. But the approach itself is wrong. For Chekhov is analyzing these points of view without giving preference to any of the contrasted characters; instead he is making Kovrin and the Pesotskys suffer in an identical way at the hands of life and fate.

What are the real reasons that lead to the havoc—the reasons that correspond to the author's logic and not the "logic" of any of the characters' accusations? The overriding cause, once again, is to be found in delusions, identical and equally distributed between both parties, and not in the evil intent or mistakes of one party alone.

Again, these mistakes and delusions are epistemological in character: they are linked with attempts to understand the real world and orient oneself within it. Of primary importance in "The Black Monk" is one of the most universal delusions (for in spite of the individual and somewhat unusual accompanying circumstances, the story of Kovrin and the Pesotskys is a commonplace one, as Kovrin himself perceives in his reflections). This delusion is the inability of each individual to form a correct (fair) judgment of a situation or another person, especially when the person judging is involved in the situation and in a close relationship with the person being judged.

The "it seemed . . . it turned out that" situation plays a defining role in the story of the characters in "The Black Monk."

In the relationship between Layevsky and Nadezhda Fyodorovna in "The Duel," and in the attraction that Zinaida Fyodorovna feels in "The Story of an Unknown Man" for Orlov and later for the unknown man himself, Chekhov had already explored the love and family conflicts that arise when the chosen person turns out to be not what he first seemed.

Similar to this is Kovrin's strange blindness at the moment of his decisive declaration to Tanya:

> She was stunned and bent forward, hunching her shoulders, and in a moment she seemed to have aged by ten years, but he found her beautiful and exclaimed rapturously in a loud voice: "Isn't she lovely?"

When making this declaration of love, which marks the beginning of the Pesotsky family's tragedy, Kovrin is not in a fit state to take responsibility for his words and actions: just before this he has seen the black monk for the second time, and on this occasion the apparition has spoken to him. Having received apparent confirmation of his genius and ability to perform great deeds for the benefit of humanity, Kovrin does not immediately come out of his state of exaltation. At that very moment he meets Tanya, and although he seems to be talking to her about the two of them, in fact he is thinking and talking only about himself.

But Tanya will also later recognize—albeit too late—that she has made exactly the same kind of mistake: "I took you for an unusual person, a genius. I fell in love with you, but you turned out to be mad."

The fact that Kovrin, as the Pesotskys subsequently (and belatedly) discover, was not the man he had first seemed, is in no way the result of his attempt to deceive them or create a false impression, nor is there any conscious self-deception on their part.

Because the garden is the be-all and end-all of his life, Yegor Semyonych does not want it to fall into the hands of strangers. With peasant bluntness he tells Kovrin that he would like him and Tanya to produce a grandson, a future horticulturist. But as events turn out, the price that Pesotsky pays for this total self-absorption is the ruin of his garden, and in a moment of senseless animosity Kovrin refers to the "improper role" that Pesotsky has played in the romance between him and Tanya.

Tanya's mistake follows just as naturally from her essential character. It seems at first glance as if Pesotsky has cultivated his daughter as successfully as a new variety of apple. But in her conversation with Kovrin about the garden, Tanya confesses: "It's a good thing, I know, and it's useful, but at times I feel the wish for something more to add variety to my life." If Yegor Semyonych had heard these words, he would scarcely have understood what more his daughter could need, any more than he can understand anything about Kovrin's irritability.

Pesotsky is the product of a different, "positive" epoch; he is firmly rooted, whereas Tanya is much closer in her spiritual questioning to her future husband. She is even more sincere in her blindness than her father. If Tanya is to be thought of as a victim, she is certainly not a victim of Kovrin alone—with whom she has joined her fate on the strength of how things "seemed" to her, only for them to "turn out" quite differently—but also of her father, who has been storing her to manage the estate, whereas she felt "the wish for something more."

"She was . . . but he found her"; "I took you for . . . but you turned out to be. . . ."

A relationship with illusions of that kind at its source is bound to have a fatal outcome. The blame attached to the characters and the reason for their downfall is to be found in these illusions, but if there is blame it is mutual, and the delusions are inherent in each person, they are not peculiar to especially "negative" characters.

One special motif made it possible for Chekhov to refer to "The Black Monk" as a "medical" story. What gives everything that happens a fateful coloring, what makes Kovrin think of the "unknown force" that has wrought such havoc, is the difficulty of drawing the line between mental or psychic normality and disease.

In interpreting the author's attitude toward his hero, it is often overlooked that Chekhov describes his master of psychology as sick from the very outset—he is anxious to engage his characters in the action long before Kovrin's madness becomes public knowledge. That Kovrin is a maniac remains hidden from the Pesotskys until it is too late for anything to be done about it.

There is something fateful about the way in which a destructive illness insinuates itself into the everyday relations between completely unsuspecting people. The reader already knows about Kovrin's madness: the black monk has appeared to him for the first time and pronounced the first part of his "ravings" . . . then straightaway "Tanya was walking across the park to meet him," Tanya who suspects nothing and is dreaming of marriage to Kovrin as the supreme happiness of her life; and Yegor Semyonych is naively sharing with Kovrin his dream of the grandson to whom the garden, his whole life's work, can be entrusted.

Fatal, universal blindness! But who is most to blame?

Should one blame a sick person for being sick, hallucinating, and raving? Or blame the Pesotskys for failing to notice what no one could have noticed?

Among the mistakes and unsuccessful attempts to "find one's bearings in life," Chekhov gave special consideration to those of his characters who are doomed in advance: doomed for natural, anthropological reasons. Chekhov the scientist saw the tragic element in human existence that arises from the imperfections and limitations of our biological nature ("I'm convinced that only bad things can be expected from this life—mistakes, losses, illnesses, weaknesses, and all kinds of dirty tricks").[4] Without dabbling in biological determinism, and with the norm as his ideal, Chekhov by his own admission very often turns to pathology, "the abnormal," and the boundaries separating pathology from the norm (including the biological/medical norm). As artist and as scientist, Chekhov never ignores human nature, those natural qualities which sometimes exercise the strongest influence on his characters' social functions and the real process of their lives in society.

But on the other hand, Chekhov never places exclusive emphasis on the problem of human nature; man for him is never presented as nothing but a "natural individual." In "The Black Monk," a "medical" story, Chekhov shows, alongside the natural foundations of mistaken ideas and actions, those mistakes that are purely social in

4. *Letters*, 5:117.

character and can be seen as predisposing or aggravating factors. Mistakes of this kind, we should emphasize again, are characteristic of both sides.

They consist of those false doctrines, including decadent ideas, which have become widespread in society and determine how individuals think in a normal state, as well as the character of their hallucinations in time of illness ("he recalled what he himself had learned and taught others, and decided that there was no exaggeration in the monk's words"). Here too it is useful, of course, to determine the specific sources of Kovrin's "ravings" (Schopenhauer, Minsky, Merezhkovsky), so long as one does not forget that alongside his characters' lack of philosophical originality, Chekhov also wants to show their total sincerity and sense of personal conviction.

The mistakes, then, consist of "general categories" applied unthinkingly by the characters to their own individual situations in life ("We're little people, but you're a great man"; "the thought would come to her out of the blue that she was small, petty, and insignificant, and unworthy of such a great man as Kovrin"). Among other general categories (those labels and stereotypes legitimized by general opinion), that of "the unusual man" or "the great man" was of special interest to Chekhov in the first half of the 1890s ("The Grasshopper," "Big Volodya and Little Volodya," "The Story of an Unknown Man").

To say that Chekhov's ultimate aim in "The Black Monk" was to show the tragic impact on his characters' lives of involuntary and conscious mistakes does not go far enough. Alongside the characters' ignorance of the "truth" and deviations from the norm there are other contrasting indications by the author of how the question of real truth and the norm should be posed correctly. Avoiding the didactic solution of making one side in the story represent his own views, Chekhov finds purely artistic ways of drawing the reader's attention to the norm from which his characters' lives are deviating.

As in several previous works, this is done by reminding the reader of the beauty that surrounds the characters and which they usually fail to notice. All through the story there runs a lyrical motif connected with the beautiful garden. The whole of the action in the first half of "The Black Monk"—the period of the characters' happiness—takes place in the garden, and when he is dying, Kovrin calls upon "the large garden with its magnificent blooms all sprinkled with dew, the park and the pine trees with their shaggy roots." Yet this garden is going to ruin . . . and it is not a question of the ill will of one person, Kovrin. The garden's creator and owner, Pesotsky, as has often been pointed out,[5] values the commercial side of the garden; everything else he "referred to contemptuously as trifles." Not to see or value the beauty around them is a fate common to many Chekhov characters, beginning in 1886 with "The Witch," "Agafya," and "The Requiem."

Another subtle motif colors the whole of the story, that of dying love. The apparently prosaic description of the disastrous wedding celebrations is full of an underlying sadness: "The food and drink cost three thousand rubles, but because of the inferior hired band, the noisy toasts, and the waiters scurrying about, because of the din and crush, no one appreciated the taste of the expensive wines or the remarkable hors d'oeuvres ordered specially from Moscow." In the same way no one noticed the first snow in "The Nervous Breakdown."

Chekhov was able to use these reminders of the beauty that his characters pass by or destroy, and the creation of a certain mood in the reader, as a very effective aesthetic means of expressing his own ideas of what ought to be, of "real truth."

Critics of "The Black Monk" have often pointed out that "the possibility of interpreting the image of Kovrin in different ways, of justifying or condemning him, is contained within the story itself."[6] You can indeed find evidence in the text to justify or condemn both Kovrin and the Pesotskys. But to understand the author's idea cer-

---

5. Thomas Winner sees in Pesotsky's practical activities a comment "on the fruitless intellectual efforts of Kovrin. . . . Do we have, in the old man, an inverted picture of Kovrin?" (op. cit., p. 117).

6. E. M. Sakharova, " 'Chyornyi monakh' i 'Oshibka' Gor'kogo" in *A. P. Chekhov. Sb. statei i materialov* (Rostov-on-Don, 1959), pp. 233–252.

tainly does not mean that one must come down in favor of one character and take a biased view of another character, refusing to see any contradictory elements.

The presence in each of his characters of heterogeneous features does not obscure the author's idea, but, on the contrary, is a prerequisite for its clear and unambiguous expression. For Chekhov's conception of human relations does not consist in contrasting bad people with good, those who have gone wrong and those who are innocent, but in just this: that living people, because of their inherent qualities and aspirations, may make mistakes and come to grief. To show how people may commit irreparable mistakes and ruin their own lives and other people's, Chekhov did not need to make some characters positive and others negative, to contrast their merits and demerits, or to prefer some over others.

No, to fulfill his aims it was enough for Chekhov to show his characters as self-absorbed people, each seeking to realize his conceptions and "general ideas," and each convinced of the absolute value of his "personal view of things." Here is the novel feature of conflict, to be demonstrated subsequently with great clarity in his plays. When in the early 1900s Chekhov was advising dramatists of the next generation, Gorky and Naidyonov, "not to contrast" some characters with others,[7] he was thinking not of the characters' relative qualities or of assigning to all of them equally "positive" features in the everyday sense, but of transferring the play's center of gravity from the contrasting of characters to different conflicts of an all-embracing, equally distributed kind. So far as Chekhov was concerned, to bring dramatic conflict down to the level of the positive or negative qualities of this or that character was old-fashioned—the drama of a bygone age.[8]

This principle of "equal distribution" in conflicts as a comprehensive rule and basis for the unity of form and content in

7. *Letters*, 10:96; 11:244.
8. For more details, see my article "O literaturnykh predshestvennikakh 'Vishnyovogo sada'" in *Chekhovskiye chteniya v Yalte. Chekhov i teatr* (Moscow, 1976), pp. 145–146.

Chekhov's plays was brilliantly demonstrated by A. P. Skaftymov in his article on *The Cherry Orchard.*[9] Long before the creation of that play, Chekhov had already affirmed the same principle in his prose: in "Enemies," "Ward No. 6," "The Duel," and "The Black Monk."

9. A. P. Skaftymov, "O yedinstvye formy i soderzhaniya v 'Vishnyovom sade' A. P. Chekhova" in *Uch. zap. Sarat. ped. inst.*, 1946, no. 8, pp. 3–38; *Nravstvennye iskaniya . . .* , pp. 339–380.

# 16

## Chekhov's General Conclusions

Chekhov was not setting out, then, to support any opinion his characters might express or course of action they might choose, nor was he taking sides in their conflicts or trying to solve any of the "specialized" problems at the center of their arguments and reflections. Of far greater interest are the principles he adopted for examining each problem, irrespective of its "specialized" nature.

The same can be said of the various ethical values that, it is sometimes claimed, Chekhov's work sets out to champion: such values as personal freedom, taking individual responsibility for the state of the world, self-emancipation, human dignity and self-respect, the rejection of vulgarity and philistinism, and culture understood in the broadest sense.

To highlight one or another of these themes, commentators invariably fall back on all the usual kinds of evidence: what individual characters say, their sympathies and antipathies, and how they act and behave. To emphasize the importance that Chekhov attached to work, for example, as the foundation of culture, the words of Laptev from "Three Years" are quoted ("Without work there cannot be a pure and joyful life") or of Irina in *Three Sisters* (from Act I, but not from Acts II and III, by which time her original expressions of rapture have turned sour on her); or Chekhov's protest against spiritual impoverishment is said to be "voiced by Gromov" in "Ward No. 6." We have already seen how conclusions based on that kind of evidence are quite unreliable, and how inapplicable such techniques of interpretation are to Chekhov.

Culture, freedom, humanity, scholarship, work, individual dignity: these values, it goes without saying, were absolute for Chekhov. To single out any one of them as most important would scarcely be appropriate: what struck Chekhov's contemporaries about his personality was its harmonious combination of a rich variety of human qualities. No less absolute was his rejection of vulgarity and narrow-mindedness, and his protest against the violation of freedom, the absence of culture, and violence. That Chekhov was passionate in his sympathies and could be highly critical is beyond doubt, just as he undoubtedly had his own decided views on the "specialized" problems that confronted his heroes.

So what is it that constitutes Chekhov's distinctively new and unique contribution to world literature? What at the end of the day did he leave behind as a writer that has guaranteed constant and growing interest in him in the modern world? Was it nothing more than the affirmation or defense of certain moral values, the sum total of ideas he expressed on individual subjects, or the combination of certain positive moral recommendations?

No, it is the particular kind of artistic thinking embodied in Chekhov's work that constitutes its chief value. Chekhov's particular way of examining things takes in moral problems that vary considerably in their nature, importance, and contemporary relevance, and this represents another sphere in which his characters must orient themselves. The point at which other writers would think they had completed their task—by making the hero break or intend to break with his social milieu, or by registering their protest against vulgarity and their support for humanity, culture, dignity, and personal independence—is the very point at which the real problem and investigation begins for Chekhov.

The orientation of Chekhov's characters in the moral sphere is a particular instance of their orientation in the world.

More than any other writer before or since, Chekhov was the poet and investigator of a specific range of experience: making sense of life, orienting oneself within it, choosing a course of action or a way of behaving. In Chekhov's world these processes are all-inclusive, and to a large extent his distinctive literary forms are determined by this angle of vision on reality.

There is no question linked with how we orient ourselves and perceive our position in the world that Chekhov does not examine to see if it is posed and answered correctly. Both large-scale constructs (theories, doctrines, general convictions) and their smaller units (the ideas and opinions of particular people, forms of individual behavior) are examined to see if they are true, complete, universally binding, and fair. It is not so much the absolute sense of these epistemological constructs that is examined, as the ways in which they arise and become manifest; Chekhov is looking at the difficulties, subjective and objective, of finding true solutions.

His description of this constant, deliberately chosen range of experience guarantees the unity of Chekhov's artistic world. Thus, in his humorous and his "serious" works, he treats differently—either comically or tragically—exactly the same set of phenomena: the multiplicity of "truths," "general theories," sign systems, and rules, along with the absence of satisfactory guidelines, which prevent people from making sense of a hostile reality.

Another constant is Chekhov's approach to his material, his principle of "treating each individual case in isolation." He is not simply recording various attempts to find one's bearings in life and "solve the problem": he and his heroes are not searching for its own sake but in order to find out. All the problems to be solved by Chekhov's heroes can be correlated with the search for "real truth." This central Chekhov concept is not to be thought of as an a priori eternal truth, the same for everyone and long since known, but as a truth to be sought, in many respects unknown and most often to be defined negatively, by contrast with the "norm," how things ought to be.

Like Tolstoy and Dostoevsky, Chekhov is speaking of universal processes in which all persons are involved. Hence the general human significance of his work. Chekhov's "trademark" shows a variety of human efforts, all relating to a single, inalienably human process—the search for "real truth." But unlike his predecessors, Chekhov never generalizes the ideas and solutions that his characters arrive at; he individualizes each case, stressing that any answer is conditional and indicating the limits to which it can be applied. There are no general, final prescriptions and solutions, Chekhov is saying, and one should not be taken in by one's "personal view of things" and by "false conceptions," or attach absolute significance to "general ideas." In other words, what is most important in his opinion is that the solution of general problems should come about through unique individuals and in unique circumstances.

Thus the system of coordinates upon which Chekhov's artistic world is built consists of a special range of experience, i.e., how human beings orient themselves in the real world, and a special way of looking at that experience, i.e., treating each individual case in isolation. Chekhov's "absolutes," his general conclusions, are contained within these limits. But while he insists that "each case should be examined in isolation," Chekhov at the same time leads us to certain general conclusions of permanent and universal human significance.

These general conclusions are in the first place negations. The relative, conditional nature of ideas and opinions, and of stereotyped ways of thinking and behaving; the refusal to regard any individual solution as absolute; and the baselessness of various claims to the possession of "real truth": these are constants in Chekhov's world. They show a side of Chekhov that was uncompromising and incapable of being satisfied by any illusion, however sanctified it might be by tradition and authority. None of Chekhov's heroes knows the "real truth"; in each of his stories, illusion after illusion is shattered and rejected, and the falsity of various general and individual ideas is revealed. Yet the correlation of the characters' words and behavior with "real truth" is not purely negative.

Chekhov may have opposed attaching absolute value to "truths" that are bound to be inconclusive, individual, and partial, but he saw nothing absurd in the urge to obtain the end products of our thinking and our orienting/cognitive activity generally. His work never fails to convey the idea that the attempt to "make sense of life" and find the truth is something inescapable, an inalienable part of belonging to the human race. "Real truth" is unknown, or is understood wrongly and in different ways, but the search for it is a sure sign of Chekhov characters as different from each other as Nikitin in "The Teacher of Russian," the hopelessly entangled Sofya Lvovna in "Big Volodya and Little Volodya," and Ivan Terekhov, the innkeeper in "The Murder." Thus illusions are not simply destroyed: each work provides a standard by which to judge the degree of their falsity, shakiness, and inadmissibility.

General conclusions of these two kinds recur in Chekhov with the greatest regularity. After each of the significant events and turns in his own life, they invariably became deeper, reinforced by life itself. Thus after Sakhalin, Chekhov writes predominantly about human disunity and how judgments and verdicts that may appear sound turn out to be unfair ("Gusev," "The Duel," *The Island of Sakhalin*), as well as about the ineradicable human urge, in spite of appearances to the contrary, to try to define one's position: to question life, challenge fate, and ask oneself previously unanswered questions ("The Duel" and "Gusev" again, "In Exile," "Ward No. 6"). But it is not difficult to discover the same motifs in "Lights," "An Unpleasant Incident," "The Nervous Breakdown," and "Thieves," written before Sakhalin.

We know that Chekhov insisted on making a distinction in literary criticism between solving problems and posing them correctly, regarding only the latter as obligatory for the artist. How did Chekhov, while not claiming to solve problems about the essence of the "norm" and "real truth," and rejecting wrong solutions, satisfy himself that he had posed such problems correctly? What did he consider essential to this task?

In addition to negative general conclusions and affirmative conclusions with regard to "searching for truth" and the "thirst for truth," in Chekhov's work there is always another structural element, another variety of general conclusion. This consists of the criteria and measures against which ideas and theories, fixed opinions and forms of behavior, are tested, and which Chekhov establishes as an indispensable condition of "posing problems correctly." Each work by Chekhov indicates the factors to be taken into account if the problem of "real truth" is to be posed correctly. "Real truth" is not the solution of some specialized problem. No definition of it is given, nor is it even supposed to be. But Chekhov introduces into each story and play the *criteria* which this unknown and sought-after truth ought to satisfy.

Chekhov laid down his own distinctive criteria of "truth" (a concept common to Russian realism in general) once and for all in his works written in the 1890s.

The first is the requirement of completeness: taking the fullest possible account of all the circumstances and "complications" connected with this or that phenomenon, event, or problem. Truth in Chekhov is above all a synonym for complexity. And most often the Chekhov hero does not know the *whole* truth.

"Why should a little one have to suffer so much before dying?" the grieving Lipa asks the old man "from Firsanov" ("In the Ravine").

"We can't know all the whys and wherefores," he replies. "A bird's meant to have two wings, not four, because two's enough to fly with; same thing with man, he's not meant to know everything, but only a half or a quarter. He knows as much as he needs to know for getting through life." This is a very rare example in Chekhov of a character who accepts not knowing "everything" calmly, as the inevitable lot of human beings.

Far more often Chekhov's characters are either tormented by not knowing "everything," or else pass off their "half" or "quarter" of the truth as the whole truth. The author, in assigning qualities of this kind to his characters, is trying on each occasion to build a picture of the world in all its colorful complexity and variety.

Thus for Chekhov an essential component of truth in all its completeness is always beauty. The beauty that people very often fail to notice is present even in his most tragic works. (In the world of "Ward No. 6," where reality is symbolized by the prison, the fence studded with nails, and the madhouse, there would seem to be no place for a bright spot, but suddenly at the end, in the vision before his death, Ragin sees a herd of deer flash past, "unusually beautiful and graceful.") An image of "austere and beautiful Russia"—austere and beautiful at the same time—arises from Chekhov's pages, and reveals a degree of complexity in its comprehension of the outside world that was new in Russian literature.

But "not knowing the real truth" is very different from "not knowing the whole truth." The concept of "real truth" must satisfy beyond dispute those criteria in Chekhov's world other than completeness.

A further requirement of "real truth" is that it should be *universally significant.* This is a criterion that Chekhov's characters who claim to possess the truth often fail to meet. If the most ardent and sympathetic confession leaves its listeners unmoved ("No Comment," "The Nervous Breakdown," "The Head Gardener's Story"), or if the lessons of one person's life are inapplicable to dozens of other lives, then the "truth" being affirmed by the hero looks to be nothing more than a "personal view of things." Whenever a delusion is widespread and general, the method of treating each individual case in isolation is used to expose its falsity.

Finally, truth for Chekhov is inseparable from *fairness.* We know that he thought of "absolute and honest truth" as the aim of literature.[1] The criteria of completeness and universal significance correspond to "absolute truth." But for "honest truth" there are few indications that truth in its logical or philosophical sense satisfies. "Honest truth" is essentially an expression of moral values. His letters and fiction constantly make it clear that the highest moral criterion for Chekhov as a man and as a writer was fairness, which is "more vital than air for an objective writer."[2]

So these criteria of "real truth," always expressed with unam-

1. *Letters,* 2:11.
2. *Letters,* 4:273.

biguous clarity through the actual structure of a literary work, represent another kind of Chekhov general conclusion, his message and sermon to the reader, the expression of his "conception of life."

Chekhov's general conclusions may be negative ("no one knows the real truth") or affirmative (seeking the truth is an inalienable part of human nature), or they may take the form of indicating the criteria and conditions necessary for establishing real truth. But never once can they be expressed by a particular Chekhov hero: the opinions, behavior, and position of any character are to be seen as particular instances of more general phenomena. They are examined from a higher point of view, as material for the author's comprehensive analysis.

There is one other important aspect of Chekhov's general conclusions: they are inseparably connected and are to be found at the same time in each of his works.

In Chekhov there are no negations without an affirmation, just as there are no affirmations without a negation. It is from seizing upon only one kind of general conclusion that the most typical mistakes in interpreting Chekhov may be said to derive. If we speak, for example, about Chekhov's sympathies for his "searching" or "protesting" heroes, we should not forget that in each case Chekhov shows that these heroes do not know the truth—the "absolute" or "honest" truth.

Or conversely, if we speak of a "cruel" Chekhov, who destroys illusions and is coldly ironical about one unsuccessful attempt after another to find one's bearings in life, we should not fail also to explain why Chekhov took such an unfailing interest in these attempts.

In the same way we should not think of Chekhov setting out to affirm particular "specialized" truths connected with a specific phenomenon, and forget that he steadfastly refused to consider "the specialized," that his general conclusions apply to all people at all times, and that he discovered principles for assessing each idea, form of behavior, and position irrespective of its specialized content.

Chekhov's negative and affirmative conclusions are not in conflict; instead, by complementing each other, they introduce an element of harmony into Chekhov's artistic world and belie simple, one-sided conceptions of humankind. This sense of measure and harmony marks the boundary that separates Chekhov's work from the searchings of writers of later generations.

The reflections and conclusions that Joseph K. comes to in the last chapters of Kafka's *The Trial* might be seen as a variation on the theme of the heroes' discussions in "Ward No. 6." It is as if Chekhov had looked into the future and foreseen the nightmares of human existence that were to preoccupy the artists of the twentieth century. Nothing new, in effect, would be said after Chekhov about human loneliness, the inability of the individual mind to come to terms with the world's complexity, the despotic power of "general conceptions," or about human noncommunication and disconnectedness. Chekhov's discoveries determined the conclusions of many artists in the twentieth century, so that the creators of the *nouveau roman* and of the theater of the absurd are happy to recognize in Chekhov a kindred spirit.

Yet for all the well-known similarity between Chekhov and the modernists in their perception of life and their assessment of the possibilities open to the individual, the conclusions to which they lead us are completely opposite.

" 'What am I to do?' or 'Why should I do this?' are not questions they ask round here": this is how Kafka in "The Railway Passengers" concludes his comparison of life with a train crash in a tunnel. For Kafka, the tragic irony of human existence lay in the impossibility of getting to the bottom of what was going on in the world, and in having to remain no more than a passive observer of "the passers-by." The urge of people in Kafka's world "to look into the depths of the Law" is itself absurd.

For Chekhov, who is writing about the meaninglessness or inadequacy of all manner of human activities, and whose characters also have no idea of the final aims of their strivings and searchings ("if only we could know . . ."), one of the most frequent and definite conclusions is that in spite of everything, one should not do nothing, that it is impossible not to try to make something out "in this world," in which most of the time "you can't make sense of anything."

The similar fates of the two heroes in "Ward No. 6" confirm Ragin's words about the impossibility of breaking out of the "vicious circle." But the bankruptcy of the passive, contemplative position is shown not only by the logic of the plot; the narrator's voice in "Ward No. 6" is that of a stern judge of Ragin's indifference. In "Ionych," speaking of his character's sad fate, Chekhov shows that his downfall was almost inevitable: the forces that turn a carefree young man into an insensitive money-grubber are too strong to be resisted by one person on his own. Chekhov shows that a human being who wishes to remain human in a hostile world must harbor no illusions: neither health, nor work, nor contempt for the local philistines could provide an effective antidote against the transformation of Startsev into one of the philistines himself. The final conclusion that Chekhov invites us to draw, however, is not one of hopelessness or pessimism, but of sober honesty. Contempt for what Ionych has become is expressed so openly ("greed has got the better of him," "he leads a dull life," "not a man, but a pagan god") that even in spite of the obvious inevitability of the hero's moral collapse, it is the urge not to become reconciled but to resist the pressures of society that the story stimulates in the reader.

L. Shestov described Chekhov as the murderer of human hopes.[3] But Chekhov was not killing hopes, he was killing illusions. He was against attaching absolute value to inconclusive, partial "truths," and he spoke of the difficulties of attaining real truth, but he was not claiming that the urge to know and to act was in any way absurd. In Chekhov the questions "What am I to do?" and "Why should I do this?" *are* constantly being asked, and it is because they are asked so unfailingly that they are not meaningless.

In modernist and avant-garde literature, individual Chekhovian motifs can be identified, showing that Chekhov was ahead of his

3. Leon Shestov, *Chekhov and Other Essays* (Ann Arbor, 1966, reprint of the 1916 translation), pp. 4–5.

time and had a premonition of the problems that would reverberate in the second half of the twentieth century. But the modernists have inflated and seen as exclusively important what is only one side of Chekhov, one general conclusion. His work is distinguished from the disharmony and one-sidedness of modernism primarily by its sense of harmony. The secret of this harmony was held by the last of the classic nineteenth-century Russian writers.

# Right in One's Own Way:
## *The Seagull* (1896)

In his comedy *The Seagull*, Chekhov continued the development of a new dramatic language that he had begun in his first plays. He was very conscious of writing a play "in defiance of all the rules of dramatic art."[1] What constituted the originality of this play, a play about people in whose lives art and love are inseparable?

The Chekhov type of hero and event had already been defined in *Ivanov*. The originality of the new play revealed itself in another very important area, that of *conflict*.

If "orienting oneself" in life is to be understood as Chekhov's central theme, this might seem to restrict the main interest of his work to the realm of consciousness, to purely thinking processes. But in fact it is their "personal view of things" that determines how Chekhov's heroes behave and the relationships among them. The initial events in Chekhov's plays that are invisible and "unsubstantial" lead to actions, collisions, and outcomes that are fully perceptible.

The first plays tended to monodrama: one central character was selected and came into conflict with the others. In *The Seagull*,

---

1. *Letters*, 6:100.

Chekhov tried using the construction he had worked out for his stories, whereby the conflict is *equally distributed*: characters who would seem to be at opposite poles in their attitudes to love and art turn out to have hidden features in common. As a result, the author's ideas on life are revealed not by one central hero but by several characters equally or by all of them at once. Attentive readers of *The Seagull* were struck by the "hidden dramas and tragedies of each figure in the play."[2]

The first glimpses of *The Seagull* in Chekhov's notebooks show that to begin with, in the autumn of 1894, he was thinking about the image of a young artistic rebel (Kostya Treplev in the play): "It's the naive and pure-minded who can anticipate new directions in art, whereas conservatives like you—you've grabbed all the power, you accept only your own art as legitimate, and everything else you squash."[3]

This note is the germ of a very important theme in *The Seagull*, that of youth, forever making bold experiments in art and rebelling against what it sees as obstacles standing in the way of its artistic vision. The rebellion is both just and blind at the same time; it raises its hand against idols and fetishes . . . and yet it obeys the eternal laws of art; it not only has a shattering effect on the forces of routine and moderation that are hostile to talent, but it can result in disaster for the rebel, who spares neither the people around him nor himself.

This initial theme of *The Seagull* took the form in Chekhov's mind of a Shakespearean/Hamlet situation. From the start he was thinking both of the young rebel and also of his opponents—the usurpers who had grabbed the best places in art, the "conservatives" (his actress mother and her lover), and the teacher (Medvedenko in the play), who was evidently intended to emphasize the contrast between the search for "new forms" in art and something more down to earth, the struggle against life's adversities. What is surprising is

2. V. I. Nemirovich-Danchenko to Chekhov, April 25, 1898. *Perepiska A. P. Chekhova*, 3 vols. (Moscow, 1996), vol. 3, p. 64.
3. *Works*, 17:35.

that in the original conception of *The Seagull*, the seagull herself, the play's heroine, was not there; there are no notes about Nina Zarechnaya.

In July 1895, when he was still mulling over the play, Chekhov made an unexpected trip to see his friend, the artist Levitan, who had tried to shoot himself after an unhappy love affair. The lake, the bird that had been shot down, and the attempted suicide now became part of the play. And it was only in October 1895, when Chekhov began writing, that the heroine took her place alongside the hero. A note appears about an actress recalling her lost past: "For play: actress, seeing pond, bursts into tears, recalls childhood."[4] With Nina's appearance, the theme of new directions in art becomes firmly linked with the theme of love.

Nina Zarechnaya, the play's young heroine, dreams of becoming an actress; she is attracted most of all to the glamour and celebrity of being an artist; to be loved by someone her own age is pleasant enough until a genuine passion comes along. Kostya Treplev, the apprentice writer, thinks "new forms are necessary," he finds the modern theater dull and boring; he hates those who hold the leading positions in art, and suffers first from humiliation, then from jealousy.

But before the last act a change takes place in Nina and Kostya, and it is this change that constitutes the main *event* in *The Seagull*. Everything that happens in the first three acts—the failure of the play about the World Spirit, the start of the relationship between Nina and Trigorin, Kostya's suicide attempt—only leads up to and prepares the way for this fundamental change.

Chekhov carried out his plan boldly and confidently. The whole melodramatic "collection of incidents" (Aristotle) is transferred offstage: like the messengers in classical tragedy, other characters supply us with information—and even then, only casually and in passing. For a mass audience or readership, what happens to Nina between Acts III and IV would have provided several interesting

4. *Works*, 17:39.

separate topics: her life as an actress, her affair with the writer, the death of her child . . . not to mention what has been happening in the lives of the other characters.

But for Chekhov there is nothing at all new in what has happened to Nina: "it's the same old story." The attention of audience and readers is directed firmly toward the main event. The "collection of incidents" in *The Seagull* may be colorful, but there is only one basic event. This event or change is the *discovery* that each of the young heroes makes after setting out in the world and coming into collision with life. These discoveries are identical in type.

In the last act both young heroes sum up the way in which the secrets of art have become more comprehensible to them. They speak of their discovery and take issue with their previous ideas, which have been overturned by life and their own experience. Both Kostya and Nina have covered the ground from "it seemed" to "it turned out that," just as dozens of heroes from Chekhov's stories had done before them.

"I used to talk so much about new forms": this was the starting point of Kostya's rebellion, how he understood his artistic goals. But now—"I'm becoming more and more convinced that it's not a question of old and new forms. What matters most is to stop thinking about forms altogether, and to write just because it comes pouring freely from your soul." Nina, too, acknowledges the falseness of her previous ideas on art: "I know now, Kostya, I've come to see, that what matters in our work—whether we're actors or writers—is not the fame or the glamour, not all the things I used to dream of, but just learning how to keep going. Learn how to bear your cross and have faith."

The path from "it seemed" to "it turned out that" is similar for both of them, the collapse of their former illusions is inevitable. But here another principle of Chekhov's artistic world takes over, that of "treating each individual case in isolation." With people like this, who do not separate life and love from art, simply to *understand* the secrets of literature and the theater is not enough to enable them to go on living.

Kostya now knows how one ought to write. But in order to write and to live, he *needs love*, and his feelings are not reciprocated. He takes Nina's rejection as a final verdict.

Nina now knows how one should act. But in order to survive and to believe in herself, she must *rid herself of her love* for Trigorin, who does not believe in the theater and in her talent. Nina runs away to save herself, but there is nowhere she can hide from Trigorin, because she loves him "even more than before," loves him "with a desperate passion."

As always in Chekhov, there are no universally binding prescriptions for how things should be in art and in love; no general solutions are to be found, and each person's fate, the course of each life, is unique. The critics who accused Chekhov of vagueness of purpose and shaky composition failed to see this precise, unambiguous dramatic construction. In writing about his contemporaries wearing jackets and drinking tea, Chekhov was making use of a type of drama close to that of the classical theater, in which the heroes' fates are determined by forces they are bound to be incapable of overcoming.

Chekhov is writing about those tragic regularities in art and in life that are repeated with each new generation. He does so by showing how very different characters, who would seem to be at opposite poles in the conflict (Nina and Arkadina, Kostya and Trigorin), turn out to have hidden features in common.

In the very first idea for *The Seagull*, the rebel is contrasted with the conservatives, who have achieved success and taken leading positions in art. The victors are pitiless and indifferent to those who have not found themselves. Kostya is humiliated by his actress mother while Trigorin unthinkingly insults him by his indifference or condescension.

But it is Nina who finally destroys him. At their last meeting, after they have summed up the consequences of their collisions with life ("I believe . . .", "I don't believe . . ."), Nina inflicts three cruel and pitiless blows on Kostya: she again scorns his love, she acknowledges once more her desperate passion for Trigorin, and she reminds him of the play that was the beginning of all his subsequent misfortunes. After this, nothing is left to bind Kostya to life.

Having experienced Trigorin's cruelty toward herself, Nina is no less cruel in her attitude to Kostya, who cruelly fails to notice the hopeless infatuation of Masha, just as she in turn scorns the love of the teacher Medvedenko. The same roundabout of hopeless admissions and cruel rejections is to be found in another age group (Dorn, Shamrayev, Polina Andreyevna, and Sorin). Here not only love and jealousy form part of the general chain but also a doctor's indifference to a patient, who hopes to be told how to ease his sufferings.

Even such a perceptive critic of Chekhov as J. B. Priestley saw it as one of the weaknesses of *The Seagull* that the characters obey a single principle—A loves B, B loves C, C loves D—with the result that "it has too large a circle of unrequited lovers."[5] But it is this general involvement of all the characters in a single circle of relationships that provides the entire foundation for the play.

It is not simply that they are all subject to identical feelings. Of far more importance is that all their mutual relationships are illuminated by the light of a single understanding. The play's analysis of the reasons for the misfortunes yields an unexpected result.

Why is it that in one way or another, for a time or absolutely, all the characters are unhappy? Who are the victims and who are the authors of this suffering? It turns out that it has nothing to do with anyone's "ill will"; it is simply that each person is acting in accordance with his own conviction, idea, view, or nature. In one of the early versions of *The Seagull*, this is alluded to directly.

"Each person is right in his own way," says Sorin, "each person has to follow his own inclinations." To which Dorn replies: "It's just because each person is right in his own way that they all suffer."[6]

In the final text these words do not appear: Chekhov was moving consistently away from the traditional approach of using a char-

5. J. B. Priestley, *Anton Chekhov* (London, 1970), p. 75.
6. *Works*, 13:263.

acter as a mouthpiece for the author's point of view. It is through the logic of the characters' interrelationships and fates that Chekhov's own point of view is revealed.

Chekhov's characters become the authors of other people's misfortunes "simply" because they are trying to realize their own ideas on happiness, love, art, how to run things, etc. Being the author of other people's misfortunes is not the lot of particular individuals who are evil, heartless, and immoral. Each person is subject to it. Having one's personal view of things, being preoccupied by that view and incapable of understanding another person's "truth"—this is what leads to misfortunes and broken lives in Chekhov.

Most theatrical and critical interpretations of *The Seagull* have been based on the contrast between one set of characters and another, or on highlighting one character at the expense of the others.

Very often Nina is contrasted with Treplev, since she moves away from him, in Yermilov's words, "onward! and—upward!"[7]

Sometimes the attention is given to Treplev, who acquires a certain wisdom toward the end of the play.

Sometimes the two young hero-innovators are jointly contrasted with the older conservatives.

Sometimes emphasis is placed on "wise old" Dr. Dorn, who speaks of the need for clear, consciously perceived goals in art.

Thus some interpretations see the play as nothing more than a statement in favor of realism against decadence in literature, or of ideological content as opposed to formalism in art, or as an attack on conservatism and vulgarity. The preoccupations of the characters are taken to be synonymous with the ideas of the author.

But the principle of contrasting one character with another does not apply to *The Seagull*. The negative qualities of *these* characters as opposed to the positive qualities of *those* characters—Chekhov had firmly rejected this tactic as a source of conflict. His deeper insight leads to an understanding of what is concealed in everyday life, what escapes notice and does not wish to be recognized. His play shows

7. V. V. Yermilov, *A. P. Chekhov*, p. 336.

how each person's thinking and behavior can become a link in the chain of general misfortune.

This equal distribution of conflict has nothing in common, of course, with any sort of leveling of the characters' personalities, psychology, or behavior. On the contrary, Chekhov makes every effort to individualize each person's "truth" to the highest degree and to show how "each person has to follow his own inclinations." The more expressively and uniquely each character pursues his own "line," the more striking the cumulative effect.

One should not forget, moreover, that although all the characters are made equal in relation to the conflict and causal sequence, Chekhov characterizes them in two distinct ways. The cast of *The Seagull* can be divided into two unequal groups, depending on whether their characteristics change or not over the course of time.

Most of the characters do not change. Each possesses a permanent feature or set of features. Each has his own "inclination," his partiality, his limitation.

Medvedenko: his small salary, the hard life of a teacher, "it's a tight squeeze."

Masha: adoration of Kostya, unrequited love, that "intolerable creature," as Kostya calls her.

Shamrayev: the estate, stale anecdotes about the theater.

Polina Andreyevna: jealousy of any woman who appears alongside Dorn.

Sorin: at sixty he has not yet lived; "*l'homme qui a voulu.*"

Dorn: has lived for pleasure, a medical man's cynicism combined with "an inclination toward philosophy" and an ideal attitude toward art.

The same principle, of fixity and permanence, applies to Arkadina and Trigorin. Each of them has a broader range of features and inclinations, the oxymoronic principle is widely applied to both of them, and each in his or her own way is a "psychological curiosity." As a result, especially in Arkadina's case, their stability has an extremely rich and varied quality. But the principle is still the same—stability, fixity, and permanence.

In Act IV, two years later, the characters each repeat themselves and appear with the same features or set of features. Changes, of course, have occurred in each of their lives: Sorin has had a stroke, Masha has married Medvedenko out of desperation, Dorn has traveled abroad, Trigorin has had a liaison with Nina, Arkadina has gone on new tours and had new successes, etc. But their essential qualities are unchanged, and so too is Chekhov's way of depicting them. What Trigorin says can be applied to each of them: "It's the same old story."

This fixity and permanence is superficially akin to the way in which characters are depicted in the comedy of masks or in classical comedy, but there is an unmistakable difference. Each of the figures in *The Seagull* has an individual character formed by his individual fate. Actor and spectator can easily picture the "prehistory" of each feature or set of features. The reasons behind these characteristic features are as lifelike as the ways in which they are expressed.

Only the two young heroes—Nina and Treplev—occupy a different position and are differently depicted; and it is how they are portrayed that links *The Seagull* closely with Chekhov's earlier prose and with the basic coordinates of his artistic world.

In the first three acts they are depicted on equal terms with the other characters, and each of them "is following his own inclinations." In the final act, after each has made his discovery, they are changed people.

Nina's words, "Learn how to bear your cross and have faith," are often seen as the ultimate wisdom, the ideological core, of Chekhov's play. Does this mean, then, that to convey the point of *The Seagull* the author is using one of his characters as a mouthpiece after all? That would be an entirely traditional way for an author to express his ideas, and would negate one of Chekhov's most radical "heresies" as a dramatist.

One must not forget that Nina's words are a quotation, one of several to be found in her closing speeches. She recites from Treplev's play about the World Spirit, then she recalls Trigorin's words from long ago about "a subject for a short story," and she also quotes from the classics, from Turgenev's *Rudin*. This heightened

sense of reference in Nina's final speeches is psychologically motivated: the quotations create a world that is different from her present life. Through them she is either returning to her bright past or,
as in the case of the words from Turgenev, finding a poetic equivalent for the harshness of her present situation.

The words about a cross and faith are also a quotation, or more
accurately a paraphrase from the Bible. Christ's appeal to the
disciples varies slightly from gospel to gospel: "And he that taketh
not his cross, and followeth after me, is not worthy of me"
(Matthew 10:38); "If any man will come after me, let him deny himself, and take up his cross, and follow me" (Matthew 16:24; Mark
8:34; Luke 9:23); "And whosoever doth not bear his cross, and come
after me, cannot be my disciple" (Luke 14:27). Moreover, Christ's
words immediately before this, demanding allegiance to a higher
cause—"I am come to set a man at variance against his father, and a
daughter against her mother. . . . And a man's foes shall be they of
his own household" (Matthew 10:35–36)—directly recall Nina's
own situation in life.

The fact that Nina's thought about a cross and faith is not her
own but a quotation is enough in itself to give her words a special
coloring. A commonplace, a well-known saying adduced as an example, needs to be uttered in a different tone of voice from an independently formulated conviction.

At the same time there can be no doubt of what Nina has had to
endure and suffer in order to attain faith and not to lose heart. Her
next words—"I have faith and I don't suffer so much now, and when
I think of my vocation, I'm not afraid of life"—are an answer to her
own words earlier: "He didn't believe in the theater, he was always
laughing at my dreams, and gradually I also stopped believing and
my spirits fell." Nina has had to pay a high price for her faith, and it
is this faith alone that enables her to go on living.

Although couched in the language of the Bible, Nina's thought
is self-evidently devoid of any religious content. "One's cross" here
is a symbol of life's burden, of the lot that befalls a person. Her belief is a belief in herself, in her vocation, in the possibility of making
her dream come true, in her ability to stand up against the coarse-

ness of life. "I have faith" has a wider meaning, because it includes an awareness of the need to go on living in spite of everything, and to keep in mind those higher values that underlie the idea of "real truth."

The "beliefs" of two of Chekhov's other heroines—"I believe, Uncle, I believe, ardently, passionately" (Sonya in *Uncle Vanya*); "man should have a faith or be seeking one, otherwise his life means absolutely nothing" (Masha in *Three Sisters*)—are different in content from that of Nina. Everything depends on the concrete circumstances that give rise to each declaration.

Thus, "learn how to bear your cross and have faith" is at the same time a quotation, a commonplace, and the heroine's personal conviction. Clearly, Chekhov was not setting out to use Nina as the mouthpiece of an impressive phrase proclaiming the play's main idea but was trying to achieve maximum individualization—to show, in other words, the complexity of the circumstances that accompany what the heroine formulates as an absolute assertion.

We know the nature of Nina's "truth" now and what her present bearings are in life, but how does this truth impinge on the life around her? Nina's faith is her salvation, but it does nothing to warm Kostya's heart. She has found her way in life, but at the same time she destroys the disheartened Treplev. A victim herself, she inflicts mortal suffering on someone else. And so on. To discount these overtones accompanying Nina's melody in the finale means ignoring the author's generalizing conclusion in favor of a particular idea of the heroine's.

The original approach to conflict in *The Seagull*—apparent opposition combined with concealed similarity—also contains within it the source of the comic in the play: the revelation of similarities in what is (seemingly) different.

Among theater producers and literary scholars, Chekhov's classification of his plays as "comedies" has provoked disagreement, incomprehension, and the urge to prove that when Chekhov spoke of "comedies" he actually had something quite different in mind.

All options have been tried: rejecting the idea that Chekhov's plays are in any way comic; treating individual characters or scenes as comic and everything else as dramatic; and, conversely, attempting to read Chekhov's plays as pure comedy or vaudeville. Even those who adopt the author's classification often do so from a crudely sociological standpoint: Chekhov's laughter is interpreted as mockery of the members of particular classes, the decadent movement, etc. It has also been suggested that instead of trying to classify Chekhov's plays, we should simply regard them as drama in the most general sense.

Each of Chekhov's great plays has so many facets that it would undoubtedly be hard to find a genre that was not represented. There is much in them that is dramatic and even tragic. It is clear also that what constitutes a genre in modern times is very different from Aristotle's classifications, and that each great work creates a new genre of its own. Nevertheless we need to fathom the logic of Chekhov's classification, since we can assume that he *did* know how comedy differs from tragedy and drama.

To start by saying that Chekhov's plays contain a mixture of the comic and the serious would be breaking no new ground. Is there any great dramatist in whom the sad and the cheerful are not intermingled, as in life itself? In the matter of genre, as in the other elements of drama, Chekhov was both adopting ancient traditions and striking out on his own. What exactly was the nature of his new departure, and how much was he adopting?

As we have seen, it is Chekhov's single focus of interest that determines the distinctive nature of the comic in his works.

All the characters are shown from a single point of view—in their attempts to "orient themselves," to assert their own truth, their "personal view of things." They are all made equal by a single painful dependence on life, by ignorance of the real truth. But this also provides an inexhaustible source of the comic. How people fail to notice or deny the hidden features they have in common is, after all, an age-old source of laughter.

The humorous may consist of an absurdly constructed phrase, a pun, an unexpected altercation. There is considerable humor of this kind in *The Seagull*. Shamrayev's theater anecdotes are amusing in their own way. Arkadina's guile is comic when, after the stormy scene in which she wins over Trigorin, she then offers him with apparent nonchalance the right to choose. Medvedenko's "clever" phrases are comic. All this might be called comedy of instant effect.

But if the comedy is to be found in the characters' lines of conduct or constantly visible pattern of relationships, that kind of comedy is evident all the time and in every section of the play.

In the first three acts of *The Seagull*, the depiction of the characters is unconditionally comic, and this applies to them all without exception. Each character in Chekhov's comedy is not a single instrument that keeps playing one monotonous note. Put them all together, each with their characteristic features, and they are more like a small orchestra—but one where the instruments and the melody are prescribed and unchanging for the greater part of the play.

Unchangeability and repetition: these underlie the way in which the essential nature of each character is revealed in the first three acts of *The Seagull*. There is repetition of Medvedenko's "It's a tight squeeze" and Polina Andreyevna's "Our time is passing"; of Sorin complaining about his unrealized dreams and Masha about her hopeless love; of Nina's enthusiasm when she speaks of art, and Dorn's skepticism when he listens to his patient's complaints, etc. Each of these characters—embodying his truth, his grievance against life—is absolutely sincere. These truths and complaints vary in quality: some are an extension of their bearers' shortcomings and even perhaps vices, while others are a consequence of good qualities, noble aspirations, or misfortunes. Chekhov bore in mind that the comic playwright has a responsibility not to lapse into caricaturing the virtuous: "better to leave the picture unfinished than to spoil it."[8]

But it is an implacable law of stage comedy that if you repeat something, if you constantly assert even something praiseworthy or

8. *Letters*, 3:113.

moving, you make it funny. However much we may sympathize with the teacher Medvedenko's complaints about the hardships of his existence, their constant repetition only makes us laugh at his inertia. In the first three acts of *The Seagull*, as soon as almost any character opens his mouth, we can foresee how he will behave and what he will talk about—and because we recognize him so easily, we laugh.

Treplev and Nina are most often portrayed in Acts I to III in light of their subsequent unfortunate fates. But presenting them in that way from the very start does not follow at all from the text. Treplev is sometimes shown as some kind of Hamlet, whereas at first he is more of an unhappy Pierrot. In principle it is possible to see everything that happens to him in the first three acts in a comic light. That includes his constant moaning about being rejected in love and not being understood. That also includes the unsuccessful attempt at suicide by a young man who comes to grief twice, in art and in love. In so far as Acts I to III are dominated by each character's easily predictable repetition of his theme and by the concealed similarity between characters, they can and ought (if the play is correctly interpreted) to be accompanied throughout by the audience's nonstop laughter.

But in Act IV all this appears in a different light.

We now realize that much of what seemed comic or amusing was actually terrible. True, most of the characters have not changed at all: "It's the same old story." But out of the trifling details that were comic to begin with, a whole life has been built, like a mountain from grains of sand. The same pitilessness, the same impossibility of happiness for each person that were present earlier on in the lives of the older characters are repeated in the lives of the younger ones—in other words, there is no end to sorrows and sufferings. . . .

This effect—a sobering one—is produced by the interval of two years between Acts III and IV. Laughter is still to be found even in Act IV, but it strikes a different note. As for the ending—Kostya shooting himself—that is a very clear reminder of "how coarse life is." And it makes one think of Chekhov's idea for a vaudeville where the hero dies at the end: after all, it's "true to life. Isn't that the way it happens? People are joking and laughing, and suddenly—bang! Curtain!"[9] That was just the kind of comic structure that appealed to Chekhov most.

From the outset, *The Seagull* was compared with Ibsen's *The Wild Duck*. The "Ibsenism" of Chekhov's play was seen primarily in its symbolism.

Chekhov's symbolism is far removed, however, from the inflexibility of Ibsen's allegorical approach. Theater and literary critics argue to this day about whether Nina or Kostya is the seagull that has been destroyed. As in Ibsen, the text can suggest in what sense each of the young heroes might be identified with the seagull that is shot. But the role of symbolism in Chekhov's play is much wider than that of a commentary or an indirect analogy with the events taking place. The seagull is also a symbol of purity, youth, freshness, and love that have disappeared beyond recall or have perished. It is also a symbol of the dream before it comes into collision with the coarseness of life. These wider meanings of the symbol throw light on the fates of *all* the characters. Like the garden/orchard in "The Black Monk" and *The Cherry Orchard*, like love in "The House with a Mezzanine," it symbolizes a beauty that perishes. It perishes while the characters are trying to work out their problems and asserting their "truths." This is another reminder by Chekhov that personal truths are relative, that "everyone suffers" because "each person is right in his own way," and that each of us is responsible for the general course of events.

9. See *Chekhov i teatr* (Moscow, 1963), p. 55.

# 18

# Arguments About Arguments: "The House with a Mezzanine" (1896)

Most critics of "The House with a Mezzanine" concentrate their attention on the problem of "small deeds," which form the subject of the argument between the artist and Lida Volchaninova in Chapter 3 of the story.[1] To understand the place of this argument and of the problems arising from it is indeed important, as we shall see, but one must not lose sight of the fact that the argument is only part of the story of the unrealized love between the artist-narrator and the girl with the strange and delightful name of Misyus.

The artist relates how once, it seemed to him, he had felt happy and in love; and how being in love and the feeling of happiness passed away. As usual, Chekhov traces the appearance and disappearance of being in love in a certain kind of person by casting light on that person's own perception of his behavior, and by correlating the forms of his awareness with the actual state of affairs.

---

1. In the 1880s and 1890s a large part of the Russian intelligentsia adhered to the ideology of "small deeds." After the collapse of the grandiose schemes of previous years (the "Going to the People" movement and the revolutionary organizations of the late 1870s and early 1880s), they believed they could best fulfill their "duty to the people" by means of more modest but specific schemes: building village schools, setting up medical centers and libraries, etc.

But the story of unrealized love is itself placed within a wider framework. Chekhov is concerned to show us his hero's emotional state before he felt himself to be in love, and the state he arrived at once he had lost Misyus forever.

Of the initial state the narrator says he felt himself then to be "hopelessly lonely and unwanted," and "alone, exasperated, and dissatisfied" with himself and other people. From this state he moves to one of love. At the end, after his hopes of happiness have been dashed, he returns to his initial state: "a sober, everyday mood took possession of me . . . and I felt as bored with life as before." So the plot of the story may be broadly summarized by saying that the hero moves from an "oppressive" earlier state to one of love, and finally returns to his initial state. This denouement links "The House with a Mezzanine" with similarly constructed Chekhov stories, where the conclusion marks a return to the beginning, to initial states and unresolved questions ("Neighbors," "The Murder," "My Life").

Love appears and disappears so quickly in the story that some critics pay it no attention and concentrate on the argument about the usefulness of "small deeds," whereas others declare the love of the artist and Misyus to be unreal and look for hidden clues that the hero is really in love with . . . her elder sister Lida, whom they consider a more worthy object of love.

But the sudden, fleeting, fragile, and commonplace feeling described in "The House with a Mezzanine," and at the same time its special charm, become comprehensible only if one can put aside preconceptions (that love, for example, ought to be of such a kind and run such a course, or that the petty love of unexceptional people is meaningless) and try to enter into the logic of the author's thoughts as reflected in the way the story is constructed.

Love—or, more accurately, being in love with Misyus—is first of all an escape for the artist, from an "oppressive" state of loneliness and dissatisfaction with himself and other people to snugness, naiveté, and mutual sympathy: all those things that the Volchaninovs' estate, their house with the mezzanine, come to mean to him.

Yet the artist-hero is not the kind of person who would be satisfied with purely family happiness. For a man of his mentality, even had Lida not intervened, family happiness would have provided a brief and temporary calm and refuge, a starting point for the conscious work of "new thoughts" (as in the case of Nikitin, the teacher of Russian), and then he would have wanted to "run," the more so since the story touches briefly on all of Misyus's potential defects.

But the hero of "The House with a Mezzanine" is not even granted Nikitin's period of family happiness. In contrast to "The Teacher of Russian," this is not a story about how the hero is deceived by one of life's stereotypes, that of family happiness, but about a happiness not realized. A sad reflective melody of unjustified hopes and unrealized love runs throughout the story.

Leaving aside for the moment Chekhov's treatment of the love theme, it is worth noting that apart from the artist and Misyus there are two other characters in the story whose personal happiness is not realized and whose fate does not work out: Belokurov, who is too lazy to fall in love and marry, and finds it much more peaceful to cohabit with the lady "who resembled a fattened goose"; and Lida, who scorns the idea of personal happiness and imagines herself to be the center of civic activity in the district. This universality and equality of distribution make it impossible to claim that the author intended to accuse one side and defend the other. It is not a case of "being consumed by one's environment" or of "wicked people" (Lida, for example) being guilty. Rejecting such traditional explanations, Chekhov uses the individualizing approach to consider various forms of the same phenomenon: how people so easily let life slip by, renounce their own happiness, and extinguish the "spark" within their own souls.

And as usual in his prose works of the 1890s, Chekhov invests those characters who are incapable of finding their bearings correctly in the real world and of "making" their lives (this applies in different ways to the artist, to Lida, and to Belokurov) with a passion for trying to solve the most general and significant problems.

On this occasion the argument turns on whether the activities of the zemstvo are necessary or not, and, more widely, on the relationship between the intelligentsia and the people.

What is the function of the debate within the story?

Some critics directly link love with the discredited, historically worthless notion of "small deeds" by saying that the two are incompatible: Lida destroys the love between her sister and the artist precisely because she is preoccupied with "small deeds." In the words of one critic, "she mercilessly tramples underfoot the touching love between Misyus and the artist. Chekhov shows very subtly that Lida's convictions, activities, and spiritual qualities are in complete accord: only a narrow, shallow, and insensitive person could be so fanatically devoted to such a false idea."[2] Why "small deeds" and love should be incompatible is impossible to explain without straining the point.

As usual with Chekhov, what is at issue is not, of course, the specific, "special" nature of the doctrine under discussion (as much is said in favor of "small deeds" as against them, and neither protagonist in the argument makes the slightest impression on the other). Here it is worth mentioning the contradiction that many critics of "The House with a Mezzanine" have pointed out: how can one reconcile a critique of "small deeds" with the well-known fact that Chekhov himself was engaged in similar "small deeds" in his own life?

Among the manifestations of Chekhov's active humanism were such ambitious undertakings as carrying out a census on Sakhalin, or organizing the erection of a monument to Peter the Great in Taganrog (Chekhov's birthplace). But he did not shun more modest projects, like surfacing the local road at Melikhovo, building schools, giving the peasants free medical treatment, making loans to famine victims, etc. What does all this have to do with the fact that in "The House with a Mezzanine" the champion of "small deeds," Lida Volchaninova, is given full credit for her energy, honesty, and

2. M. Ye. Yelizarova, *Tvorchestvo Chekhova*, p. 117.

consistency, yet this "slim, beautiful, invariably severe girl" is herself not eulogized?

In their efforts to resolve this contradiction, some critics refer to Chekhov's notorious "diffidence" about expressing his own views, while others argue that Chekhov was secretly sympathetic to either Lida or her opponent. But the contradiction will remain unexplained as long as we go on trying to discover Chekhov's sympathies for one side at the expense of the other, or giving Chekhov credit for solving this or that specific problem—in this case, the problem of "small deeds" and the attitude of the intelligentsia toward the people.

What Chekhov finds unacceptable is not a doctrine as such but its claim to absolute status as a sole and universal truth. Supporters and opponents of a doctrine are alike absorbed in their own points of view, and each protagonist is confident of having a monopoly on "real" truth, whereas the author convinces us of the impossibility of accepting any of the given positions as a universal truth. The principle of equal distribution of conflict is fully realized in the way the verbal clashes are presented in "The House with a Mezzanine."

We said earlier that in presenting these debates Chekhov's aim was twofold. On the one hand, arguments and opinions are deprived of any absolute significance and turned into a means of characterizing the heroes' consciousness and psychology; at the same time it was part of Chekhov's artistic design to show that the problems raised were important, often of universal and epochal significance, and that the protagonists' arguments should be serious, passionate, and appropriate to the characters' belief in the importance of the problems under discussion. Chekhov achieved the required effect by assigning to his characters ideas and positions that he himself or one of his remarkable correspondents might have held in private, or that were to be found in articles in the periodical press or in public pronouncements. In composing speeches for these characters, Chekhov had recourse to the art of stylization.

"The House with a Mezzanine" was written in 1896. In 1891–1892, when the outbreak of famine was at its height, Tolstoy's remarkable articles were published (see Volume 29 of the Jubilee Edition), including the one entitled "About the Famine." Chekhov's artist repeats the content and form of Tolstoy's ideas in this article almost literally.

The artist's words about the terrible conditions in which "all these Annas, Mavras, and Pelageyas" are living ("millions of people are living worse than animals") correspond to the words of Tolstoy, who wrote with exceptional boldness about the inevitability of famine given the conditions in which the people were living— "overtaxed, short of land, neglected by the rest of society, and allowed to run wild." The artist speaks of a "great chain" in which "the people are entangled"; Tolstoy writes of a "string" which is "too tightly stretched."

Referring to the false, superfluous attempts made by the administration and the zemstvo to help the people by means of philanthropic "small deeds," Tolstoy wrote: "These individuals persuade themselves and others of their deep concern for and love of the people. All that is untrue. . . . Why deceive ourselves? The people are necessary to us only as a tool. What is of benefit to us . . . is always diametrically opposed to what is of benefit to the people." This is echoed by the artist: "You try to help them with schools and hospitals, but in so doing you don't free them from their fetters—on the contrary, you enslave them still further . . . they have to pay the zemstvo for their books and their plasters, which simply adds to their burden." At this point the argument between Lida and the artist is very reminiscent of the one between Sviyazhsky and Konstantin Levin in *Anna Karenina* (Part 3, Chapter 28) about whether village schools do more harm than good.

Both Tolstoy and Chekhov's artist say it is better to do nothing than deceive oneself with the lie of "small deeds." "When nothing is undertaken, a lie remains a lie and is not especially harmful" (Tolstoy). "In my opinion a medical center at Malozyomovo is quite unnecessary. . . ." "What is necessary? Landscapes?" "No, they're not necessary, either. Nothing at all is necessary" ("The House with a Mezzanine").

The artist's positive program also copies Tolstoy's and shares his utopian illusions. Tolstoy hoped that each representative of the ruling class would say to himself: "My conscience tells me that I am guilty before the people, that the disaster that has struck them is partly my fault, and for that reason I cannot go on living as I have done but must change my way of life so as to become as close to the people as possible and to serve them." The artist dreams of the possibility that "we shall all, town and country dwellers alike, all without exception, agree to share out the work between us."

All these juxtapositions show that in "The House with a Mezzanine" one cannot talk of an original solution to the problem of the intelligentsia's attitude toward the people, or of the novelty of the artist's thoughts, though everything he has to say is no doubt striking and significant. In attributing to Chekhov and giving him credit for the critical spirit and utopian tendency of the artist's speeches, we pay the author a doubtful compliment.

Lida says in answer to these speeches: "I've heard all that before." So had the reader in the 1890s. Objectively speaking, there were two opposing viewpoints then on the zemstvo: that of the zemstvo members themselves, and Tolstoy's. Chekhov divided them between his characters. He had no thought of solving the problem of the zemstvo or putting forward any new point of view; he was trying in the debate scene to expound the two existing viewpoints as vividly as possible. He assumed that the reader would relate these arguments to the structure of the story as a whole and understand their artistic function in characterizing the heroes' mental worlds.

But the question arises: does the fact that the argument is about "small deeds" have any relevance to the plot of "The House with a Mezzanine"? Suppose they had been arguing instead about "freedom of educational instruction" or "disinfecting the prisons"? Would nothing be changed and the story of the artist's love for Misyus remain the same?

The answer would seem to be, yes: there is no direct link between the theory of "small deeds" and the love that was destroyed. The argument ends inconclusively, neither participant convinces the other of anything, and both stick to their own opinions, having expressed some correct ideas and some incorrect ones. But the substitution of another topic for "small deeds" would be far from irrelevant to the expression of the author's complex conception.

What was said in the debate does have a bearing on the "correct posing of the problem" of why love was not realized. It was precisely this debate (with that range of questions and those arguments) and not any other that was needed. For it is in the debate about "small deeds" that a great deal is made clear about the reasons for the artist's initial and final "oppressive" state, which forms the contrasting background to his central state of being in love.

An integral feature of that "oppressive" state is the artist's refusal to work, his idleness. The idleness motif occurs at the very beginning of the story, is repeated with variations in the early stages, and for a long time remains quite unexplained. We read that the hero was "condemned by fate to constant idleness," that he ought to seek "some excuse for his constant idleness," that he was ready "to go about like that all day and all summer with nothing to do and no aim," and that the time he was willingly spending on the Volchaninovs' estate left "the impression of a long, long idle day." These repetitions are obviously intended to attract the reader's attention, but for the time being nothing is said about the reasons for this idleness and for the artist's initial psychological state as a whole. He is "condemned to it by fate"—and that is all.

Only in the debate about the "millions of people living worse than animals" does the artist discover (or guess or acknowledge—he is not, after all, aiming to analyze his attitude systematically) the original sources of his dissatisfaction with himself and his work, his unwillingness to work and his idleness: "In those conditions an artist's life has no meaning, and the more talented he is, the stranger and harder to understand his role becomes, for it turns out that he is working for the amusement of a dirty rapacious animal and supporting the existing order. And I don't want to work, and I won't work."

No theoretician and certainly no dogmatist, the hero of "The House with a Mezzanine" belongs to that breed of people, frequently described by Chekhov, who are bored with life, "dissatisfied with themselves and other people," and exasperated because life as a whole is set up wrongly and unjustly, and in particular because of the false relationship between the intelligentsia and the people, and of the artist's false position in society. So (without, of course, presuming to solve the problems being discussed by his characters) Chekhov makes the content of the debate anything but irrelevant, linking this part of the story with strong threads to the main story of unrealized love.

In Chekhov's works of the 1890s the system of criteria for "real truth" becomes more and more complicated. Among the elements that Chekhov considers it necessary to include for the "correct posing of problems" are some that are directly social in nature: not only is man's individual life badly set up, so too are "existing social conditions."

In "A Woman's Kingdom," "Three Years," and later "A Case History," the soul-searching of characters with whom we sympathize is seen against a grim and terrifying background: of a steel foundry, which creates "an impression of hell" and where the workers "live worse than convicts," or of the degeneracy of the owners of a rich trading company, whose employees call them "exploiters," or of a factory where you feel "as if you're in a prison." The characters in stories like "The House with a Mezzanine" or "At Home" have little or no connection with the factory owners and their subordinates. But the prevailing mood of both the artist and Vera Kardina in "At Home," their "constant dissatisfaction with themselves and other people," is also determined in the final analysis by wrongly established social relations, and by the faulty position of the intelligentsia in relation to the millions of oppressed peasants and workers.

In stories from Chekhov's final years like "On Official Duty," "At Christmas," "The New Dacha," and "In the Ravine," the characters do not know the "real truth" any more than they do in "Lights" or "A Dreary Story." But while he does not make them discover any final truths, Chekhov depicts their attempts to orient themselves in life against a broad canvas of "peasant misfortune" and popular notions of justice.

Let us emphasize once again the place and function of the social theme in Chekhov's works, whether it be in "The Wife," "Ward No. 6," "A Woman's Kingdom," or "The House with a Mezzanine." The social theme is mediated through the epistemological theme; it forms part of the analysis of the correlation between the real world and the hero's ways of perceiving his situation and his resulting action or inaction. But it is significant that social factors now come in as the prerequisites, initial impulses, and background for the characters' conscious activity, as a condition for correctly posing the problems of what is happening to them. It would be as wrong not to be aware of this extension of the role of social factors as it would be to ignore the deeply mediated nature of the way in which they are used, and by so doing to simplify and coarsen the link between the basic structural elements of Chekhov's world.

# 19

# Wasted Lives:
## *Uncle Vanya* (1897)

In *Uncle Vanya* (published in 1897, but exact dates of composition unknown), as in *Ivanov*, considerable importance attaches to an event that took place *before* the action begins. Once again, this event is a *discovery* that the hero makes.

All his life it *seemed* to Uncle Vanya (Voinitsky) that his late sister's husband, Professor Serebryakov, was a remarkable scholar ("I was proud of him and his learning, I lived and breathed for him!"), and he and his niece Sonya worked on the estate "like slaves" on his behalf. But now he has discovered that Serebryakov is a sham, that "he's been reading and writing about art for the past twenty-five years without understanding the first thing about it." Uncle Vanya decides he has been deceived ("You duped us!") and has sacrificed his life to a nonentity. The idol turned out to be false; Vanya's life has been wasted.

This belated discovery leads to endless regrets and complaints ("I can't sleep at night for anger and frustration that I've been such a fool and missed the chance of having everything that now I'm too old for!"), and later to Vanya's absurd attempt on the life of the man he sees as the chief architect of his failure. In the conclusion, though, everything reverts to how it was at the beginning. Completely broken, Uncle Vanya can only repeat: "Must work, must work . . ."—in other words, go on doing the same as he has done for the past twenty-five years. He is consoled by Sonya: "We shall find rest! We shall hear the angels, we shall see the whole sky sparkling with diamonds . . ."; and this sounds both like a consolation and like a requiem for a wasted life.

A significant question arises: how true or false is Ivan Petrovich Voinitsky's discovery? *Uncle Vanya* is a good example of how the discoveries made by Chekhov's heroes (unlike the discoveries in Dostoevsky or Tolstoy) are certainly not bound to be a simple journey from falsity to truth. Having discovered for themselves the falseness of their previous ideas or actions, Chekhov's heroes may fall straight into a new delusion, taking on ideas that are just as questionable as the ones that went before. This is what happens to Uncle Vanya: freeing himself of one mirage does not become his salvation; his new ideas, alas, are no less imaginary.

"For us you were a superior kind of being": this is how Vanya now defines the essence of the delusion that possessed him for twenty-five years. It is the same kind of false idea that is so widespread in Chekhov's world—seeing someone as "an unusual person"—and it invariably leads to a bitter reckoning. Chekhov had investigated the nature of this mirage on several occasions, in "The Grasshopper," "The Story of an Unknown Man," "Big Volodya and Little Volodya," and "The Black Monk." As Tanya Pesotskaya wrote in her last letter to her husband in "The Black Monk": "I took you for an unusual person, a genius. I fell in love with you, but you turned out to be mad." Her belated feeling of hatred, which solves nothing, is very reminiscent in its origins of Vanya's hatred for Serebryakov—someone who was until recently not only his idol but his friend.

But Vanya also shares with the unfortunate Tanya Pesotskaya her subsequent conviction/delusion. They both put the blame for the misfortune that has occurred, the "havoc"—whether it be the ruin of the garden or their own lives that have been wrecked to no purpose—fairly and squarely on their "unusual person," who has now been turned into a hateful enemy.

Tanya: "My father has just died. I can thank you for that, since you killed him. Our garden is going to ruin. . . . I can thank you for that, too. I hate you from the bottom of my heart and hope you die soon."

Vanya: "You've ruined my life! . . . Thanks to you I've torn up and destroyed the best years of my life! You are my worst enemy!"

Alas, as had already been pointed out in "Enemies" (1887), unhappy people are least of all capable of being just and fairly assessing themselves and other people.

The madman Kovrin in "The Black Monk" was scarcely planning to ruin the garden or bring his father-in-law to the grave; the terrible "havoc" wrought in his life and the lives of those surrounding him was their responsibility as much as his. In the same way, Serebryakov may be accused of various sins but hardly of planning to ruin his brother-in-law's life—and moreover by deceit. Voinitsky's many years of service to his idol had not been given under duress but quite voluntarily and consciously. Serebryakov had not "duped" him—Vanya had duped himself all his life.

The mistakes in Vanya's ideas and the absurdities in his behavior do not reduce—and may even strengthen—the sympathy that readers and audiences feel for him. Chekhov makes use of a powerful technique already tried out by Gogol. After a series of increasingly absurd actions, the hero of Gogol's "The Diary of a Madman" suddenly cries out: "Mother, save your poor son! . . . there's no place for him in the world! He's being persecuted! Mother, have pity on your sick little child!"—and this abrupt shift in tone is calculated to change our attitude toward him. "I'm going mad. . . . Mother, I'm in despair! Mother! . . . Mother! What am I to do?"—exclaims Chekhov's unhappy hero, appealing, like Gogol's madman, to his mother at his moment of greatest despair. It is the plaintive cry of a helpless child confronted by an incomprehensible and hostile world, and his previous absurd fantasies appear in a different light.

(Chekhov goes a step further than Gogol: the unhappy hero's mother sides with his enemy, and instead of easing his pain, is capable only of increasing it.)

We sympathize with Vanya and can even agree with him that the behavior of the people around him is no less abnormal than his own. But this does not make his judgments look any less suspect; it does not rule out the possibility that what has happened may be explained differently from his view of things.

Although its title would seem to point to the central position of one character, the play cannot, after all, be regarded as his story only; the fates of the other characters are equally important in the play's overall conception and in the general picture of life portrayed.

Among theater people, drama critics, and literary scholars, Voinitsky's view of his own situation and Serebryakov's part in it is widely accepted. "An old fossil, an academic trout," "he chews over other people's ideas, he's been working in a vacuum," "a writing *perpetuum mobile*," "a pathetic old man with gout," etc.—all these characteristics attributed to the professor by Voinitsky provide a rich basis on which to create a sharply defined negative interpretation of the professor's role. Often the colors are deepened still further: Serebryakov is presented as a creature who stifles beauty and youth (Yelyena), as some kind of spider sucking the vital juices from Uncle Vanya and Sonya, or as a usurper appropriating what by rights belongs to others (the house and estate). Even the generalized concept of "Serebryakovism" (meaning "the personification of a deadly-dull approach to life,"[1] or, in the vulgar sociological interpretation, doctrinaire liberalism[2]) came into use. Serebryakov as anti-hero has inspired some brilliant stage performances.

At the opposite pole we have Uncle Vanya, who says of himself: "I've got talent, brains, and confidence. . . . If I'd lived a normal life, I might have been a Schopenhauer or a Dostoevsky." David Magar-

---

1. Z. Paperny, *"Vopreki vsem pravilam . . .*", p. 104.
2. V. Ye. Khalizev, "O prirode konflikta v p'ese A. P. Chekhova 'Dyadya Vanya' " in *Vestnik Moskovskogo un-ta. Seriya VII. Filologiya, zhurnalistika* (Moscow, 1961), no. 1, p. 152.

shack contrasts Serebryakov's "selfishness and vanity" with the "mild and inoffensive" Uncle Vanya, proud in his belief that "by sending Serebryakov his regular allowance he was helping the intellectual advancement of his country,"[3] while V. Yermilov sees the two men as representatives of true and false beauty.[4]

Good destroyed by the forces of evil, the true contrasted with the false—these are the kinds of polarities that critics like to use when sorting out the characters in *Uncle Vanya*. But this is the same convention of traditional theater that Chekhov so firmly rejected! Even after his first plays, with their fairly traditional division of characters, the critics wanted from Chekhov a clear answer to the question, "Who is in the right and who is to blame?"[5] By the time of *The Seagull*, Chekhov was elaborating a radically different type of conflict, one in which it was important to discover the resemblance between antagonists, to see what seemingly very different characters and their situations had in common.

From the very beginning of *Uncle Vanya*, motifs can be heard which obviously do not fit a complete polarization of the characters—or, more precisely, which remind us that any division of the characters is relative.

When he wishes to comment sarcastically on his opponent's behavior, Vanya uses a quotation: "With brain o'ertaxed and furrowed brow . . ."[6] In *The Seagull*, Treplev, who has tried to shoot himself because of unrequited love, makes the same sarcastic use of a quotation when Trigorin appears: "Words, words, words . . ." In *The Seagull* it is obvious that all of Treplev's sarcastic descriptions of his rival are dictated by jealousy alone and cannot be taken at face value. We are offered other ways of forming an opinion about Trigorin. Similarly in *Uncle Vanya*: objectivity is not to be expected from a character who is consumed by hatred and makes no secret of the fact. A true portrait of the man whom he sees as the embodiment of

---

3. David Magarshack, *Chekhov the Dramatist* (New York, 1960), pp. 206, 210.
4. V. V. Yermilov, *A. P. Chekhov*, p. 348.
5. See *Works*, 12:391.
6. See *Works*, 12:393.

evil is built up only slowly and turns out to be more complex than Uncle Vanya's one-dimensional figure.

One cannot help being struck by a particular feature of the invectives directed against the professor. Vanya seems to have copied many of Serebryakov's negative characteristics . . . from himself.

"His liver's swollen from envy and jealousy." Examples of the professor's envy and jealousy will follow later. But already at this stage, after Astrov has responded, "You seem to be envious," Vanya frankly confesses: "Yes, I am envious!" Later it becomes evident that the professor is not the only person of whom he feels envious and jealous. And which character in the play is "forever complaining about his misfortunes"? Vanya himself—and to a far greater extent than the professor. As for his next accusation—"What conceit! What pretensions!"—could this not apply to the parallels Vanya draws between himself and Schopenhauer and Dostoevsky? True, the professor likewise puts his own illness on a par with Turgenev's, and these two passages in the play neatly echo each other. In an outburst of irritation, Voinitsky accuses his mother, and then the professor again, of devoting the whole of their lives to the same futile and meaningless activity. But could not the term *perpetuum mobile* be used of the whole of Vanya's life's work, even though it has nothing to do with writing or reading pamphlets?

Envy, jealousy, inordinate conceit, fruitless activity . . . thus, from the very start, in Act I, Vanya fires off a whole salvo of negative epithets at his opponent, and almost equally at himself. It is as if, looking at himself in the mirror of Serebryakov, Vanya sees not lost opportunities, as he thinks, but his own weaknesses and shortcomings that are much more visible from outside. Chekhov is showing the extent to which everything we hear about Serebryakov from Voinitsky must be regarded as partial and therefore relative, and is warning us that apart from the contrast between the antagonists, we must not forget their concealed similarities (concealed from them, but not from readers and audiences).

The same principle of concealed similarity can be extended to the characters of *Uncle Vanya* as a whole.

To Yelyena Andreyevna—someone from outside—this similarity is more noticeable than to the others. She says to Voinitsky about her husband: "he's the same as everyone else. No worse than you." And later, in response to Astrov's speech about the forests, she develops this theme of general similarity: you're "all of you" destroying the forests; in just the same way "you" destroy a person; there's a devil of destruction lurking "in all of you." In Act II, in her speech beginning "Things are all wrong in this household," she lists those who are contributing to the general atmosphere of irritation, spite, and hatred: "Your mother . . . the Professor . . . Sonya . . . you . . . me . . ." Very soon after, in his conversation with Sonya, Astrov offers *his* list of those who are responsible in equal measure for poisoning the general atmosphere: "your father . . . Uncle Vanya . . . your grandmother . . . your mother-in-law . . ."

More often, of course, we hear something different: it is not similarities but contrasts that are most apparent to each of the characters, and in its way this also makes them all equal. "All the people round you [and by implication "me"] are freaks," Astrov says to Vanya. Both Astrov and Serebryakov refer to the people round them as "stupid"; for Yelyena "there are just grey shapes wandering about instead of people." On the day when he gets drunk, the people surrounding Astrov seem to him like "little insects . . . microbes"; to Serebryakov, no doubt, they seem like this every day. The fits of misanthropy that Astrov admits to are familiar to Yelyena also: "How I wish I could fly away from you all as free as a bird . . . forget you all exist."

Another general theme runs through different speeches: the acknowledgment of one's own degradation, of changing for the worse. Astrov: "I've become a different person. . . . I've become a freak, Nanny"; Voinitsky: "I'm the same as before, worse maybe"; Serebryakov: "I've become repulsive to myself." To this series of self-reproaches can be added Yelyena's admission—"I'm just a tiresome character, an incidental figure"—and her later conjecture that "you and I are probably such good friends, Ivan Petrovich, because we're both boring, tiresome people!"

But it is not primarily by their characteristics, or in verbal coincidences and utterances, that the similarity between characters is revealed. It is in their fates that the similarity becomes most noticeable.

Alongside Voinitsky's "wasted life" are several other unfulfilled lives: those of Yelyena, Sonya, and Astrov. Dr. Astrov, unlike his friend Vanya and the professor, is not chasing illusions: he treats the sick and plants forests. But in a moment of frankness he admits: "I'm disappointed with life. . . . I'm fond of life as a whole, but this petty, provincial life of ours in Russia—that I can't stand, I despise it utterly. . . . I've aged, I'm overworked, I've become coarse and completely insensitive to everything." Once again there are hidden features in common between characters whose external behavior would seem to be completely different.

Unlike Khrushchov, his direct predecessor in *The Wood Demon*, who said, "at last I've found my light ahead," Astrov comments bitterly, "for me there is no light shining in the distance." No light shining in the distance: what that means, again, is not knowing the truth, not having any reliable guidelines, being without hope. Astrov retains all the qualities of a "nonwhiner," but now, in contrast to *The Wood Demon*, this expresses itself not as courageous optimism but as indifference to "the blows of fate."

In *The Wood Demon* the suicide of one of the characters is the event that forces the others to make a discovery and change their attitude to life. By the 1890s it was the drama of the people who had *not* departed from life and were condemned to a long and meaningless existence without "a light ahead" that began to seem more important and more terrifying. In this way *The Wood Demon* grew into *Uncle Vanya*.

In *Uncle Vanya* two types are contrasted, the "whiners" and the "nonwhiners." "Uncle Vanya is crying but Astrov is whistling!": this was how Chekhov explained the difference between the two characters to the actors.[7] Astrov's whistling in response to "the blows of

---

7. K. S. Stanislavsky, *Collected Works*, vol. 1, p. 232.

fate" is an outward manifestation of his "nonwhining" indifference. But by comparison with the earlier plays, the nature of the conflict is now different again: both whiners and nonwhiners are made equal by their suffering dependence on life. "Our position, yours and mine, is hopeless," Astrov says to Vanya.

Harvey Pitcher defines the general meaning of *Uncle Vanya* accurately, in my opinion, when he considers failure and frustration to be the play's basic theme. It is important to understand the genuine nature of what has gone wrong in the characters' lives. Voinitsky is not deceived:

> He has made a foolish if well-intentioned mistake, which it is now too late to rectify. Reluctant to accept that he himself must bear full responsibility for what he has made of his life, he seeks to turn the Professor into a scapegoat. His plight is real enough; but in his anguish he ceases to be entirely honest with himself and begins to dramatize his situation. . . . And in his impulsive decision to take his revenge on the Professor, he is still refusing to accept the ordinary little truth. How much easier to think of himself as a victim than as a fool!

It was Chekhov's intention "to show the plight of a man who is not only frustrated but who really has no one but himself to blame for the mess that he has made of his life. This gives Voinitsky's frustration much greater depth than if he were simply the innocent victim of a cunning exploiter." Chekhov was not concerned to accuse some characters and justify others. The theme of frustration embraces all the characters. "In *Uncle Vanya* there are no winners, only losers."[8]

Among these losers is Serebryakov, and it is interesting to look at the methods used by Chekhov to acquaint us with this man whom Voinitsky sees as absolutely evil.

The professor's own behavior in the course of the play is unlikely to arouse any sympathy. His difficult, capricious character and his grumbling, his tedious arrogance, the way in which he regards

8. Harvey Pitcher, *The Chekhov Play: A New Interpretation* (Berkeley, 1985), pp. 83–85.

his own concerns as of overriding importance, and his inability to understand other people's situations—it is hard to imagine anyone putting up with this for long. Everyone around him suffers as a result.

But Chekhov does not let us forget the underlying causes of his behavior. There are two of them. One is purely medical: the "intolerable pain" that he refers to at the start of Act II. The other is psychological: for a man like him, used to being in the thick of things and the center of attention, life in the country is like being walled up, sent into exile, or dropped onto another planet. Serebryakov understands and admits that behind all this there lies one thing— "damnable, disgusting old age" and "becoming repulsive to myself"—only he can do nothing to help himself in any way. This is no justification, but it does explain a great deal in his character and behavior. Old Nanny may well be the only one who understands him: "Old folk are like children, they want someone to feel sorry for them, but there's no one to feel sorry for old folk." This is another very general reminder of the "common denominator" that applies to the fates of all the characters.

That Serebryakov is not a genius, as Vanya and Sonya had imagined all his life, but an average (or perhaps rather indifferent) scholar—this we again accept as fact from his opponent's exasperated descriptions of him. True, the accuser seems to be contradicting himself when he says that there was, after all, something about Serebryakov that attracted people to him all his life and especially ensured his unusual success with women! When Vanya says of him that "not a single living soul has heard of him, he's completely unknown," his words are contradicted by the statements of other characters. Yelyena was "attracted to him as a scholar and a well-known man," and the professor himself says that he is used to "being well-known and making a stir." These contradictions further undermine our confidence in what we learn from Voinitsky about the man he hates.

In recent years these contradictions have begun to attract the attention of critics. In his analysis of the play, Pyotr Dolzhenkov concludes that Uncle Vanya's verdict on Serebryakov's scholarly activities is not simply equivocal—"there is nothing in the text that could confirm or refute Uncle Vanya's statements definitely either way." Dolzhenkov sees this deliberate vagueness as "the essential idea behind the play. The drama of Uncle Vanya is not the tragedy of a man who has sacrificed himself to a nonentity, but the drama of a man who gives up his life—but to what?" The situation presented in the play is universal: "everything that is best in us, all human lives, are given up to some unknown cause, disappearing into the yawning abyss that is called Professor Serebryakov . . . and Serebryakov begins to be understood as a symbolic figure, as the symbol of a world that is unknown to man."[9]

Dolzhenkov sees in this refusal to define Serebryakov's character in simple terms the conscious application by Chekhov of the positivist principles of "the unreliability of human judgments" and "conjectural knowledge."

An alternative explanation may be suggested.

It is indeed true that one cannot build an authentic picture of Serebryakov on the basis of what his obviously biased opponent says about him. It is also true that for every argument for or against Serebryakov in the text, a counterargument can be put forward which calls the judgment into question. Chekhov keeps us in ignorance of the professor's real importance as a public figure or a scholar. Similarly, in *The Seagull* the questions of how gifted Treplev is as a writer or how talented Zarechnaya is as an actress remain unclarified, while in "The Black Monk" one can only guess whether its sick hero is a genius or a mediocrity.

Vagueness of characterization? On the contrary: a very clear indication by Chekhov of what is truly important in these situations and what is unimportant. In all these cases, Chekhov is not creating works about talented people being stifled by the untalented, or untalented people passing themselves off as great talents, nor about genius that is not recognized by other people, nor about honest toil-

9. Pyotr Dolzhenkov, *Chekhov i pozitivizm* (Moscow, 1998), pp. 38–40.

ers who are deceived by a nonentity. Plays and stories with that kind of subject could have been written by Tanya Pesotskaya or Uncle Vanya, had they been writers.

Chekhov has a completely different kind of subject matter, in which it is pointless to look for the author's answers to incorrectly stated questions or to questions that he did not intend to ask. "Each person is right in his own way. . . . It's just because each person is right in his own way that they all suffer": this vision of the essential nature and outcome of collisions in life, as affirmed in *The Seagull* (and even before that in "The Black Monk" and other stories) is fully present in *Uncle Vanya* too. With such a vision it is important not to assess each character simply on the basis of his adherence to good or evil; it is necessary to trace how the "truth" affirmed by each person (with the simultaneous rejection of another person's "truth") leads in the final reckoning to general, overall suffering.

In *Uncle Vanya*, as in *The Seagull*, the collision between different "truths," each of which is relative, may act as the source for a comic treatment of the play—or at least of many of its episodes. Once again, *Uncle Vanya* has plenty of examples of "instant" humor: the neighbor Waffles's responses, paradoxical aphorisms, illustrations of the professor's pedantry, etc. But it is the collisions that arise because "each person is right in his own way" with the result "that they all suffer" that can be regarded as distinctively Chekhovian humor.

Broadly speaking, the situation described in Act II admits of being treated quite differently from the usual: not as drama or satire (in relation to Serebryakov) but as comedy or even vaudeville. One of the characters is ill, he is capricious and demanding, while all those around him have their own worries and interests, which gives rise to amusing collisions. This is how the action is built up, for example, in Chekhov's one-act farce *The Anniversary* (1891). There you have a sick bank clerk writing an urgent report, a director who likes to throw dust in people's eyes, the director's young wife whose head is full of romantic stories, a female visitor preoccupied by her own prosaic worry, and, as a climax, an unsuccessful attempt at murder provoked by this general discord.

Or compare these episodes from Act III of *Uncle Vanya* and from the early comic story "Notes from the Journal of a Quick-Tempered Man" (1887).

In the play, Astrov gives Yelyena a short lecture—illustrated by statistics and a map—about the destruction of the forests. But her thoughts are obviously far removed from the subject he is explaining to her so seriously: her intention is to find out "cautiously and by hints" whether at this moment "he loves anyone or not." The lecture is broken off when Astrov sees from her expression that the subject, so important to him, is "simply of no interest" to her, and she admits: "My thoughts were elsewhere."

The hero of the comic story is "a serious person with a philosophical turn of mind"; he is writing a thesis but is besieged by the young ladies from the neighboring dachas, who can think of nothing but romantic adventures and finding a husband. There are individual comic details, like the absurd title of his thesis—"The Dog Tax: Its Past and Future"—or the inappropriate allusion to Schopenhauer; but the main source of the comic is to be found in the complete absence of a "meeting of minds," as we see in the following typical episode:

> "Please do say something," she insisted.
>
> I tried to think of some popular topic which she might be capable of understanding. So after much thought I said: "The felling of forests is causing enormous havoc in Russia. . . ."
>
> "Oh, *Nicolas*," Varenka sighed, and her nose began to flush. "*Nicolas*, I see you're avoiding heart-to-heart conversation. . . . But what would you say if the girl whom you love were to offer you Eternal Friendship?"

In the story the comic effect caused by the absence of a "meeting of minds" is obvious, whereas in the play it may remain unnoticed. But it is important to realize that what gives rise to these diametrically opposed treatments is exactly the same in both cases.

A slight change of focus, and once again similar situations can be presented by Chekhov in either comic or dramatic form. This was the case with the different versions of *Ivanov*, and with the stories and vaudevilles. Only the sharp change of tone in the climax of Act III and the sad melody of the conclusion of *Uncle Vanya* determine, as in *The Seagull*, the inescapable seriousness of the final perception of the play.

Chekhov will achieve the same kind of balance of contrasts in the conclusions of his last two plays—plays in which the dramatic principles he had already formulated will become deeper and more complex.

2 0

_____

# Chekhov's "Little Trilogy": The Fourth Story

Chekhov's so-called "Little Trilogy" consists of three stories written in 1898 ("Encased," "Gooseberries," and "About Love").

Burkin, a schoolmaster, and his friend Ivan Ivanovich Chimsha-Gimalaisky, a veterinarian, are on a short hunting expedition in the country. One night, before they go to sleep, Burkin tells the story of the life and death of his schoolmaster colleague Belikov ("Encased"). Later the two friends decide to call at the estate of their friend Alyokhin, where Ivan Ivanovich relates the story of his civil service brother, Nikolai Ivanovich ("Gooseberries"). Finally, in "About Love," Alyokhin tells his own life story. Chekhov places the individual stories within a framework that embraces all three.

Critics have long pointed out an affinity between the heroes of each of the stories. The teacher whose whole life has been reduced to following rules and regulations, the civil servant whose one aim is to purchase an estate with gooseberry bushes, and the landowner who falls in love but allows his inhibitions to dominate him so completely that love itself perishes: all three have an underlying resemblance.

This resemblance is most often defined by using the concept

from the first story, that of *futlyarnost'* or "being encased." The hero of "Gooseberries" can indeed also be fairly described as encased within his all-absorbing dream of owning gooseberry bushes, while the main characters in "About Love" are similarly encased by those "conventional ideas of sin and virtue" behind which they try to hide their feelings.

"Being encased" is first and foremost, of course, an epistemological concept, linked with the problem of making sense of life and orienting oneself in it. Each of the three stories is essentially about the "false conceptions" that have taken possession of different individuals. For Chekhov, a particular way of life is an example of how people orient themselves in the world. In that sense, "being encased" is analogous to other kinds of orientation that are used to determine the whole structure of a person's life. In each instance it enables the hero to construct his life according to a stereotype, to have a single answer to all of life's possible "questions."

In the "Little Trilogy," Chekhov found a spacious metaphor within which to express a concept he had analyzed several times before. Using his "case"—his galoshes and umbrella, his ancient languages—Belikov "hid himself from real life." "Being encased" captures the whole point of such concepts—that is, one hides within them from "real life," which cannot be made to conform to stereotypes or reduced to generalizations.

How are these false conceptions brought home to the reader? Primarily through the plot. Each story shows a person's life breaking up as a result of following this or that "general idea." "Real life" triumphs—and somewhat cruelly—over any "case" that attempts to confine it. It was only in the grave that Belikov fully "achieved his ideal"; Nikolai Ivanovich Chimsha-Gimalaisky reaches his appointed goal at the cost of losing his youth, his health, and, above all, his human image; and Alyokhin has to lose his beloved forever in order to grasp "how unnecessary, trivial, and deceptive" were all the obstacles that he himself put in the way of his love. Each story presents its own aspect of the theme of "being encased."

Thus the stories themselves already contain an obvious general conclusion: a rejection of those "cases," stereotypes, and "membranes" within which the heroes tried to confine life. But the fact that the stories are placed within an overall framework, that the storytellers then offer their own assessments of the stories, and the author enables us to understand the logic of these assessments—all this makes the final significance of the trilogy appreciably more complicated. Chekhov takes the analysis further by evaluating the conclusions that his narrator-heroes draw from the lessons of other people's lives.

The "Little Trilogy" can be said to contain not three but four stories. The same epistemological viewpoint is maintained in the fourth story—the overall framework—as in the stories themselves. Through the individual storytellers, Chekhov shows three kinds of assessments, three kinds of reactions to the negative phenomena of life that are at the heart of each story. As in "The Duel," behind each assessment lies a particular orientation to life.

There's nothing we can do, "how many other encased men have been left behind and how many more are still to come!"—Burkin, the narrator of "Encased," twice repeats.

"It's impossible to go on living like this," we must do something, we must "jump across the ditch or build a bridge across"—this is the reaction of Chimsha-Gimalaisky, the narrator of "Gooseberries."

Having made a mistake and renounced the hope of love "forever," Alyokhin, the narrator-hero of "About Love," has condemned himself to going round and round on his estate, "like a squirrel in a cage."

These reactions are quite different: each is inseparable from, and conditioned by, the particular narrator's personality. The possibility of misinterpretation (all too common, unfortunately, in criticism of the "Little Trilogy") arises if any one of these reactions is regarded as absolute. Most often the phrases uttered by the second narrator, Chimsha-Gimalaisky, are seen as the ones that Chekhov intended to highlight. The reasons for this identification are understandable, but they are always extraneous, both to the story and to the author's actual position. As usual, the author does not show a preference for one reaction over another, he "merely" establishes and individualizes each one. And his conclusions are on a different plane from those of any of his heroes.

The framework of "Encased" is no less essential, therefore, than the actual story that Burkin tells. As in "The Head Gardener's Story" (1894), it reveals the individual, relative nature of the narrator's reactions and conclusions. Belikov has died, his story is finished, but life around goes on, never-ending and remote from the story just told. At the end as at the beginning, there is a reference to the village recluse Mavra, who repeats Belikov but somehow differently. This approach is familiar from "Lights": a story, from which the narrator is inclined to draw a simple finite conclusion, is placed by the author within the context of the never-ending panorama of life.

Another technique used in "Encased" had also been tried out in "Lights." Burkin concludes by saying that there always were and always will be other Belikovs, and that there is no hope of improvement. But his listener, Chimsha-Gimalaisky, who is more expansive, excitable, and radically inclined, draws a much bolder conclusion: "It's impossible to go on living like this!"—and widens the interpretation of *futlyarnost'* to such an extent that Burkin objects: "Now you're on to a different theme, Ivan Ivanych." Whether he is or not remains unanswered; what evidently matters to Chekhov is to show how very different conclusions may be drawn from the same phenomenon, depending on differences in temperament, mood, and attitude.

The second story, "Gooseberries," contains the most outspoken conclusions. "Why do we go on waiting?" asks the narrator, Chimsha-Gimalaisky. We ought not to stand "above the ditch," he asserts, "we ought to jump over it or build a bridge across."

Any phrase in Chekhov, as we know, can acquire a different meaning and emotional flavor depending on context. "No, life is intolerable!" decides the "young, ginger-colored bitch, a mixture of dachshund and mongrel," in "Kashtanka." "Life has become intolerable!" says Dezdemonov, the office spokesman, screwing up his courage outside his chief's door ("The Spokesman, or How Dezdemonov Came to Lose 2 5 Rubles"). Literally the same form of words is used by one of the narrators in the "Little Trilogy," and to explain his remarks the overall framework is no less important than the gooseberry story itself.

It is already clear from "Encased" that Ivan Ivanych Chimsha-Gimalaisky differs from his friends Burkin and Alyokhin, and the outspokenness of his conclusions may be attributed to his temperament and intense preoccupation with radical ideas. "I'm old and past fighting," he says in "Gooseberries," "I'm not even capable of hating any more. I just grieve inwardly, I feel exasperated and indignant. At night thoughts crowd in on me, so that my head burns and I can't sleep. . . . Oh, if only I were young!"

Again, as in "Encased," we are told that "Ivan Ivanych's story did not satisfy either Burkin or Alyokhin"; listening to a story "about a wretched little civil servant who ate gooseberries was tedious." Again, Chekhov is not concerned either to associate himself with Chimsha-Gimalaisky's assessment of the story or to discredit it; what matters most is that the narration and the sermon fail to achieve their goals. The thoughts that enter the listeners' heads, "of elegant people and of women," and the presence of the beautiful Pelageya—"these were better than any stories."

The listeners' nonacceptance of Ivan Ivanych's point of view is also indicated by different means. When he cites other examples of individuals obsessed with money, Burkin replies, as in "Encased": "Now you're on to a different theme, Ivan Ivanych." As for Alyokhin, he simply cannot make out "if what Ivan Ivanych had just said was wise and fair or not." The possibility of adopting a critical attitude toward Chimsha-Gimalaisky's point of view is indicated here but not expressed.

Finally, although the qualification is not made specific, it is clear from a careful reading that Ivan Ivanych's thoughts may themselves be illogical and contradictory. This is the technique that Chekhov had used for Shamokhin's speeches in "Ariadna" (1895). Exactly the same passionate conviction and aphoristic style may be used by a character to make assertions that are true or, immediately alongside them, ones that are known to be untrue.

Thus Ivan Ivanych speaks of how town dwellers are drawn toward life in the country. To begin with he speaks of this approvingly, but then he immediately condemns it. "If you've ever caught a ruff or watched migrating thrushes swarm over a village on a clear, crisp autumn day, you won't feel you belong to the town any more and you'll be yearning for freedom until the day you die." Here the wish to exchange town for country is treated sympathetically, as a longing "for freedom." (Chekhov himself had earlier adopted the same kind of tone in his letters to justify his wish to buy an estate and move out of Moscow.) But Ivan Ivanych completely reverses his judgment only a few sentences later: "To escape from the town, the struggle and the hurly-burly, to hide away in your own place in the country—that's not life, that's selfishness, laziness." And he uses the aphorism that became famous, about the six feet of earth that are needed by a corpse, while a human being needs the whole world.

This is a suitable place to recall those famous Chekhovian "antinomies" which made such an impression on the people he talked to. Bunin recalled that Chekhov "sometimes used to say" that writers should be beggars, because then they could not indulge in idleness and would have to write nonstop, "but at other times he would say the exact opposite," claiming that each person and especially the writer needs the whole world.[1] Or, talking of religion,

> he would say very earnestly on many occasions that immortality, life after death in whatever form, is complete nonsense.
>
> "It's superstition. And any kind of superstition is terrible. One should think clearly and boldly. We must go into this thoroughly some time. I'll prove to you as clearly as twice two is four that immortality is nonsense."

1. *Literaturnoye nasledstvo*, vol. 68 (Moscow, 1960), pp. 670–671.

But on several occasions he would say even more firmly:

"There is absolutely no way in which we can disappear after death. Immortality is a fact. Wait a moment and I'll prove it to you. . . ."[2]

"What *did* he think of death?" was the question that Bunin not unnaturally asked himself after such conversations.

We can find out what Bunin himself thought of death from his many works in which the question is posed and resolved ontologically. But for Chekhov, "death," "God," "the meaning of life" are "special" problems. What interests him as an artist is the realm of epistemology, in particular, that "you can use words to prove anything you like," and on subjects like death and immortality completely opposing judgments are possible. The internal contradictions within Chekhov's heroes' monologues and dialogues make sense within this context. It is as if, in trying out the persuasiveness of mutually exclusive judgments on other people, Chekhov were preparing for those works in which his characters often come out unconsciously with conflicting judgments of just that kind.

Along with the other two narrators, Chimsha-Gimalaisky is interesting to the author as a representative of the sort of person who is completely absorbed by his "personal view of things." To the hero that view seems to be the "real truth," but the author lets us feel that his position is subjectively conditioned and relative, if only because to the others it does not seem like the real (only and universal) truth, and because the narrators' conclusions stem from, and are conditioned by, each one's individual personality. Given the criteria that we know "real truth" must satisfy—completeness and general significance—the relativity of their position is obvious.

In conjunction with the two earlier stories, "About Love" confirms the critical importance for the author of the epistemological aspect of "knowledge in the realm of thought." Its aim is not to offer prescriptions for being in love or to solve love's mysteries; it

2. Op. cit., p. 666.

examines how those who are in love perceive their own situation and how they behave as a result. The framework offers a perspective on the uniqueness of the story of Alyokhin and Luganovich. This is done through the story of Pelageya's love for Nikanor and the friends' reflections that all questions connected with love are a great mystery, "and you can interpret the subject how you like." Alyokhin then comes out with the assertion already quoted in Chapter 9: "The explanation that would seem to fit one case doesn't fit a dozen others. The best we can do, in my opinion, is to explain each case separately, without trying to generalize. We must treat each individual case in isolation, as the doctors say."

His own story confirms both the highly individual, unique nature of his love conflict as well as the possibility of drawing conclusions not about the "special" problem itself, but about how the problem is understood and the behavior that results. The main characters complicate their love by various "fatal questions," as Alyokhin puts it. To him it is a "mystery" why his beloved should be married to Luganovich, a husband confident of his happiness, "why she should have met him and not me, and for what reason such a terrible mistake had to occur in our lives." Alyokhin puts six other similar questions to himself. "She, too, was tormented by the question. . . ."

The story ends with a Chekhovian "discovery": the hero realizes—too late—what should govern one's behavior in love. "I realized that when you're in love, you must not make happiness or unhappiness your starting point, nor conventional ideas of sin and virtue—you must think of love as something higher and more important, or else not think about it at all."

As in "Gooseberries," the relative nature of the hero's conclusion is obvious. What this "something higher and more important than happiness or unhappiness" is, the hero never knows, and if he were to fall in love again, there is no guarantee that he would find an ideal solution of every problem. Chimsha-Gimalaisky's conclusions ("to jump over the ditch") are no use at all to the participants in this love drama, any more than their experience provides an answer to the problems that make his "head burn."

Thus the stories in the "Little Trilogy" contain two kinds of analysis. The stories themselves analyze the "false conceptions" to which people subjugate their lives and which they even cultivate, while the overall framework analyzes and individualizes those conclusions that claim to be universally binding but are shown to be relative and unacceptable to other people.

Both kinds of analysis come to negative conclusions. Chekhov cannot accept any kind of "case"; he shows the impossibility of enclosing "real life" in any sort of "membrane." At the same time the verbal solutions put forward by the narrators are also deceptive: though natural and persuasive in some situations, in others they seem to belong "to a different theme." The image of "the man with the little hammer" in "Gooseberries" is most applicable to Chekhov himself, refusing to let us accept a single illusion.

But as before in Chekhov, these negative conclusions, important as they are, are not exclusively so.

As well as a similarity between the stories in the "Little Trilogy," there is also a link among the storytellers. They are all ordinary people, occupied with the ordinary business of living and granted the kind of average will and unstable mind of the average person. Yet for all their natural limitations it is clear that these three characters—Burkin, Chimsha-Gimalaisky, and Alyokhin—are intended to evoke our interest and to make us feel that the problems disturbing them are close and comprehensible to each and every one of us. What they have in common, like the heroes of "The Teacher of Russian" and "The House with a Mezzanine," is "a sense of dissatisfaction with themselves and other people," and the principal source of this dissatisfaction is once again the way in which life is currently organized; they cannot understand why the real world is so absurd, and they yearn for a different life that would correspond to the norm, the way things ought to be. This norm is sensed dimly, in the most general terms: "Freedom, freedom! Even a hint, even a faint hope of its possibility, makes the spirit soar, doesn't it?" (Burkin); "Happiness does not exist," says Chimsha-Gimalaisky, "it ought not to exist, and if life has any meaning and purpose, they are not to be found in our happiness, but in something loftier and more rational. Do good!"; and Alyokhin's words also belong here, that in questions of love "you must not make happiness or unhappiness your starting point, nor conventional ideas of sin and virtue, but something higher and more important."

These are people "searching for real truth," suffering setbacks, caught in dead ends, but refusing to calm down and evoking our sympathy for that reason. They are sensitive to "deviation from the norm," reacting against it and dimly conscious of what the norm should be. It is not only illusions and delusions that the people in Chekhov's world have in common, it is also a longing for "real truth," for "the norm." This is a positive generalization on Chekhov's part, though closely linked with a negative one.

Finally, it is not only the logic of events, of characters and narrators' pronouncements that lead the reader to general conclusions. In the framework of the "Little Trilogy" are elements outside plot and characterization that act as markers, pointing to the essentials of a complete picture of the world, of the "real life" in which the characters are trying to find their bearings.

As always in Chekhov, it is the motif of beauty present in the world that fulfills this function. In the description in "Encased" of the village sleeping in the moonlight, the repetition three times of the word "quiet" and the concentrated effect of "gentle, sad, and beautiful . . . with tender kindness . . . all is well" shift attention from the ugliness of life to the harmony that may be divined in the beauty of nature. A sentence like the one at the beginning of "Gooseberries" provides a keynote for all the narration to follow: "Now, when the weather was calm and the whole of nature seemed in a gentle, thoughtful mood, Ivan Ivanych and Burkin were filled with love of this open country, and both of them thought what a vast and splendid land it was."

The quiet beauty that usually passes unnoticed and inspires the dream that "evil is no more and all's well in the world," the allusion to the "vast and splendid" land—all this not only sets the keynote, like a tuning fork, it also bypasses the plot and affects the reader directly, pointing to what the author sees as essential signs of the norm that are absent from the characters' ideas and actions.

The vagueness of Chekhov's characters' ideas about how things should be is often attributed to the vagueness of the author's own ideas, as if he had intended to depict the norm but had not been equal to the task. But the immediate explanation of this lack of clarity is to be found in his characters' unstable minds and wills, and in dozens of circumstances (both depending on the characters and independent of them), each of which the author pinpoints.

To reduce Chekhov's lessons to these admittedly vague daydreams (and to speak in this context of his failures and partial successes) is to impoverish the content and to undervalue the artistic and social significance of those valid general conclusions to which Chekhov boldly leads the reader. The writer had uncovered an illness—trusting in illusions and subjugating yourself to them—in places where his contemporaries had not suspected it. This sober outlook was unprecedented in Russian literature, but it does not mean that Chekhov lacked faith in the norm and was not ceaselessly preoccupied with searching for it throughout his work.

## 2 1

# "This Is a Great Mystery": "The Lady with a Little Dog" (1899)

Th="hey felt that this love of theirs had changed them both."
Numerous critics and readers of "The Lady with a Little
Dog" rightly see these words from the concluding section
as a key point in the whole story. But "changed" in what sense? This
is where opinions begin to differ.

The kind of denouement where the characters are shown to undergo a change had been gradually perfected by Chekhov in a
number of stories. One of his earliest attempts was in "Thieves"
(1890), where the hero, Yergunov, gives up his stereotyped existence for a new life based on diametrically opposite principles.
Then came "The Duel" (1891), in which Layevsky undergoes a similar change. In "The Wife" (1892), Chekhov took on an even more
difficult task. Here the domestic conflict between Asorin, a man in
the Karenin mold, and his young wife unfolds against the grim
background of a national disaster: the famine. In Asorin's character
there seemed to be no glimmer of light: the hostility and hatred of
the people around him, in whose eyes he was "vermin," the universal rejoicing when he left his own house—none of this applied to
Layevsky, who was accused by some and defended by others. But
even in Asorin's case, after a "strange, crazy, unique" day in his life, a

change occurs, as a result of which he feels himself to be "a different person."

But Chekhov makes it clear that these changes are not to be seen as the successful conclusion of the hero's searchings or the discovery of answers, but as the beginning of new questions. In "Thieves" the final reflections of Yergunov, whose life has been shaken completely out of its rut, consist of question after question. Layevsky's final reflections about people's searches for real truth seem to be affirmative, but they too contain the question, "Who knows?"—a question that concerns the fate of human searching in general, quite apart from the problems that directly confront the changed Layevsky. Asorin's memoir ends with the phrase, "What the future holds, I do not know."

This kind of denouement, showing how the hero changes after rejecting certain stereotypes and is then faced with new questions, is what Chekhov uses to conclude the story of Gurov and Anna in "The Lady with a Little Dog." In contrast to the "resurrection" and "rebirth" endings well known in Russian literature from the works of Tolstoy and Dostoevsky, no solution is found in the conclusion to the problems that have been raised in the story, and no light of truth is revealed.

One should not therefore assume that Chekhov is endorsing Gurov's reflections that "each person" must inevitably lead "a double life." Chekhov shows that for people like Gurov, leading a double life may be the only way out, but he also notes that Gurov "judged others by himself" and always assumed that everyone else's life followed the same course as his own. A person's "real, most interesting life" more often than not runs its course in secret; that is so, and Chekhov points it out with regret, but he does not go on to say: that is how it ought to be.

The relative and individual nature of the character's opinion is further demonstrated by Chekhov's usual method: we simply see that other people view the subject differently. In the last chapter of "The Lady with a Little Dog" this is done with special subtlety. In a story where Gurov's point of view prevails (on everything, including their love affair), the author occasionally introduces Anna's "voice," and we see that "this love of theirs" has united two very different people. They take different views of their secret life. For him, "everyone's private existence is maintained in secret," whereas for her, "why could they meet only in secret, hiding from people like thieves? Hadn't their lives been ruined?" But then we come to see that he is adopting her point of view (and this is one of the features of the "new" Gurov). Previously he has used "all kinds of arguments," like the inevitability of a secret life, to reassure himself. But the new Gurov can experience "deep compassion," sincerity, and tenderness, feelings that force him not to object to Anna's logic, as he had done several times before, but to stand up for her point of view. That double life, which the old Gurov might have found interesting and piquant, now seems a life of "intolerable bonds" to him as well as to her. What was no more than an interim conclusion even for Gurov cannot, of course, be regarded as a final conclusion by the author.

No questions are resolved for Gurov and Anna once "this love of theirs had changed them both." On the contrary, only then does the full seriousness of the problems become truly apparent. What stands in the way of their love is not simply "bourgeois morality" or social opinion (in contrast to *Anna Karenina*, society, in so far as it is shown at all in "The Lady with a Little Dog," is completely indifferent to Gurov and Anna's affair). Even if they had managed to overcome the complications of a divorce and to negotiate the problem of the family left behind, etc., questions still remain. "Why does she love him so much?" What is "love" if you can have no conception of it even after participating in dozens of love affairs? Why has love come to them when "his hair had turned grey" and her life is beginning to "fade and wither"? And why does fate compel the two of them, who were destined for each other, "to live in separate cages"? Four more question marks follow in the story's final sentences.

Clearly, no answer is given to these questions which the characters find agonizing and cannot resolve—questions that will always accompany love, for "this is a great mystery"; everything "that has been written and said about love is not a solution but only the posing of questions that remain unresolved," "the causes are unknown," and "we must treat each individual case in isolation, as the doctors say." The solution envisaged, say, by the hero of "About Love," Alyokhin, who was drawn into a similar situation and asked himself similar questions—bitter experience had taught him to take the general view that one ought not to "decorate" love with "these fatal questions" but to cast them aside as "unnecessary and trivial"—is obviously unacceptable to the characters in "The Lady with a Little Dog."

Chekhov's changes to the text show how he rejected any form of words that could be taken to mean that the characters' searches were over and their problems solved. He corrected his first version, "Love had made them both better," to "Love had changed them both for the better," before finally deciding on "This love had changed them."

But if the conclusion of "The Lady with a Little Dog" evidently has little in common with the "resurrection" or "rebirth" sort of ending, or with the discovery of answers, what exactly is this "change" that has taken place?

The answer is to be found in the way that Chekhov constructs the story. How Gurov's ideas change (for he is the focus of the author's interest) is expressed by means of certain links that are revealed on careful reading. Most prominent among them are two pairs of opposites: "it seemed"/"it turned out that" and "ending"/"beginning."

"It seemed"/"it turned out that" is familiar from a whole series of works, starting with the "stories of discovery," in which Chekhov describes the disappearance of illusions and the rejection of stereotypical thought and behavior.

"Ending"/"beginning" is linked with the particular stereotype that is being rejected in a given story. Both pairs are closely linked from the beginning and run right through the text like musical themes with variations, to merge in the conclusion.

As the reader quickly discovers, the "multiple experience" that Gurov has acquired in his past love affairs stamps its mark straightaway on his affair with the lady with a little dog. This experience has determined his mindset toward all such episodes, of which he is sure there are many more to come ("What strange encounters one has in life!").

The central point in this mindset is that sooner or later all the affairs come to an end (so that new ones can take their place). The first half of the story—the Yalta and Moscow chapters—is designed both to bring out the nature of this stereotype and to show how at first everything develops in full accordance with it. As soon as Gurov's affair with Anna is related to the past, the "seeming" chain of words begins to unfold, and parallel with it a similar chain of "ending" words and phrases.

"It *seemed* to him that he had learned enough from bitter experience . . ."—this is how the story of Gurov's past conquests is introduced (italics added here and subsequently). In line with this experience, each intimacy was pleasant "*to begin with*," but "*in the end*" it became oppressive. New encounters, however, then followed, past experience was easily forgotten, and "everything *seemed* so simple and amusing." In the first half of the story "seeming" and "ending" are the dominant themes and variations. The course taken by each of Gurov's previous affairs is also a kind of "seeming" game in which both parties accept the conditions. Each intimacy always "*seemed* such a delightfully easy adventure"; Gurov (we learn later) "always *seemed* to women different from what he really was"; and when the affair was coming to an end, the women would become loathsome to him, "and then the lace on their underwear *seemed* to him like the scales on a fish."

Should one of the parties break the rules of this game—by adopting, for example, a serious instead of a playful attitude toward "love" and "passion"—Gurov immediately alludes to this (everything being seen from his point of view) by the use of "seeming" words. These are intended to indicate his unwillingness to take seriously what—as far as he is concerned—are infringements of the rules. For example, we are told that certain women made love to Gurov "insincerely, with superfluous conversations, in an affected, hysterical way, and the expressions on their faces seemed to say that this was not love, not passion, but something more significant." This additional theme accompanies the main one.

Gurov's new affair promises to develop "according to the rules." He and Anna quickly become intimate and with obvious signs of willingness on her part ("when men spoke to her, they had one secret aim in mind that she could not fail to divine . . ."; " 'Let's go to your place,' he said quietly. And they set off quickly together"). That the other party in the affair then behaves "strangely and inappropriately" also seems to him like a generally familiar and annoying deviation from the rules: "Anna Sergeyevna, this 'lady with a little dog,' treated what had happened in a curiously personal, very serious sort of way, as if she looked upon it as her downfall. . . . She struck a thoughtful, despondent pose, like some fallen woman in an old-fashioned painting. . . . 'You seem to be trying to justify yourself' . . . had it not been for the tears in her eyes, he might have thought she was joking or playing a part." But taken as a whole the Yalta affair has evidently not broken the stereotype: the theme of "seeming" and "ending" in the background becomes more and more audible in the description of the farewell and of Gurov's first days in Moscow, where Chekhov puts great emphasis on "seeming" and "ending" words:

"We are saying farewell *forever*"; "it was as if everything had conspired to bring that sweet trance, that madness, to a swift *end*"; "So that had been another escapade or adventure in his life, he thought, and now it too was *over*. . . ."; "this young woman whom he would *never* see again, had not after all been happy with him . . . he must have *seemed* different to her from what he really was"; "A month or two would pass, and his memory of Anna Sergeyevna, it *seemed* to him, would cloud over and only occasionally would he dream of her and her touching smile, just as he dreamed of the others."

So the first phase of the story finishes with an idea belonging to

Gurov: it seemed to him that everything had come to an end as usual.

But then the new phase begins: in Moscow, memories of "the lady with a little dog" pursue him relentlessly. At first his thoughts are framed in the usual way: "she *seemed* lovelier, younger, and more tender than she had been; and he even *seemed* better in his own eyes than he had been back there in Yalta."

But when for the first time in several months Gurov catches sight of Anna in the crowd at the provincial theater, "his heart missed a beat, and he saw clearly that she was the nearest, dearest, and most important person in the world for him now." Like an echo of the earlier melody, several "seeming" words appear briefly (the husband "*seemed* to spend all his time bowing"; "people *seemed* to be looking at them from every box"). But in contrast to all the earlier "seeming" words, the phrase "and he saw clearly" is heard here for the first time and strikes a distinct and unmistakable note. For Gurov this marks the start of his new life, of his new relationship to life.

Then, at the very center of the composition, the earlier melody returns ("He suddenly recalled that evening at the station, after seeing Anna Sergeyevna off, when he had said to himself that it was *all over* and they would *never* see each other again"), only to be at once reversed: "But how *far* they still were *from the end!*" From now on the two melodies will be heard inseparably together. (The chapter about their meeting in the theater finishes with a paragraph which reverses the old Gurov's stereotyped attitude toward women: "She kept looking back at him, and he could tell from her eyes that she was *truly* unhappy.")

In the last chapter there is a complicated interplay between the story's main themes. The new melody strikes a confident note at first, simply reversing the previous "it seemed, it would end": "It was *obvious* to him that *the end* of this love of theirs *was not near*, was not even in sight." The old Gurov's way of thinking is twice briefly recalled: "And it *seemed* strange to him that he had grown so old and ugly in recent years"; "he always *seemed* to women . . ." But here this is done solely to point up the contrast with his genuine new feeling, for "it was only now, when his hair had turned grey, that he had fallen *well and truly* in love—for the first time in his life." This first real love forces Gurov, who had earlier thought of his feeling of superiority over "the inferior breed" as perfectly natural, to renounce his self-absorption. To underline the two lovers' oneness of thought, Chekhov writes: "*it seemed to them* that they had been destined for each other by fate itself." "Seemed" here seems to mean "self-evident."

So we come to the last sentence of all. Even in the rich musicality of Chekhov's prose, this last sentence of "The Lady with a Little Dog" is a rare miracle of harmony. The contrasting melodies running right through the story, enriched in meaning and sound by numerous subtleties, are linked in an inseparable harmony at the end:

> And it *seemed* that in a short time the solution would be found and then a beautiful new life would *begin*, and it was *clear* to both of them that the *end* was still a very long way off, and that the most complicated and difficult part was only just *beginning*.

"It seemed, it would end (easily)"—"it turned out that (the most difficult part) was beginning." This is how Chekhov sums up the change that his hero has undergone. Contrary to his old stereotype, according to which the only prospect ahead of him was a succession of love affairs, Gurov has attained his one and only love and feels that it alone is real. This is the essence of the transformation from the old Gurov to the new; it is the source, too, of "the most complicated and difficult part," but these will be complications arising from "this love of theirs." His one and only love turns out to be not less but more complicated than his previous multiplicity of "escapades or adventures."

Chekhov's last sentence may be misinterpreted. One might suppose that doubt is being cast on the heroes' hopes that "a beautiful new life would begin." This is not so: if a solution is found, "a beautiful new life" will begin without fail. The element of doubt is raised by a different illusory hope: "it seemed that *in a short time* the solution would be found." This, indeed, can only seem to be so; what is clear beyond doubt is "that the end was still a very long way off, and that the most complicated and difficult part was only just beginning."

The transition from "it seemed, it would end" to "it turned out that . . . was beginning" constitutes the essential change in the hero's consciousness. But it does not in itself explain why the stereotype should have been rejected—a stereotype that seemed so firmly fixed in Gurov's consciousness and determined his behavior, and which was only reinforced by each new "escapade or adventure"—including, so it seemed, the affair in Yalta.

Why this particular adventure with the lady with a little dog should have become this inveterate cynic's one genuine love does indeed remain the kind of riddle that forces one to say of love that "this is a great mystery" and "the causes are unknown."

Chekhov does not set out to prove that the mystery of love does not exist. On the contrary, the mystery is what he is writing about. Love is a mystery for Chekhov's characters because there are no general solutions and each case of love is unique. As Masha says later in *Three Sisters*, "when you read some novel or other, it all seems so stale and obvious, but as soon as you fall in love yourself, you realize that no one knows the first thing about it and you've got to work it out on your own."

Chekhov's characters know and have read about "what love is" in general, and the philosophy of love contains nothing new or interesting for them. The mystery begins with the individualization "of each separate case." Why in that way? Why at that time? Why that particular person? Chekhov's characters in love ask these and dozens of similar "why?" questions. The impossibility of "finding one's bearings" in love is a particular but frequent instance of not being able to find one's bearings in life as a whole.

So it remains a riddle and a mystery why "this quite unremarkable little woman, swallowed up in the provincial crowd, holding a vulgar lorgnette, now filled his whole existence, was his joy and sorrow, and the one happiness that he now craved in life." What we find out about Anna from her speeches of repentance makes us feel sympathetic toward her. But being dissatisfied with one's husband, complaining about the boredom of life, and feeling repentance—all this sort of thing Gurov must have heard many times before in confessions from women. One of the explanations she gives ("*I wanted to live!* To live, to live . . . I was burning with curiosity . . .") sounds so much like Gurov's own usual motivation ("and *he wanted to live,* and everything seemed so simple and amusing") that one would expect his stereotype to be strengthened by all this, not weakened. It is easy to be ironic at Anna's expense, but she is the one who succeeds in becoming Gurov's only true love.

Evidently the reasons for the change depicted in the story are to be sought in Gurov himself. In order to correlate his character's thoughts and actions with the "norm" and "real truth," Chekhov again introduces certain markers—unobtrusively, in passing—that make this correlation possible.

Where do these markers first appear in "The Lady with a Little Dog"? Is it at the moment when Anna, after referring to her "lackey of a husband," feels no need to explain herself, since both she and Gurov understand what is meant—and this sounds less like the coded language of lovers than a simple exchange of messages between two people oppressed by their lack of freedom? Or even earlier, in the reference to Gurov's wife as "plain-spoken, sure of herself, imposing, and in her own words, 'a thinking person'"? (Both the "thinking wife" and the "lackey husband" clearly base their lives on certain stereotypes and "general ideas" that are bound to remain unshaken.)

Another marker appears later, in the Oreanda episode: "Gurov reflected on how beautiful everything in the world really was when you stopped to think about it, everything except our own thoughts and actions when we lose sight of the higher aims of existence and our human dignity." This allusion to "the higher aims of existence," like the allusion in "Gooseberries" to "our splendid land," would seem to have no connection with the course of the narrative or the demands of the plot. But these allusions are not fortuitous, they are vital. Introduced into a character's train of thought, what they indicate above all is the author's intention to raise a specific individual story to the level of something universal—not known to the characters, but dimly sensed—that would be able to unite everyone. At the start of Chapter 3 the same kind of higher, general note is struck by the reference to "recalling the years of one's youth."

The thoughts that come to Gurov about "the higher aims of existence" are not peculiar to this story. Almost the same feelings that overcome Gurov when he is spellbound by "those magical surroundings of sea and mountains, of clouds and open sky," had been experienced by another Chekhov hero, Dmitry Startsev, on that unique occasion in his life in the moonlit cemetery. Layevsky, Ionych, Gurov—each is moved at a given moment by higher thoughts and reflects on what is eternal. Their thoughts about "the higher aims of existence" come and go, but the "escapade or adventure" continues.

Also outwardly unrelated to the development of the characters' attitudes is the episode in which Gurov tries to strike up a conversation about his affair in the summer, and receives the famous reply:

> "You were quite right just now about the sturgeon, it *was* a bit off!"
>
> For some reason these everyday words suddenly roused Gurov's indignation, and struck him as coarse and degrading. What barbaric manners, what ugly people!

Then follows the indignant Gurov's monologue about our "barren, uninspiring life."

This monologue is often seen by critics as an indication of Gurov's rebirth and regeneration under the effects of love, or of the "rebellion" that will give rise to such a regeneration. It is also cited as proof of the social significance of Chekhov's story. Such an interpretation needs to be closely examined, otherwise the whole love story looks like no more than a makeweight addition to the hero's speech of protest.

For a start, Gurov has not yet visited Anna's town and fallen "well and truly" in love. That will happen later; for the moment "he himself had no clear idea" of what was happening to him and what to do; all he wanted was "to see Anna Sergeyevna and speak to her, arrange a meeting if possible." And in the long chain of "how it seemed" expressions, this "struck him as," especially in combination with "suddenly" and "for some reason," looks like a familiar Chekhov example of inconsequential human thoughts, with their unexpected leaps and indiscriminate conclusions. Finally, Gurov's emotional outburst contains nothing that is new or that we have not heard before from other Chekhov characters.

One might suppose that Gurov's companion, who failed to see that love and sturgeon do not go together (especially when the sturgeon is a bit off), was intended by Chekhov to represent a hopelessly crass typical member of society. This is not necessarily so. It is quite clear, after all, from what the companion says, that Gurov himself has just been talking about sturgeon. But right now, at this particular moment, Gurov is someone else, someone who feels in great need of sympathy and of being understood (just like the cabby Iona Potapov in "Yearning"), whereas his companion is too self-absorbed to understand—to be able to understand—him.

Chekhov's characters are submerged in everyday life. There are moments when they expand spiritually and want to break out of the circle of everyday vulgarity, but they do not do this collectively, or at the same time, or even with someone else, but on their own. At each of these moments they are lonely, they are not understood, they obtain no response. This constant Chekhov theme had been expressed very poignantly in "Ionych" (written a year before "The Lady with a Little Dog"), in the scenes of the two declarations of love that are not understood. In "The Lady with a Little Dog," Chekhov describes with a certain amount of irony how this world of everyday vulgarity is suddenly revealed to Gurov, and the latter explodes with indignation against "these barbaric manners and ugly people . . . these days of unrelieved boredom." What is revealed for a moment to Gurov is shown to be an inescapable constant of human relations.

There is no reason, therefore, to regard this episode as almost more important than the whole of the love story and the change in

Gurov's attitude toward the "inferior breed." Such an approach is favored by critics seeking to establish the important social message of "The Lady with a Little Dog." But of far deeper and more genuine social significance in Chekhov's world than any words of protest or indignation uttered by one character is the author's unfailing preoccupation with distinguishing the true from the false, the "genuine" from the "nongenuine" in human ideas and actions.

Nevertheless, Gurov's indignant inner monologue *is* important—important in characterizing Gurov. An average man and one of the crowd, he remains so till the end of the story; at all events, nothing is said about a "break" with the society that made him so indignant. But we find out something else about him. Somewhere deep in his soul he carries a feeling of discontent, an awareness that "ordinary" life is a deviation from the "norm" (everything is beautiful "except our own thoughts and actions"), and a consciousness of "the higher aims of existence."

Gurov's monologue repeats almost word for word what Dmitry Startsev, already halfway to becoming Ionych, said about everyday life in the town of S.: "You ask what kind of life we have here? No life at all. We grow old, we get fat, we let ourselves go. Days and nights flash past in a dull blur, without thoughts or impressions. . . . Making money by day and spending the evening at the club, surrounded by gamblers, alcoholics, and vulgarians, whose company I detest. What's good about that?" Both monologues contain the note of "dissatisfaction with oneself and other people" that is felt by so many characters in Chekhov. The outcome of such speeches varies considerably according to the particular individual. It may be, as in the case of Ionych, that everything comes to an end with this surge of indignation, and the "spark in the soul" goes out; or it may lead, as in Gurov's case, to his one and only true love. But these speeches, these thoughts and moods, are like a mark, a sign—a sign of one more ordinary person being drawn unconsciously toward the search for "real truth."

## 2 2

# Last Stories of Discovery:
# "A Case History" (1898),
# "On Official Duty" (1899)

In "The Lady with a Little Dog" the "easy ending" theme is displaced by that of the "difficult beginning." This is a variation on the well-established type of Chekhov story—about overturning illusions and rejecting stereotyped ideas and ways of behaving—at the heart of which is the "it seemed . . . it turned out that" situation. In the works of his final period, Chekhov returns to this situation time and again, examining ever new attempts to find one's bearings in an increasingly complicated real world.

Just as the student Vasilyev in "The Nervous Breakdown" knew about brothels only by hearsay, so Korolyov, the house surgeon in "A Case History," "had never been interested in factories and never visited one. But he had read about them . . . and whenever he saw a factory in the distance or close by, he always thought that from the outside everything looked so quiet and peaceful, whereas inside there was bound to be . . ."

We know that according to the rules of Chekhov's world, the hero should now express some kind of initial idea, that the disclosure of its simplified nature will then lead to its rejection, and by contrast the genuine—i.e., incomparably more complicated—state of affairs will be shown. As in "The Nervous Breakdown," the source of the original conception is also shown: "this makes sense and can be easily assimilated only when presented in a newspaper article or a textbook."

Korolyov's a priori idea of factories, based on newspaper articles and textbooks, consists of the following: "the impenetrable ignorance and blind egoism of the owners, boring unhealthy labor for the workers, squabbles, vodka, and insects." The next phrase about the workers, in whom Korolyov sensed the presence of "uncleanliness, drunkenness, nervousness, and bewilderment," serves to confirm the second part of his conception. But after that the whole story moves on to a different aspect of factory life and concentrates on the life of the owners.

Here, as we shall see, the hero's initial conception does indeed change, although it is not overturned. The owners prove to be subject to normal human feelings: Lyalikova is in grief and despair at the illness of her only daughter, while Liza's face has a "gentle, suffering expression that was touching and full of intelligence." Both the factory owner and the heiress to her fortune are unhappy; only the vulgar, tiresome governess is in a state of bliss.

The story contains a topical social theme in that it deals with the origins of capitalism, when factories were being built in villages and it was possible to grow up in Moscow with only the most general notion of what factories were like. But as in "The Nervous Breakdown" earlier, it is not the social phenomenon itself but the sense made of it by a particular kind of individual that is being presented and studied.

Korolyov's most general initial conception clearly amounts to a resistance of capitalism and a conviction that factory life is a focus of evil. But "the case history" gives him an opportunity to ponder what the "root cause" of this evil might be.

After taking a closer look, Korolyov comes to the conclusion that Christina Dmitriyevna, the governess having a pleasant time, is only a "figurehead." The main person for whom everything here is being done is the devil. For Korolyov the devil is "the mysterious force" responsible for "that gross mistake . . . which nothing can now put right"; and twice more he refers to this "unknown" and "mysterious" force.

Korolyov's conception of life as a whole is what we have come to expect from Chekhov's typical "average man": he is powerless to find his bearings in "the muddle of which everyday life consists, in the tangle of all the small threads from which human relations are woven." As always, this conception of life and human relations—"an alien and incomprehensible world" (Vasilyev in "The Nervous Breakdown"), "a fire in the theater" (Sobol in "The Wife"), "as dark as this water reflecting a tangle of weeds" (Ivashin in "Neighbors")—is the product of a collision between the Chekhov hero and a specific feature of the real world, whether it be prostitution, the famine year, or love and family conflicts. In "A Case History" the hero concludes that everything generated by modern factory life is incomprehensible, unknown, and seemingly a product of the devil's trickery. Under capitalism, human relations themselves are "a gross mistake," "a logical absurdity," and "an incurable disease"; both owners and workers alike are deceived by the devil.

In line with this understanding of the "root cause" of the disease is the prescription recommended by Korolyov to Liza Lyalikova. She must get away from the factory as soon as possible, "get away from this devil, who looks out at night," throw everything up and go away, as "our children and grandchildren" will be sure to do.

How should we evaluate this understanding of the "root cause" and this prescription? But first, how does the hero's position accord with that of the author? These questions are bound to confront the story's interpreters.

Ilya Ehrenburg bypassed the question of a distance between the two positions ("Anton Pavlovich, or in this instance, Doctor Korolyov, says . . .").[1] But a distance exists. Everything in the story is seen through the hero's eyes, and the problems of factory life are

---

1. Ilya Ehrenburg, *Perechityvaya Chekhova*, pp. 9–10.

characterized only to the extent that they are perceived and resolved by a particular individual.

Confined within the limits of the hero's pronouncements and reflections, with all their inconsistent, vague, restricted, and other qualities, we analyze only his point of view, and Chekhov consistently underlines the fact that it is subjectively conditioned. However close the author and his character may appear to be in their attitude toward capitalism, we can obtain a full idea of the author's position only by going beyond the level of narrative analysis to investigate the author's train of thought as reflected in the story's structure.

Chekhov takes his character from "it seemed" to "it turned out that," and in so doing indicates the circumstances that are omitted when the question of factory life is posed incorrectly, and that ought to be considered when it is posed correctly. It is also worth noting that the hero's solution of the "question" is not an apotheosis rounding off the story: it sheds light and disappears. The story ends on a calm, bright note, with a feeling of confident optimism—and not only because the hero has found the "root cause" and prescription. This note in the conclusion can be attributed equally to the motif of mutual understanding that has been arrived at by two good people.

The unity in thought and mood between two sympathetic characters, Korolyov and Liza ("it was clear to him that she thought the way he did, and was only waiting for confirmation from someone she trusted"), is a further indication by Chekhov that the problem has been "posed correctly."

This surmounting of disunity between characters is a very infrequent event in Chekhov's world. Whether he is talking about family ties, love, or the relations between people living in the same town, Chekhov writes of how illusory these ties are and of the difficulties of establishing genuine mutual understanding, so that the theme of disunity and apartness may appear to be dominant in his creative world. But clarification is essential here. The theme of "universal disunion," however grand it may sound, is a particular theme; it is subordinated to Chekhov's all-embracing interest in the problem of man orienting himself in the real world and making sense of life. For in Chekhov's world the causes of disunity between people are to be found in the existence of many "truths," in people's absorption in their own separate "truths" which prevents them from arriving at a unified understanding, and in how even the "good thoughts" of good people may seem unacceptable to other equally good people ("now you're on to a different theme," as Burkin says to Ivan Ivanych in "Encased").

Chekhov's theme of the difficulties of human fellowship and understanding stops short of the purely modernist theme of the impossibility of establishing contact, of absolute noncommunication. But before "A Case History" there are perhaps only two stories, "Beauties" and "The Student" (and partly "The Lady with a Little Dog"), which are devoted entirely to the theme of overcoming disunity, to finding a single common understanding of "how things are." Elsewhere this motif appears rarely and serves only to highlight universal disunion and the incredible difficulties in the way of genuine mutual understanding; so that when Chekhov introduces the motif of discovering unity, it makes that much stronger an impression.

Only by recognizing that the hero's outlook is subordinate to the logical development of the author's thought can we then ask about the value of Chekhov's views on the special problem of "factory life."

What is revealed by the assessment of factory life that Chekhov attributes to the hero of "A Case History"? Many critics make the direct or indirect assumption that it is economically and socially naive. "The reasons are unknown" is the usual conclusion that Chekhov's heroes draw when confronted by the most varied aspects of life (think of Vasilyev's judgments in "A Story Without an Ending" or those of Alyokhin in "About Love"), so that the idea of the devil as the prime cause of the evil of capitalism may indeed deserve the reproach of vagueness and naiveté. But in characterizing Chekhov's social assessments it is far more fruitful not to overlook another, more important, conclusion.

First and foremost, this is to be found in the consistently accurate and tough-minded assessments of capitalism that are delivered in the second half of the story, corresponding to the "it turned out that" phase ("an incurable disease," "a gross mistake," an absurdity like something from the time of "pile-dwellings" and "the stone age"). The same uncompromising honesty applies in the assessment of the "various improvements" called upon to smooth over the defects of capitalism but incapable of changing its "diabolical" essence; and equally with regard to the naive attempts to make rich men change their minds: "any conversation on the subject usually turns out to be embarrassed, awkward, and lengthy."

So in speaking of Chekhov's position, one should concentrate on the accuracy and tough-minded honesty of these assessments, to be found not simply in the hero's own conclusions but in all the story's descriptive material and the logic of its development. This artistic accuracy and honesty supported everything that could be said at the time of the story's composition: a time when "hopelessly incurable" social relations had not yet become openly and manifestly explosive, when "the workers stood back timidly and deferentially to let the carriage pass" on its way to the big house, and when Christina Dmitriyevna was still justified in saying, "The workers are very pleased with us . . . they're really quite devoted." The subsequent development of class relations after 1898 would very quickly render this position out of date. Yet what the new state of affairs demanded was not the abandonment of Chekhov's artistic assessments but their further development; so far as 1898 is concerned, their accuracy and honesty are beyond dispute.

Where Chekhov takes up a particularly insistent polemical position in "A Case History" is in relation to the features of factory life to be found "in a newspaper article or a textbook." The hero's journey from "it seemed" to "it turned out that" shows that Chekhov, the creator of this artistic world, was not satisfied with too generalized an approach in which abstractions are drawn from "the muddle of which everyday life consists," and which fails to penetrate "the tangle of all the small threads from which human relations are woven." Remaining loyal to his familiar method of individualization, Chekhov the artist-investigator champions the need for the greatest consideration of social micro-elements: of each individual existence, of individual situations and individual relations. In "A Case History" he shows that at this micro-level any general law "is no longer a law at all but a logical absurdity."

Why is it that whenever Chekhov broaches the subject of capitalism in Russia, he does not write about central figures but chooses those who are somehow incidental and secondary: Fyodor, son of the dying head of the Laptev trading company in "Three Years"; Anna Akimovna Glagoleva, niece of the late founder of a commercial enterprise in "A Woman's Kingdom"; and the widow and daughter of the late factory owner Lyalikov in "A Case History"? Those who once created these trading companies and enterprises are either handing them over or are remembered by others as they look down from their portraits on the walls. Their heirs, on the other hand, the stories' active characters, do not create or increase capital but find it a burden. Chekhov's capitalists—Anna Akimovna, Laptev, Liza Lyalikova—are sensitive, restless people who find their position inappropriate and incomprehensible, and would like (but are unable) to cast off the burden of their inheritance, power, and wealth. The last of their number is Lopakhin in *The Cherry Orchard*, who exclaims: "Oh, if only all this could be over quickly, if only this unhappy, disjointed life of ours could somehow be transformed."

These characters' features are directly linked with Chekhov's method of "individualizing each separate phenomenon." One of this method's first requirements, derived from the Zakharin school of medicine, was that in establishing the picture of a disease (and in "A Case History" capitalism is actually described as an incurable disease), all the phenomena that accompany, complicate, and individualize the basic process must be taken into account. In preferring to present figures who were "untypical" of Russian capitalism,

Chekhov deliberately complicated the picture of the phenomenon he presented. The consistency with which he stuck to his principle of "individualizing each separate case" should not be regarded as evidence of the writer's economic and social naiveté but as a manifestation of his artistic and humanist extremism.

Chekhov was fully aware, of course, that in dealing with large-scale categories the task of accounting for the peculiarities of each individual existence is unbelievably complicated. But as an artist and humanist—and an extraordinarily tough-minded one—he could not be satisfied with less. The greatness of Chekhov's artistic world can be defined by his readiness to consider these extreme cases.

The examining magistrate Lyzhin in "On Official Duty" is another person attempting to make sense of life. What preoccupies him (as it did the heroes of "Lights," "The Wife," "My Life," "A Case History," and many other works) is the search for a connecting principle in life.

Thrown into the depths of the provinces "a thousand versts from Moscow," Lyzhin keeps thinking that "this isn't life here, but scraps of life, fragments, everything is accidental and you can't draw any conclusions"; whereas in Moscow and St. Petersburg, he thinks, in a cultured environment, "nothing is accidental, everything hangs together and obeys certain laws, and any suicide, for example, is comprehensible, you can explain why it happened and what significance it has in the general cycle of life."

This initial conception of the author's is accompanied by a characteristic commentary: "He supposed that if the surrounding life here in the wilds was incomprehensible to him and he could not see it, that meant there was no life there at all." Such an outlook, when the hero imagines that he can judge the life and the people around him by his own standards, is one of the commonest kinds of delusion and false conception in Chekhov's world (remember what was said about Gurov: "He judged others by himself, did not believe what he saw, and always assumed that in everyone else's life . . .").

Here too, in taking his hero from "it seemed" to "it turned out that," Chekhov makes him aware of the falsity of his earlier conceptions.

In Chekhov's late works, the "jolt"—an essential structural element in the story of discovery—is usually spread out and prepared for by building up information in the hero's consciousness that overturns the initial stereotype. In order to understand that a universal link exists between the phenomena of life, Lyzhin needed to explain the connection between the suicide of the unfortunate Lesnitsky, a rural insurance agent, and the difficult life of the peasants among whom he had to live. Lyzhin's conversation with Loshadin, the village policeman, is highly significant, and the final jolt comes in his dream, in which Lesnitsky the suicide and old man Loshadin are walking across the fields in a blizzard, "side by side, supporting each other," and singing: "We know nothing of rest, we know nothing of joys. . . . We carry on our backs all the burden of this life, of our life, of your life. . . . Ooh-ooh-ooh! We go on, we go on, we go on. . . ." It is this dream that forces Lyzhin to think about the link between "the suicide and peasant sorrow."

The jolt leads to the discovery.

And now . . . it seemed to him that . . . some link, invisible yet significant and vital, existed between these two people . . . and between everyone, everyone; nothing is accidental in this life, even in the back of beyond, everything is filled with one common idea. . . . The unfortunate "neurasthenic," as the doctor called him, who had broken under the strain and killed himself, and the old peasant who spent every day of his life trudging round from one person to the next, were accidents, fragments of life, only if you thought of your own existence as accidental, but they were parts of a single organism, wonderful and rational, if you thought of your own life as part of this whole.

Having seen the link in what at a superficial glance seemed accidental, Lyzhin felt that this discovery itself was not accidental but natural, "it was a secret thought that he had long harbored and that only now had unfolded fully and clearly in his consciousness."

From the truth revealed to him, Lyzhin draws a moral conclusion: it is wrong, it is immoral to desire happiness and contentment for oneself when other people have "shouldered the burden of what is darkest and most oppressive in life."

At the beginning of the story, when the hero is thinking about "the real Russia," he supposes that real intelligible life is to be found only amid the noise and lights of the capitals. The author makes him see the universal connection of "how things are" after his life has collided with the fates of people "who have been crushed by toil and cares, or of weak abandoned people, who are only ever discussed occasionally over supper in an irritated, sneering way, and to whom no help is offered."

Thus Chekhov not only leads his hero to pose correctly the question of what is accidental and what is natural, but also the question of "the real Russia"—a Russia that is now inseparable in his mind from "peasant sorrow" and the anonymous fates of sufferers like Lesnitsky, scattered over the vast Russian spaces, far from the cultured island-capitals.

For the hero (and the reader too) new markers are established for the correct presentation of the questions that disturb him.

# 23

# "If Only We Could Know!": *Three Sisters* (1901)

Three Sisters was the first play written by Chekhov especially for the Moscow Art Theater. Scholars have observed that it is also the first play by Chekhov to exhibit features that are broadly characteristic of the advanced theater of his day, of the European "new drama." So it is all the more interesting to see how Chekhov's familiar creative principles were incorporated in the play.

According to his own testimony and Stanislavsky's memoirs, Chekhov conceived the idea for writing the new play after attending a 1900 Art Theater performance of Hauptmann's play *Lonely People*. Chekhov's drama, it is true, may be seen as a development of certain elements in the form and content of Hauptmann's play.

A careful analysis of these elements shows, however, that they had all been present earlier in Chekhov's prose and drama, long before the Art Theater production and even before the writing of *Lonely People* in 1889. Perhaps it was not so much a case of imitation as of creative rivalry, of Chekhov's urge to reaffirm in dramatic form the position he had already staked out in *Ivanov*, *The Seagull*, and *Uncle Vanya* in his battle against the lack of comprehension shown by the old theater and by audiences and critics. *Lonely People*, one might say, acted as a stimulant and reawakened Chekhov's taste for writing a play (he had been insisting that he would never write for the theater again), but the initial data for its composition had been in existence much longer.

The theme of *Lonely People*—the family life of a contemporary member of the intelligentsia, his loneliness within the family, the lack of communication between husband and wife—also constitutes a large part of the external pattern of events in *Three Sisters*, and strikes a no less tragic note.

All the main characters of *Three Sisters* are lonely.

Those who are lonely within the family are Masha, Andrei, and Vershinin.

Those who are lonely in love are Tuzenbach, Solyony, and Chebutykin.

Those who do not find love are Irina and Olga.

The motif of a contemporary man's loneliness within the family, of how existing family arrangements are inimical to his mind and feelings, is graphically developed in *Lonely People* and in *Three Sisters* as a source of dramatic conflict. But the familiar motif is very much deeper and more complex in Chekhov's play.

The chorus of lonely people in *Three Sisters* does, after all, include Natasha and Kulygin, who are both lonely in their own way. Those things which cause joy or grief to the unintelligent Kulygin are absolutely alien to his wife. Natasha strives singlehandedly—albeit armed to the teeth—to become the sole mistress of the household.

Disunity and loneliness are the distinguishing features of all the characters in *Three Sisters*. There are no firm ties, whether of family, love, or society. Do the characters have elements in common? They do, but not of a kind that might give us cause for rejoicing.

However much the problems of family and of love (around which all the characters of *Three Sisters* are grouped in one way or another) may seem of immediate importance to the characters, each of them is confronted by the more general question: "how to live?" The basic Chekhov theme of orienting oneself in life can be heard distinctly throughout the play and is repeated by almost every character—in reflections, arguments, or behavior.

In Act I the joyous affirmation of the youngest sister, Irina, is heard: "When I woke up this morning, got out of bed, and had a wash, it suddenly *began to seem* as if everything in the world was clear to me and I knew the right way to live" (italics added here and subsequently). The naiveté and emptiness of this affirmation becomes clear in Act II. Irina moves from disillusionment to disillusionment, looking all the while for new guidelines in life (working hard, moving to Moscow) that prove either too difficult for her or unattainable. ". . . But *it turned out to be* nonsense, all nonsense."

Her sister Masha likewise moves from "it seemed" to "it turned out that" in her own element, that of love. Of her husband she says: "At that time he *seemed* terribly learned, clever, and important. But *it's not like that anymore*, unfortunately." Of Vershinin she says: "To begin with he *seemed* odd, then I felt sorry for him . . . and then I fell in love." At the end she says: "My life hasn't worked out. . . . I don't want anything now." Olga, too, has her guidelines and her dreams, and speaks of the divergence between her ideas and reality. The course of Andrei's life is similar: "When I got married, I thought we'd be happy. . . . I thought we'd all be happy. But oh my God! (*cries*)"

Perplexity, mental confusion, disillusion, and the awareness of having been cheated by life are common to all the main characters. Their individual exclamations merge into a common stream: "How time flies! Heavens, how time flies!" (Vershinin); "If one could start one's life all over again . . ." (Vershinin); "What a fraud life is!" (Andrei); "My life's gone past like a flash of lightning" (Chebutykin); "I don't know anything and neither does anyone else" (Chebutykin); "What a happy life I could see ahead of us then! Where did it all go?" (Tuzenbach); "Time keeps going by and I feel I'm moving farther away from the real, beautiful life" (Irina); "No one knows the first thing about it, and each person has got to work it out on his own" (Masha); "Oh, where did it go, my past life, what became of it . . ." (Andrei); "Nothing ever happens as we'd like it to" (Olga); "If only we could know!" (Olga). The rough drafts contain the exclamation already familiar from "Lights": "You can't make anything out in this world!"[1]

These heroes, then, do not know "how to live," or if they think they do, this is disproved by the course of life, by life's irony. Natasha, Solyony, and Kulygin know, but the author's ironic attitude toward their "knowledge" is unmistakable.

All the central characters are drawn into these reflections on the meaning and course of life. How Chekhov uses the individual fates of "average people" (Hauptmann's heroes, Johannes and Anna, stand out by comparison as exceptional personalities) to address universal human problems is an essential feature of the play.

This is powerfully underlined by two images that are built up from discrete but consistently developed allusions: time and nature. These images provide a background to the heroes' fates.

In Chekhov it is not only that people talk about the relentless passage of time. Nature exists in time, it surrounds the characters and is often recalled by them. Nature and time are blended in the allusions to migrating birds, trees, flowers, the falling snow, and the wide, open sky. Within this blending, individual phenomena and fates can be distinguished. The migrating bird that has grown old, the tree that has withered, the avenue of trees that is to be cut down, the philosophers appearing among the flocks of birds: these are like separate drops taken from an indivisible stream, examples that people use to explain the course of their lives.

The individual phenomena of nature and time do not affect those general laws and processes that are fixed for eternity: of arrivals and departures, flowering and fading. Nature and time are indifferent, their laws are unchanging, to them "it's all the same." Counterbalancing this calm indifference are people, who may be happy or unhappy, who laugh or are miserable, assert themselves or break down, hope or despair, make the best of life or become irrec-

---

1. See *Works*, 13:299.

oncilable. Thus the fates of Chekhov's characters are built up in a way that blends and contrasts with the background of nature and time. Their absorption in everyday life and simultaneously in the eternal motion of nature and time underlines the general significance and universality of Chekhov's conception.

This breadth in the posing of questions is matched by the breadth and comprehensiveness of the generalizations and conclusions to which Chekhov leads his audience and readers.

The main characters in *Three Sisters* are unhappy, but to criticize Chekhov, as his contemporaries did, for failing to do more than depict the unhappy lives of unhappy people completely misses the point. The author enables us to penetrate deeply into the reasons for his characters' misfortunes.

For a long time the Prozorov sisters—beautiful, poetic, and exalted—were seen by critics as a positive force standing up to aggressive vulgarity. Natasha might have appropriated the house, Solyony might have killed Irina's fiancé, and their brother Andrei might have gone downhill—but even at the end of the play the sisters are still adamant in their rejection of philistinism, and are still gazing steadfastly toward the future. In this interpretation, Vershinin and Tuzenbach are the sisters' allies. (Not a few studies, incidentally, have been written to show who is the superior of these two and to decide which of the incorrigible debaters has Chekhov's approval: the "gradualist" Vershinin or the more radically thinking Tuzenbach. The mutually exclusive proofs are derived from the characters' speeches, from their absolute, out-of-context meaning.)

Then came a time when the sisters, Vershinin, and Tuzenbach began to be seen as high-minded but ineffectual dreamers. Their words and hopes might be attractive and poetic, but as individuals they lacked the strength to defend themselves against vulgarity or to bring the dreamed-of future any closer. No outsider was responsible for their misfortunes; they themselves were.

This second interpretation takes much fuller account of certain Chekhov principles: the distance between what a character says and the author's own position, and the inner resemblance between different characters. But it too continues to contrast certain characters with other characters, assigning unconditionally positive qualities to some and equally negative qualities to others. For Chekhov, however, this way of contrasting and sorting out conflicting forces belonged to the drama of the past. For him the characters within the conflict are related differently.

It is easy to see how Natasha's aggressiveness, Solyony's coarseness, Chebutykin's indifference, and Kulygin's lack of intelligence may become the cause of other people's misfortunes. By comparison the sisters, Andrei, Vershinin, and Tuzenbach embody higher moral qualities, and it is easy to perceive them simply as victims, or, in the other interpretation, simply as protesters against vulgarity, coarseness, ignorance, etc.

It is often claimed that the essence of Chekhov's work (including *Three Sisters*) boils down to the affirmation of certain ethical values. But how Chekhov's characters orient themselves in the moral realm is a particular instance of how they orient themselves in life.

Can the conflict in *Three Sisters* be reduced to the confrontation between some characters and others, and the point of the play to the affirmation of the sisters' moral superiority over Natasha, or of Vershinin and Tuzenbach over Solyony? This superiority is too obvious, it requires no special proof, and to reduce everything to those terms would be to narrow the significance of the conflict and the author's conclusions.

In *Three Sisters*, again, what makes the conflict distinctive is that in showing a clash between different characters or groups of characters, the author reveals the features they have in common but do not themselves recognize. Many of the characters are unhappy and at the same time are the cause of unhappiness in others. This had been so in *Ivanov*, *The Seagull*, and *Uncle Vanya*, and in Chekhov's prose.

Critics have often drawn attention to the scene at the beginning of Act I, when Olga and Irina's joyful affirmations that they will soon be moving to Moscow are interrupted by the remarks of Chebutykin and Tuzenbach, who are preoccupied with their own conversation ("Not a hope in hell!"; "Absolute nonsense, of course"), and by their laughter. The glow of enthusiasm is extinguished by a cold wind; life responds mockingly to hopes and dreams.

These interruptions are clearly not introduced by Chekhov for the sake of reproducing the "random" flow of life. The insistent regularity with which he makes use of this device is a direct indication of the author's conscious design.

A careful reading of the play shows that literally the whole of it consists of interruptions of this kind. Every speech in *Three Sisters* is invariably accompanied by the equivalent of "Not a hope in hell! . . . Absolute nonsense, of course." This by no means applies only to the most obvious examples, like Andrei's confessional speeches, which the deaf Ferapont is not listening to and Natasha cuts short, or Solyony's "Tseep, tseep, tseep . . ." in response to Tuzenbach's speeches. Natasha, Solyony, Chebutykin, and Kulygin are subject to this rule as much as the other characters are. At this level the principle of equal distribution prevails.

Each of the characters has his own plan for life, guidelines, and idea of happiness. Each of them at this moment or that shares his "truth" with the others. But to the others this "truth" seems alien, absurd, comic, or strange. The confession is received by those present with ridicule, coarseness, indifference, or coldness.

When Olga says that she would be happy to give up work and get married, this sounds like a confession. Immediately we hear Tuzenbach say: "What a load of rubbish you're talking, I'm tired of listening to you." But when Masha comes to confess her love to the same Olga, the latter calls it all nonsense.

Tuzenbach, who dreams of working and having his love reciprocated by Irina, is constantly running up against her indifference. Irina responds even more coldly on the one occasion when Solyony confesses his loneliness and his love for her.

Bursting with happiness, Kulygin is constantly distressed by Masha's mocking replies, but in answer to the drunken Chebutykin's bitter confession he himself can only laugh: "You're pretty far gone, Ivan Romanych." The cold response of the beloved, from which

Tuzenbach and Solyony suffer, has been experienced in his time by Chebutykin, after which he has become cynically indifferent to everything, including Tuzenbach's passionate outbursts.

Natasha has her own "truth," but when she is not being "made fun of" by the sisters and Chebutykin, she must listen to Solyony's incredibly coarse remark about frying her baby in a frying pan.

Everything that Vershinin is made to say in the play is devalued in advance by Tuzenbach's ironic description of him.

Sometimes these interruptions are produced by "accidentally" superimposing parallel dialogues, and sometimes they are found in the same dialogue. The effect is identical: to devalue or pour cold water on the words spoken. The textual history of *Three Sisters* shows that Chekhov consistently strengthened this "interruption principle": many of the mocking, indifferent replies to the confessional speeches were introduced in the final stages of revision.

These phenomena are all similar in kind: absorbed in their "personal view of things," the characters are incapable of putting themselves in another person's position, and their own outpourings and frankness are received with incomprehension. Which of them is the most cruel, the most indelicate, the least responsive? Whose ridicule, coldness, indifference, or coarseness causes most suffering to other people?

The bourgeois Natasha is often presented as the person chiefly responsible for the misfortunes of the Prozorov household. To what extent is her role like that of traditional dramatic villains who engineer the downfall of those who stand in their way? If one thinks of Shakespeare's Lady Macbeth (Chekhov let drop the comparison in a letter to Stanislavsky, when he suggested that in Act III Natasha should "walk across the stage in a straight line, not looking at anyone or anything, holding a candle à la Lady Macbeth—it'll be quicker and more terrifying done like that"[2]), a certain similarity does exist between the two. They are both fond of power, and they both usurp authority and a house/kingdom, bringing harm to others.

---

2. *Letters*, 9:171.

The difference between them is not only that the actions of Shakespeare's heroine are more monumental and more bloody. Natasha, of course, operates on an everyday level, like all of Chekhov's characters (cf. Vershinin's "My kingdom for a glass of tea!" and Shakespeare's "A horse! A horse! My kingdom for a horse!" from *Richard III*). The basic difference lies elsewhere.

Evil is the substance of Lady Macbeth's character (". . . unsex me here,/ And fill me from the crown to the toe top-full/ Of direst cruelty!"). In order to realize her plans, she consciously embarks on a course of evildoing, which she carries out in secret.

Natasha does not organize plots or cunning traps. She carries out evil unconsciously, without malicious intent. She is simply following certain "general ideas." These ideas may not be very elevated, but society grants them full recognition: that children should be healthy (her main idea) and that a household should have one mistress. They represent her "truth," and she can talk about them with pride and dignity, for all the world to hear. As for her "little affair with Protopopov," that is also one of the accepted, or in any case forgivable and well-known, options for a married woman with a "muff" of a husband. (The fate of Andrei Prozorov is very reminiscent of the story of the marriage and family life of Pavel Beshmetev, the hero of A. F. Pisemsky's tale "The Muff" [1850].)

Natasha's plan for life, consisting as it does of the most standard components, is terrifying precisely because it is so clear, sincere, and incontrovertible. Who could possibly object to the idea that children should be surrounded by care, that one person should be in charge of a household, or that a child's smile should give pleasure to onlookers?

What is "negative" in Natasha is not these "ideas"of hers but her turning them into absolutes, her completely unshakable confidence that she is right. The qualities that are valued by the others—delicacy, tolerance, charity—are swept aside and crushed by what she regards as higher values. Her categorical approach to life is an extension of her sincerity; her cruelty comes from being faithful to her convictions, from her integrity.

Thus the evil that Natasha brings with her results from following her own "truth." She is totally convinced of the justice of certain commonly accepted guidelines and values, and follows them sincerely. Like other "negative" characters in Chekhov's plays, she is not an absolute "villain" but, so to speak, a functional one. Evil in Chekhov's plays is a function of having blind confidence in the rightness of one's convictions or beliefs.

But if that is the case, Natasha is no more than a heightened version of all the other characters, and embodies the kind of self-assertion that is found most commonly in Chekhov's world.

Solyony also bases his conduct on a specific model—a literary one—and in following it he commits murder in a duel.

Chekhov was well aware that all-conquering bourgeois women and duelists who see themselves as diabolical figures had already appeared in literature, including his own work. The usurping Natasha and the dueling Solyony both look like veiled literary allusions (to such sources as Shakespeare, Pisemsky, Turgenev's "The Duelist," and Lermontov's *A Hero of Our Time*). Chekhov was not so much creating new types as making the types created by his predecessors more complicated. His work was intended to throw new light on the hidden reasons for well-known phenomena.

It is too simple to see Natasha as the embodiment of evil, as someone absolutely alien to the other characters in the play. This is how she is seen by the sisters, and one can understand them. But in one of his letters Chekhov reminded the Theater that his play contained "four intelligent women," and that includes Natasha.[3] Chekhov shows the danger of Natasha by more subtle, nontraditional methods. He turns the characters around in such a way that they reveal, if only briefly, what puts them on an equal footing with Natasha.

In Hauptmann's play the forces in conflict were divided along traditional lines: questing, out-of-the-ordinary heroes were contrasted with their hostile, stagnant environment. In Chekhov's play all the characters, without exception, are drawn into processes that

3. *Letters*, 9:175.

cause suffering to others, or, at the least, they respond to a passionate outburst, fanciful dreams, or an outpouring of joy with mockery, coarseness, indifference, or a lack of delicacy. All the characters have in common hidden features that they do not wish to recognize.

The conclusion drawn by Chekhov in relation to Sakhalin—"we are all guilty"—is extended here to the realm of everyday relationships, to the misfortunes that normal, "average" people cause each other. For Chekhov it is more important to show how each person is responsible for the general state of affairs than to heap all the blame on an evil outside oneself, on "red-nosed prison governors" who can be seen as separate bearers of evil.

Chekhov's lonely people are either unhappy because their illusions (their previous hopes and guidelines) have collapsed, or they make other people unhappy by turning their "truth," their "general idea," into an absolute. Thus the interest within the play of such qualities as egoism, indifference, lack of delicacy, cynicism, cruelty, and coarseness is not self-contained. These qualities are shown to be the result of following a particular kind of orientation, a "personal view of things" or "general idea." In other words, the ethical theme is mediated through the epistemological, philosophical theme.

In the earlier chapter on *The Seagull*, the comic element in Chekhov's plays was said to be based on the constant repetition by a character of his "idea" ("Each person follows his own inclinations"), and on the hidden features in common between characters who would seem to be quite dissimilar. Both of these techniques are fully present in *Three Sisters*. Chekhov, as we know, "was convinced that he had written a cheerful comedy, but at the reading everyone took it for a drama and wept as they listened to it."[4] It may not be a coincidence that among the many literary quotations in the play, two are from works by Gogol, "The Tale of How Ivan Ivanovich Quarreled with Ivan Nikiforovich" and "The Diary of a Madman," both of which make use of the "comic and sad" principle of composition—

4. K. S. Stanislavsky, *Collected Works*, vol. 1, p. 235.

laughter all through the work and a melancholy sigh or a cry of despair at the end—that was also close to Chekhov's heart. In light of these parallels, the nature of the genre to which Chekhov's play belongs may perhaps be understood differently.

"Positive" types and happy endings to reassure the reader are impossible in Chekhov. His refusal to create happy endings is one of the main features of his plays.

Chekhov's conclusions are not tragic denouements coming at the end of a fateful chain of events, so much as a refusal to bring the action of the play to a happy conclusion: a conclusion to which everything would seem to be tending and for which the foundations are laid in each of his plays.

For example, in *Ivanov* it would seem possible to conclude with the wedding of Ivanov and Sasha, and in *The Seagull* with a union between Nina and Kostya after all their adversities. In *Uncle Vanya* one could imagine a similar happy outcome: Serebryakov is disgraced, Uncle Vanya joins with Yelyena, or at least Astrov with Sonya; or in *Three Sisters* Natasha is banished, Irina joins with Tuzenbach and Masha with Vershinin, Olga has to make do with Kulygin, the long-awaited departure for Moscow finally occurs. . . .

Playwrights very often use the technique of putting their characters through all manner of trials, then rewarding them and the audience with a happy or at least partially happy ending. Not so Chekhov. He confounds such expectations, pitilessly rejecting any happy ending that the course of action might lead us to expect. It is not an unhappy ending so much as the refusal of a happy ending that is the denouement common to all Chekhov's plays. In his endings Chekhov was not "killing hopes" (Shestov), he was killing illusions, pointing out the genuine complexity of the problems of human existence.

The uncompromising courage of Chekhov's approach in *Three Sisters* dumbfounded and depressed his contemporaries. In showing once again that no one knows the real truth, and in destroying illusions, Chekhov was denying them the possibility of any kind of re-assurance or consolation.

This denial seemed especially pitiless in the case of *Three Sisters*. Here was Chekhov showing up the illusory nature of the kinds of fixed concepts that literature had traditionally held sacred, such as the family and concern for children, or the intelligentsia's faith in honest toil and in suffering for the sake of future generations. Critics, audiences, and readers protested against the play's pitilessness, its refusal to console or to appease.[5]

But Chekhov is not simply writing plays with unhappy endings; he is tracing the pathways that lead to people's misfortunes. In *Three Sisters*, as before, the author is unmerciful toward illusions and complacency, but he is not indifferent or pitiless toward people. He is pointing out the deeper and usually unrecognized reasons for their misfortunes; and in that sense he is opening new pathways to understanding.

A careful examination of the surface text of *Three Sisters* shows that it is filled with allusion and quotation.

The story of Andrei's absurd marriage to Natasha looks like an allusion to Pisemsky's "The Muff," and Natasha herself is a particular variation on Shakespeare's usurping heroines. Kulygin makes liberal use of quotations from Latin. Solyony claims to be a Lermontov figure. Chekhov's very title alludes to I. Yasinsky's "epistolary tale," "Three Sisters" (1891).

Masha and Vershinin's love affair is woven out of quotations. It begins and ends with Pushkin's lines: "A green oak by a curving shore, / And on that oak a golden chain." In the middle of the play the characters joke in quotations ("My kingdom for a glass of tea!") and confess their love in quotations from Hauptmann ("apart from you alone, I have no one, no one") and especially from Tolstoy. When Vershinin says to Masha, "It's dark here, but I can see your

5. See *Works*, 13:446–463.

eyes gleaming," he is paraphrasing the words from *Anna Karenina*, which Chekhov referred to with such emotion to Bunin: "I'm scared of Tolstoy. Just think what he wrote—that Anna herself could feel and see her eyes gleaming in the darkness."[6] Their famous declaration of love—"Tram-tara . . . Tara-ra"—is reminiscent of Levin and Kitty's declaration in *Anna Karenina*, which they alone can understand, when instead of whole words they spell out the first letters only.

Why so many quotations? And what contribution of his own is the author making?

"Quoting" words and actions serves to underline the sense that Chekhov's characters are living in an old world that was established long ago. What happens to them has long since been known: these are "old stories," "dreary stories."

How do the characters orient themselves in this "old" world? What do they resort to or lean upon, what guides them when life makes it essential for them to act, behave, choose a certain path? It was here, in studying this aspect of life and reality—how the "average man" orients himself in a hostile, incomprehensible world—that Chekhov displayed his originality. In his creative consciousness he was building characters, situations, and conflicts that did not bear a simple relationship to the literature of the past but were constantly debating with it and reinterpreting well-known solutions.

The "general ideas" advanced by literature, social opinion, and tradition turn out to be false or powerless when confronted by the real complexity of life. As Masha comments: "When you read some novel or other, it all seems so stale and obvious, but as soon as you fall in love yourself, you realize that no one knows the first thing about it, and you've got to work it out on your own."

Masha is talking about the absence of general solutions that can be applied at any time to any person in love. "This is a great mystery," and there is only one way out: "We must treat each individual

---

6. I. A. Bunin, "Iz neokonchennoi knigi o Chekhove" in *Literaturnoye nasledstvo*, vol. 68 (Moscow, 1960), p. 658.

case in isolation, as the doctors say," which is what the heroes of "About Love" conclude on the same subject. Chekhov's self-appointed task as a writer was to individualize, in other words to study the complications that crop up when you consider specific instances of common situations.

The love between Vershinin and Masha, which they prefer to talk about in quotations, is so individualized that the quotations are forgotten, and it seems like the result of a unique combination of circumstances that only life itself is capable of inventing. The situation of each of them is absurd, the world in which they exist is hanging by a thread, and there is only a short time to go before it collapses completely—and yet love arises in these least likely of conditions.

*Three Sisters* is not about love or the family, though both play an important part. Love, marriage, the family are particular manifestations of the wider phenomenon of orienting oneself in the world. The play studies the orientation and behavior of contemporary man in those smaller spheres and in life as a whole, and what is revealed is everywhere the same: the absence of general solutions and prescriptions; fixed ideas that have become worn out; illusions and dogmas which the characters are incapable of rejecting.

As before, Chekhov is not only forcing his audiences to be skeptical of what is generally acknowledged and accepted. The characters' conversations in *Three Sisters* about the meaning of life and the need for faith are in sharp contrast with the absurdities of their actual situation and their day-to-day behavior, and clash discordantly with the actual course of events. This is where life's irony is most apparent.

In their dreams and what they ask from life, Chekhov's characters obviously do not wish to think about what they might reasonably expect, about whether their desires are feasible and practicable. For them, happiness is impossible given the existing ways of life, but they go on looking toward those distant horizons of space and time that they will obviously never reach. This is what constitutes their essential humanity.

By the end of the play it becomes more and more clear that all their arguments, daydreams, and hopes are an inseparable, inde-structible part of these people's lives. In spite of everything, they still have "a terrific desire to live" (Vershinin), they "must go on liv-ing" (Masha), and they "*want* to live!" (Olga). And while this desire to live remains, the urge to have faith, to seek meaning, and to try to look into the future is equally natural to them. The author's conclu-sions in *Three Sisters* are based on the indivisibility of our ignorance of "real truth" and our constant search for it.

# 24

# A Man and His Faith:
# "The Bishop" (1902)

Among Chekhov's last and most mature stories is one whose particular quiet beauty makes it stand out: a story in which the sound of the author's voice, though seemingly muted, is at the same time unusually heartrending. This story is "The Bishop." Together with the few other works that he wrote in the 1900s, it was to form part of that artistic legacy in which Chekhov rounded off many of his themes and images.

In "The Bishop" we are shown the cognitive deliberations of a man on the threshold of death, trying to find answers to the basic problems of existence and talking about this in a stern, simple way, without any self-delusion or comforting lies. As he gratefully reviews in his memory the few uniquely good things that life has given him, he is soberly aware that all this is assigned to man only once and "will not be repeated or continued," and for that reason he is both stern and tender toward people and life as a whole. Truth and beauty—those permanent accompaniments of Chekhov's creative world—are more indissolubly linked than ever in this story.

In his book on Chekhov, published in Russian in New York in 1954, Boris Zaitsev devotes a special chapter to "The Bishop." Zaitsev interprets Chekhov in a distinctive way. His book is subtitled "A

Literary Biography," but "A Religious Biography" would have been more appropriate. Throughout the author seeks to demonstrate what would seem to be undemonstrable: Chekhov's religious aspirations, the great writer's subordination to that "general idea" from which he had frequently and explicitly fenced himself off.

Zaitsev writes of Chekhov: "One must state directly that he had no faith . . . and without faith the sky can look very threatening."[1] This would seem to be an acknowledgment of what is clearly evident from Chekhov's works, the opinions he expressed, and the recollections of his contemporaries: that Chekhov was devoid of religious feeling. But Zaitsev, repelled by the generally known and incontrovertible facts of Chekhov's biography and works, distorts them in such a way as to create a portrait of a completely different writer: a split personality who was outwardly a materialist but secretly a mystic and believer yearning for God. The chapter on "The Bishop" rounds off this interpretation. Zaitsev offers no analysis of the story, only impressionistic comments, but his understanding of its meaning is nonetheless articulated very clearly: if Chekhov's previous work had somehow failed to reveal much of his hidden religious feelings, this story provides indubitable evidence that Chekhov espoused religion at the end of his creative life.

In "The Bishop," Chekhov describes the last days of a man who is a sincere believer, and as always he does so objectively, looking at this phenomenon of life through the eyes of an investigator. In the complex characterization of this religious figure, one element, naturally, is his attitude toward religion and the church. But Zaitsev asserts without qualification that Chekhov looks at everything "through the eyes of Bishop Peter." He is confusing two things: Chekhov the man, who was nonreligious in principle, and Chekhov the author of "The Bishop," who is using the literary device of "looking at the world through a character's eyes"—a device tried and tested by Chekhov on numerous occasions in stories about horse thieves and engineers, terrorists and monks, peasants and civil

1. Boris Zaitsev, *Chekhov: Literaturnaya biografiya* (New York, 1954).

servants, murderers and mental patients. Alas, this device that puts all its faith in the reader's sensitivity has not infrequently been turned against Chekhov by the critics: the words and thoughts of his characters have been misrepresented as the author's own.

Tolstoy made fun, for example, of the Orthodox liturgy in *Resurrection*, whereas Chekhov speaks of Bishop Peter's bright feelings as he offers up prayers in church. But while Chekhov is infinitely far removed from any solution of the problems of religion and the church, Tolstoy's hostility to priests and ceremonies went hand in hand with an urge to teach people the right way to follow Christ.

The calling and high office of Chekhov's central character were not, of course, without significance for the author. Making him into a bishop gave Chekhov the chance to depict a situation that was close to his own. Here is a man from the lower classes who would seem to have achieved everything he could have dreamed of; a man called upon to be a teacher in life who is himself struggling with its insoluble contradictions and riddles; and a man raised above others by his position and very much in need of ordinary human contact.

At the same time "The Bishop" is not a "narrowly specialized" story depicting the way of life of the higher clergy. What is central to Bishop Peter's feelings and experiences has nothing to do with his calling or high office. This story of a dying bishop touches on life's fundamental questions: what kinds of joys are available to man, what poisons his life, what kind of attitude does he adopt to death . . . these are all problems that concern "generic" man, man of any rank or calling, though Chekhov accurately denoted his hero's "specific" characteristics.

So it is important to be clear what position Chekhov's hero reaches before his death, what the outcome is of his agonized reflections on the contradictions and mysteries of existence.

He was someone, he thought, who had achieved everything that was open to a man in his situation, and he had faith, yet all the same not everything was clear to him, something was still lacking and he did not want to die; and he still felt that he lacked something of the greatest importance of which he had once vaguely dreamed, and he was disturbed in the present by the same hope for the future that he had entertained in childhood, at the academy, and while he was abroad.

His faith and his high office—these, then, are not everything. Bishop Peter does not wish to renounce hope, he has not yet obtained what he was hoping for in this earthly life. These are all earthly feelings natural to anyone: Chekhov does not make his hero repent his earthly activities, become one with God, or renounce "the flesh"; he merely states that all the attachments and dreams of this sincere believer are nonetheless connected with "life on earth."

Then, on the very last day, "he felt that he was a simple ordinary man again, walking quickly and cheerfully across the fields tapping his stick, with the wide sunlit sky above him, and that now he was as free as a bird and could go wherever he liked!"

"He was, of course, simply walking toward God," Zaitsev assures his readers.[2] But Chekhov is saying something quite different: death releases his hero from the bother and burdens of life; in his mother's wailing cry he has at last acquired his real name, Paul, again; he has acquired freedom!

The genuine beauty and tragedy of "The Bishop" are lost in Zaitsev's interpretation, sacrificed to the critic's preconceived, tendentious approach. Most Western critics follow Zaitsev in drawing on material from the story as evidence of Chekhov's religious or clerical sympathies, and offer no real criticism of Zaitsev's position.

Ronald Hingley attempts to take a more objective view of the problem when he writes:

> On Chekhov's religious opinions it would be difficult to find any helpful pointers at all in his literary work. He accepted the Orthodox Church as a feature of Russian life, and, in the portraits which he drew of religious people, maintained an attitude of such tolerance and detachment that they might easily be mistaken for the

2. Op. cit., p. 229.

work of a believer. This was especially true of "The Bishop," one of his finest stories, in which he drew a most sympathetic picture of a member of the clergy. Nonetheless, Chekhov's personal outlook was completely free from any religious element.[3]

Simon Karlinsky writes that Zaitsev's book created an image of "sweet, saintly, and ethereal Chekhov, seemingly made of equal parts of treacle, holy water, and cotton candy."[4]

For Chekhov, his Peter/Paul is first and foremost a man clothed in a bishop's chasuble and weighed down by a burden which he feels is beyond his strength. Everything connected with his privileged position, everything that cuts him off from the life of ordinary people, he finds burdensome, and it is no accident that in his vision before death he sees himself as a simple man who has finally cast off the burden of authority and fame, and is free to go wherever he chooses.

His mother is shy in his presence, people see in him only "the bishop" and not the human being, but he himself (and Chekhov with him) finds this a curse, an incomprehensible riddle, a tragic absurdity of life. The theme of "a man and his name," so poignantly developed in "A Dreary Story," was reborn almost fifteen years later in "The Bishop." The story is very close to Chekhov's own personal life in his final years. Loneliness, the premonition of approaching death, masses of trifling details that interrupt his work, numerous visitors and yet no one with whom he can talk openly—these are the motifs that fill his letters from Yalta, just as they do "The Bishop." The story is immeasurably sad, and the reader attributes this emotional coloring to the author himself.[5]

In his own life Chekhov persistently avoided the influence of religion, taking a detached view of the search for religious faith and of

3. Ronald Hingley, *Chekhov: A Biographical and Critical Study* (London, 1966), pp. 177–178.

4. Simon Karlinsky and Michael Henry Heim, *Anton Chekhov's Life and Thought: Selected Letters and Commentary* (Berkeley, 1975), p. 400.

5. On the autobiographical element in "The Bishop," see my commentary in *Works*, 10:458–459.

believers, and aligning himself with that part of Russian society which "has left religion behind and is moving further and further away from it, whatever people may say and however many religious-philosophical societies may be formed" (letter to Dyagilev of December 30, 1902).[6]

What is unusual about Chekhov's position is that while remaining outside religion in principle, his treatment of religious problems in his work, as of other "specialized" problems, indicates neither approval nor censure.

He is far from entering into a polemic with the seekers after God on the fundamental issues of belief and unbelief; in the same letter to Dyagilev, having firmly dissociated himself and "the educated section of society" from religious searchings, he adds a characteristic qualification: "whether this is a good thing or a bad I won't venture to say." He seems to allow that in the distant future, "in tens of thousands of years," mankind may perceive "the truth of the real God"; what he does not allow is simply that he might at present be able to accept any of the existing forms of religious outlook. Chekhov was not irreconcilably opposed in principle to people with religious convictions, and it is useless to seek evidence for this in the author's position in "The Bishop."

Understanding the pressure of social causes that may push people toward religion ("Peasants," "In the Ravine"), Chekhov bases his attitude toward believers on the general demands of morality. When he is depicting believers, he makes no attempt to show whether his characters' religious convictions are true or false; he is working on a different plane, judging people not as believers or nonbelievers but for what they are—for their characters, convictions, and behavior.

The varied assessments in Chekhov's work of priests and clergymen have nothing to do with a philosophical assessment of their religious convictions but are formed in the light of general moral criteria that apply equally well to other characters. The simple-

---

6. *Letters*, 11:106.

hearted, "rather foolish" Father Christopher in "The Steppe," Nikolai the monk in "Easter Night," "an attractive poetical man" who composed canticles, the deacon in the village of Ukleyevo who devoured four pounds of caviar at a funeral breakfast ("In the Ravine")—in the depiction of personalities like these we can find irony, sympathy, and scorn.

Closely linked though it is in theme with such a "general idea" as religion, "The Bishop" nonetheless bears out Chekhov's well-established literary principles.

# 25

# "All of Us Are to Blame":
# *The Cherry Orchard* (1903)

C hekhov's last play has become the most celebrated production of twentieth-century world drama. Actors, directors, readers, and audiences in every country have sought (and continue to seek) to discover its meaning. For that reason, as in the case of Chekhov's stories, in trying to understand *The Cherry Orchard* we should bear in mind not only the impact it had on Chekhov's contemporaries, not only the meaning and interest it has for us, his compatriots, but also its universal content for all people at all times.

It is not unusual to read or see on stage a simplified interpretation of *The Cherry Orchard*. Among the characters are the owners of a country estate, who belong to the nobility; a merchant capitalist; and representatives of the younger generation, who deny old forms and proclaim the arrival of a new life. What could be simpler than to see the play as a portrayal of the effect of historical change on socio-economic and cultural structures, as a demonstration of the inevitable collapse of some, a condemnation of others, and a welcome to the new ones arriving? But "simpler" does not mean "more correct."

Russian literature contains quite a few illustrations, after all, of a situation that was common at the end of the nineteenth century: an orchard, park, or forest belonging to the nobility falls into the hands of an ex-peasant merchant. What is new and special about Chekhov's play? It is not only that there is a difference between an Ostrovsky merchant, purposefully buying up the nobility's real estate and behaving with cruel indifference to the owners, and Chekhov's merchant, who buys the estate more by accident and has made a genuine attempt to save it for its negligent proprietors.

What is far more important is that the author of *The Cherry Orchard* has a different view of life and human relations, and speaks about them in a different way from his predecessors. We shall understand the play's meaning not by bringing it down to the level of sociological or historical explanations but by trying to grasp the method evolved by Chekhov for depicting life in a work of drama.

If the novelty of Chekhov's dramatic language is not taken into account, many things in his play will seem odd, incomprehensible, and overloaded with unnecessary details (judged by the aesthetic standards of earlier theater).

But the main point to remember is that Chekhov evolved a new language in order to express a new outlook. Behind Chekhov's special dramatic form is a particular conception of life and human beings. "Let everything on stage be just as complicated and at the same time just as simple as in life," Chekhov said. "People are having a meal, just having a meal, yet all the time their happiness is being made or their lives are being broken up."[1]

Let us start with a strikingly obvious feature. How are *dialogues* composed in *The Cherry Orchard*? Not in the traditional way, where a remark is made in answer to the one before and requires another answer in its turn. Chekhov very often reproduces an unstructured conversation (take, for example, the disorderly chorus of responses and exclamations immediately after the arrival from the station in

1. See *Chekhov i teatr. Pis'ma. Fel'etony. Sovremenniki o Chekhove-dramaturge* (Moscow, 1961), p. 206.

Act I). Characters in *The Cherry Orchard* do not seem to hear each other, or if they are listening, their replies are off the point (Anya to Dunyasha, Ranevskaya and Gayev to Lopakhin, all the other characters to Trofimov with the exception of Anya, and even she is obviously reacting not to the sense but to the sound of what he is saying: "How well you speak! . . . [*exclaiming in delight*] You said that beautifully!").

Why compose the dialogues in that way? Was it for the sake of greater plausibility—to show how things are in real life? Yes, but not only that. Disunity, self-absorption, the inability to look at things from another person's point of view: these are what Chekhov sees in human relations and is demonstrating here.

Challenging his predecessors again, Chekhov completely rejects external *intrigue*, the struggle of a group of characters around such issues as an inheritance, the transfer of money, seeking permission or being forbidden to marry, etc.

The nature of the conflict and how the characters are divided up in *The Cherry Orchard* are quite different, as we shall see later. Each episode is not a new stage in the working out of an intrigue; episodes are filled with outwardly disjointed everyday conversations, with trivialities and insignificant details, but at the same time they are colored by a single mood, which then changes to a different mood, like a musical composition without a theme.

But if there is no intrigue, what constitutes the *event* without which there can be no drama? The event that is talked about most—the sale of the estate by auction—does not take place on stage. Starting with *The Seagull* and even earlier with *Ivanov*, Chekhov had consistently made use of this technique of transferring the basic "happening" offstage, leaving behind only its reflections and echoes in the characters' speeches. Unseen by the audience, the offstage events and characters (the aunt in Yaroslavl, the lover in Paris, Pishchik's daughter Dashenka) have an importance of their own in *The Cherry Orchard*. But their absence from the stage emphasizes that for the author they are only a background, a circumstance that accompanies what is basic to the play. Along with the evident absence of traditional external "action" there is, as always in Chekhov, a rich, continuous, and intense internal action.

The main events take place in the characters' consciousness: a discovery or a clinging to habitual stereotypes, an understanding or a failure to understand—"moving concepts about in the mind and replacing them," to use Osip Mandelshtam's formula. As a result of these unseen but completely real psychological events, people's lives are broken up or their happiness is made, hopes founder or are born, love blossoms or fails to materialize. . . .

These important events in the life of each person are not revealed through striking gestures and behavior (Chekhov consistently treats all striving after effect in an ironic light) but are presented in modest, humdrum ways. They are not emphasized, attention is not drawn to them artificially, and many things are transferred from the text to the *subtext*. This characteristic development of the action in Chekhov's plays was referred to in the Art Theater as "the undercurrent." For example, in Act I Anya and Varya are talking about whether the interest has been paid on the estate, whether Lopakhin is going to make Varya a proposal, and then about Anya's brooch in the shape of a bee. "Yes, Mama bought it," Anya replies sadly. Sadly, because they both sense the helplessness of the basic situation on which their future depends.

The line of development of each character's behavior and especially of the relations between characters is deliberately not made graphic. It is more like a dotted line (actors and producers must fill in this line, which is what makes the staging of Chekhov's plays at once so difficult and so fascinating). The playwright leaves a great deal to the reader's imagination, providing basic guidelines for a correct understanding.

Thus the basic line of the play is connected with Lopakhin. His relationship with Varya expresses itself in his odd antics that neither she nor the others can understand. But everything falls into place if the actors convey the absolute incompatibility of the two characters and at the same time the special feeling that Lopakhin has for Lyubov Andreyevna.

In the famous scene between Lopakhin and Varya in Act IV, when Lopakhin fails to declare himself, the characters talk about the weather and a broken thermometer—and not a word about what is obviously most important at that moment. Why does the relationship come to nothing, why is there no declaration, no love, and no happiness? It is not, of course, that Lopakhin is a businessman incapable of showing emotion. That is roughly how Varya explains their relationship: "He's got so much on his hands, he's no time for me"; "He either says nothing or he's joking. I can understand, he's making a lot of money, he's busy with his affairs and he's no time for me." But the actors will get much closer to Chekhov's subtext, his "undercurrent" technique, if by the time of the scene in Act IV the audience has been given the clear impression that Varya is indeed not a suitable match for Lopakhin, that she is not worthy of him. Lopakhin is a man of broad vision, and in his thoughts he is capable of taking in at a glance, like an eagle, "these huge forests, limitless plains, and vast horizons." Varya, however (to continue the comparison), is a sparrow, and her field of vision does not extend beyond housekeeping, saving money, and the estate keys attached to her belt. . . . A sparrow and an eagle: it is this feeling—though he is not consciously aware of it, of course—that prevents Lopakhin from taking the initiative in a situation where any other merchant in his place would have jumped at the chance of making a "decent" marriage.

Because of his position, Lopakhin cannot hope to make a better match than Varya. But another line—broken but distinct—is indicated in the play: Lopakhin loves Ranevskaya, "like someone close—more than close." This would seem absurd and unthinkable to Ranevskaya and all those around her, and Lopakhin himself is evidently not fully aware of his own feelings. But we need only observe how he behaves, for example, in Act II, after Ranevskaya says that he should propose to Varya. It is after this that he talks irritably about life being better in the past, because then you could flog the peasants, and begins tactlessly teasing Trofimov. All this is a result of his depressed state once he sees clearly that it does not even occur to Ranevskaya to take his feelings seriously. This unreciprocated tenderness on Lopakhin's part will come to the surface several more times in the play. Among the chorus of speeches by the characters in *The Cherry Orchard* about how their lives have gone wrong, Lopakhin's unexpressed feeling can strike one of the most painful notes.

Thus Chekhov insistently repeats and exploits all these external techniques for organizing his material (how he treats dialogue, events, the development of the action), and through them his conception of life becomes clear.

But it is the nature of *conflict*—how Chekhov relates one character to another—that distinguishes his plays even more from those of his predecessors.

In Ostrovsky's plays, as we have seen, the prime mover of the action is the *difference* between characters in their class, financial, and family situations, from which their conflicts and collisions arise. Some of his plays may end not in disaster but its opposite: triumph over the petty tyrant, the oppressor, the intriguer, et al. But however varied the endings may be, the contrast within the conflict between victim and oppressor, those who suffer and those who cause suffering, is invariable.

Not so in Chekhov. His plays are based not on the contrast between characters but on unity and what they have in common.

Many interpretations of *The Cherry Orchard* go back to its first staging in 1904 by the Moscow Art Theater. This famous production concentrated on the figures of Gayev and Ranevskaya, as brilliantly portrayed by K. S. Stanislavsky and O. L. Knipper-Chekhova, and made the impoverishment of the nobility, their powerlessness in the face of the approaching disaster, into the central line of the play. The former owners of the cherry orchard were presented as complex, equivocal characters. The acting of Knipper and Stanislavsky, which combined satirical elements in its treatment of the theme of "taking leave of the past" with a lyrical strength that audiences found profoundly moving, showed the highest degree of theatrical sophistication.

The Art Theater chose its best possible actors to represent the older generation. But in spite of that (or perhaps for that very reason), the emphasis in the production was so much at odds with the author's intention that in Chekhov's words, this was "definitely not what I wrote," and the Theater had "ruined" the play.[2]

It was this production that forced the earliest audiences to interpret *The Cherry Orchard* as a play about "the change in socioeconomic and cultural structures": a process to which the characters were related in strict accordance with the author's own scale of values (either condemning them, showing their bankruptcy, or sympathizing with them). But dividing up the characters on this hierarchical basis contradicts the dramatic principles that Chekhov supported in theory and insisted on in practice when he was working on the play.

Let us take a more careful look at the text of *The Cherry Orchard*, at the author's clear and insistent pointers to the meaning of what is going on. Chekhov had moved consistently away from the traditional approach of using a character as a "mouthpiece" for formulating the author's own ideas. As usual in Chekhov, the pointers to the author's meaning are expressed primarily by repetitions.

In Act I a phrase is repeated that in various ways applies to almost every character.

Lyubov Andreyevna, who has not seen her adopted daughter for five years, says: "You're still the same, Varya," when she hears the latter taking charge of the household arrangements. Earlier on she has remarked that "Varya is still the same, she looks like a nun." Varya in her turn sadly confirms that "Mama is just the same, she hasn't changed a bit. If it was left to her, she'd give everything away." At the very beginning of Act I, Lopakhin wonders to himself: "Lyubov Andreyevna has been abroad for five years, I don't know

2. *Letters*, 12:81, 74.

what she's like now"; but a couple of hours later he is convinced that she is "as splendid as ever." Ranevskaya herself, on entering the nursery, defines her constant feature differently: "This is where I slept when I was a child. . . . And I'm like a child now"; but it is the same admission: I am the same.

"You're still the same, Lyonya"; "I see you're still the same as ever, Leonid Andreyich"; "You're at it again, Uncle": this is how Lyubov Andreyevna, Yasha, and Anya refer to Gayev's unfailing grandiloquence. Firs, too, is distressed by a constant feature of his master's behavior: "You've put the wrong trousers on again. What *am* I to do with you?"

*"You (he or she) are (is) the same"*: this is a constant, marked out by the author at the very start of the play. It is a property of all the characters, and they fall over one another to assure themselves and each other of it. "He's up to his usual tricks," Gayev says about Pishchik, when the latter makes his latest request for a loan. "You're always on about the same thing," says the half-asleep Anya in response to Dunyasha's news of her latest suitor. "He's been mumbling like that for three years. We're used to it" (said of Firs). "Charlotta was talking all the way, doing her conjuring tricks." "Every day some misfortune happens to me" (Yepikhodov).

Each character pursues his own theme (sometimes with variations): Yepikhodov talks of his misfortunes, Pishchik of his debts, and Varya about housekeeping, while Gayev lapses inappropriately into pathos and Trofimov into denunciations. Each figure in the play embodies a characteristic set of individual features, shaped by his individual fate. In Chekhov's other works this was referred to as their "personal view of things," their "truth," or their individual complaints or grievances against life (these truths and complaints vary, of course, in quality). The unchangeability of some characters is reinforced by their nicknames—"twenty-two misfortunes," "the eternal student," and by the term applied most generally of all, Firs's *nedotyopa* ("bungler").

When repetition (allotting an identical sign to everyone) occurs so many times that it cannot fail to be obvious, as in Act I of *The*

*Cherry Orchard*, this is a powerful means of expressing the author's own idea, his conception of human life, and his dramatic purpose.

Parallel with this recurrent motif and inseparable from it is another, seemingly opposite motif that is insistently repeated and can equally well be applied to everyone. Apparently frozen in their *unchangeability*, the characters every so often speak of how much has *changed*, how time is rushing past.

"When you went away, I was that high," says Dunyasha, indicating the distance between past and present by a gesture. She seems to be echoing Ranevskaya's recollection of the time when she "was a child." Lopakhin in his first speech compares how things used to be ("I remember, when I was a kid of about fifteen . . . Lyubov Andreyevna was quite a young girl then and I remember so vividly . . .") with how they are now ("I'm rich, true enough, I've plenty of money, but if you really start looking into it . . ."). "At one time . . ."—this is how Gayev begins his reminiscence, which is also about childhood, and he concludes it by saying: "now I'm fifty-one, strange as it may seem. . . ." The theme of childhood (irretrievably lost) or parents (dead or forgotten) is also repeated in various ways by Charlotta, Yasha, Pishchik, Trofimov, and Firs. The ancient Firs, like a living historical calendar, every so often returns from what is to what "used to be," what was done "at one time," "previously."

The perspective from present to past is opened up by almost every character, though to varying depths. Firs has been mumbling for three years. Six years ago Lyubov Andreyevna's husband died and her son was drowned. Forty or fifty years ago they still remembered the recipe for curing the cherries. The bookcase was made exactly one hundred years ago. The stones that had once been gravestones take us back to the depths of antiquity. . . . But the perspective is also opened up in the other direction, from present to future, and again to varying distances by different characters: Yasha, Varya, Lopakhin, Trofimov, and even Firs, locked in and forgotten inside the house.

"Yes, time is passing," Lopakhin remarks. This sensation is familiar to each character; it too is a constant, a permanent circumstance on which each character depends, whatever they may think or say about themselves and others, and however they may define themselves and their course in life. Each is fated to be a grain of sand or a splinter in the current of time.

Another recurrent motif embraces all the characters: the theme of *bewilderment* and *incomprehension* in the face of the pitiless advance of time. In Act I it is carried by Ranevskaya's questions. What is death for? Why do we grow old? Why does everything disappear without a trace? Why is everything forgotten that used to be? Why does time place a burden of mistakes and misfortunes on her shoulders like a stone? As the play proceeds, all the others echo her. For all his incorrigible insouciance, Gayev is bewildered in rare moments of reflection. "No one knows who I am and what I'm for," Charlotta says in perplexity. Yepikhodov is perplexed in his own kind of way: "I simply can't make out what direction I want my life to go in, whether I'm to go on living or to shoot myself." For Firs, the old order was understandable, "but now everything's all mixed up and you can't make anything out." Where things are going would seem to be clearer to Lopakhin than the others, but even he admits that only sometimes does it "seem" to him as if he understands the point of his existence. Ranevskaya, Gayev, and Dunyasha close their eyes to their situation and do not wish to understand it. Yasha, it seems, is the only one who understands everything, but his "clarity" appears grotesquely vulgar. Trofimov's understanding of everything also appears false. "You solve all the most serious problems with such confidence," Lyubov Andreyevna says to him, "but tell me, my dear, isn't that because you're young, because you haven't had time yet to experience any one of these problems for yourself . . . and life is still hidden from your young eyes?"

These, then, are unchanging people (each holding on to his own scheme of things) seen against a background of time which swallows up everything and everyone, bewildered people who do not understand the course of life. . . .

Finally, one may observe the following recurrent feature that is common to all the characters in *The Cherry Orchard*: they all have their hopes and dreams, great and small, comic or moving, realizable or obviously impracticable. Chekhov points out unceasingly that these hopes and dreams are formulated and expressed in an identical way: the frequency with which the *subjunctive mood* (if only . . .) occurs in the characters' monologues and dialogues is extremely high.

Varya shares her dreams with Anya: "If only we could marry you to a rich man, that would set my mind at rest, and I'd go off to a convent, then Kiev and Moscow, and I'd walk like that from one holy place to another. . . . I'd go on walking and walking." On a later occasion she says: "If I had some money, not a lot, a hundred rubles would do, I'd throw everything up and go right away. I'd go into a nunnery." Lyubov Andreyevna has different dreams and longings: "If only I could lift this heavy stone from my chest and shoulders, if only I could forget my past!" Gayev, Dunyasha, and Trofimov ("all we ought to do is work") also have their dreams. As for Lopakhin, his dreams extend from his plans for converting the orchard ("If the cherry orchard and the land along the river were broken up into plots for summer residences . . .") to ideas on what people in Russia could be like ("we, too, should be giants . . .") to his final desperate: "Oh, if only all this could be over quickly, if only this unhappy, disjointed life of ours could somehow be transformed."

What do all these and other repetitions, these insistent signals by the author, tell us? Once again they point to Chekhov's idea of how life and human relations are arranged.

The heroes of *The Cherry Orchard* frequently contrast themselves with one another. Charlotta: "These clever people are all such idiots, there's no one I can talk to." Gayev is supercilious toward Lopakhin and Yasha. Firs lays down the law to Dunyasha. Yasha in his turn reckons that he is far more cultured than any of them. And how much arrogance there is in Trofimov's words: "Everything that you all value so highly, rich and poor alike, has no power over me whatsoever." Lopakhin rightly comments on this endlessly recurring situation: "We look down our noses at each other, but life goes by regardless."

Thus Chekhov's characters are convinced of the absolute value of their opposing "truths." The author himself on each occasion points out what they have in common, the concealed similarity that they fail to notice or indignantly reject. All their mutual relationships, as we have said, are illuminated by the light of a single understanding. It is not simply that an old conflict has been given distinctive new refinements. The conflict itself is new: *apparent opposition combined with concealed similarity.*

In several of his earlier stories and plays, Chekhov had returned to situations in which opposing characters were apportioned an equal degree of mistakes, unfair attitudes, false ideas and actions. But it was in *The Cherry Orchard* that Chekhov first showed such consistency in carrying out the principle of giving the characters hidden features in common and dividing the conflict between them equally: the principle which to a greater or lesser extent determines the structure of all his main plays.

"Life is foul for everyone": this view of Russian life formulated by Chekhov in one of his letters[3] was supplemented by that other view expressed in "The Duel": "No one knows the real truth." Whatever the characters may say and think about themselves, and however subjectively meaningful, well founded, and exclusive their life situation and chosen guidelines may seem to them, Chekhov the writer makes no distinction among them in their collision with reality.

On this occasion the "not knowing" that embraces all the characters shows up in relation to the orchard. Each person makes his contribution to its eventual fate.

The beautiful orchard, which provides the background for characters who do not understand where things are going or have only a limited understanding, is linked with the fates of several genera-

3. *Letters*, 1:264.

tions—past, present, and future. As in "Ward No. 6," "Encased," and to some extent *Three Sisters*, there is an inner correspondence between the situation in the lives of individual people and the situation in Russia as a whole. The symbolic meanings of the orchard are manifold: beauty, the culture of the past, and finally the whole of Russia. One character sees the orchard as it was in the irretrievable past, while for another talking about the orchard is a way of showing off; someone else would like to save what was best about the orchard but in the event destroys it, while others welcome its destruction.

The dying orchard and unrealized love that is not even noticed: these two pervasive, inwardly connected themes give the play a quality of sad lyricism. But Chekhov insisted that what he had written was "not a drama, but a comedy, in places even a farce."[4] Remaining loyal to his principle of making the characters suffer identically in relation to a life they do not understand, and giving them hidden features in common (which does not exclude an astonishing display of external variations), Chekhov discovered for his last, great play a completely distinctive genre that was appropriate to this principle.

It is generally accepted that the task of any theater production of *The Cherry Orchard* is to strike the right balance between the sad and the comic. The play does not lend itself to a simple reading as only comic or only sad. In his "comedy" Chekhov evidently used special principles for combining the two.

*The Cherry Orchard* does not contain comic characters (such as Charlotta, Yepikhodov, and Varya) who stand apart from the rest. All the characters are assigned the kinds of limitations in thought and behavior—not understanding each other, holding opinions that clash with other people's, drawing illogical conclusions, making inappropriate replies and responses—that may be presented in a comic way.

Many of the characters seem nonetheless to be opposed to each

4. *Letters*, 11:248.

other and to form in some way contrasting pairs: Ranevskaya ("I am beneath love") and Trofimov ("We are above love"); Firs, seeing good things only in the past, and Anya, concentrating only on the future; Varya, sacrificing herself like an old woman for the sake of the family and keeping the estate going, and Gayev, who shows a purely childish egoism and has squandered the income from the estate "on boiled sweets"; the unsuccessful Yepikhodov and the brazenly successful Yasha. And so on: the comparisons and contrasts may be extended, using different characters and criteria. Never before had Chekhov been so generous and inventive in the art of individualization.

Yet for all the wealth of distinguishing nuances, the characters are linked by their hidden similarity. Each is an enthusiast for his own "truth," each is laying down his individual course in life, and the play's overall effect emerges from juxtaposing and correlating these truths and courses, and (less frequently) making them collide.

It is important to emphasize that Chekhov is not investing the simple fact of hidden similarity with any pejorative meaning. The correlation between different characters in *The Cherry Orchard* has long been noted, but how is it often interpreted? The servants, so the argument runs, can be seen as parody versions of their masters (Yasha, Dunyasha, and Charlotta of Ranevskaya, and Yepikhodov of Gayev), and this clearly indicates that Chekhov intended to satirize the former owners of the cherry orchard and to bid a mocking farewell to the past. This is a simplified, vulgar interpretation of Chekhov's principles of dramatic conflict.

Does not Anya in many ways repeat Ranevskaya, and Trofimov often remind us of the bungling Yepikhodov; and is there not an echo between Lopakhin's bewilderment and Charlotta's perplexity? In a Chekhov play the principle of repetition and mutual reflection among the characters is not directed selectively against a particular group but is total and all-embracing. To advocate one's own position, to be absorbed by one's own "truth," without noticing one's resemblance to everyone else—in Chekhov this appears to be our common fate, an inescapable feature of human existence. In itself it is neither good nor bad: it is natural. What results from the formation and interaction of different truths, ideas, and courses of conduct—this is Chekhov's field of study.

The comedy of resemblance and the comedy of repetition are fundamental to the comedy in *The Cherry Orchard*. All the characters are comic in their own way, and they all take part in a sad event, hastening its onset: this is how the correlation of the comic and serious may be defined in Chekhov's play.

Chekhov takes his example here from Gogol, with his crosscutting from the everyday to the lyrical and pathetic, from the comic to the elevated. These bold Gogolian transitions are deployed with unusual freedom in *The Cherry Orchard*, permeating the composition of the play as a whole and of each individual figure. Chekhov places all the characters in a state of permanent, nonstop transition from drama to comedy, tragedy to vaudeville, pathos to farce. This does not apply to one group of characters as opposed to another group. The principle of *permanently changing genre* is all-inclusive in *The Cherry Orchard*. Time and again the comic (the limited and relative) is deepened so that we feel sympathy, or, conversely, the serious is brought down to the level of obvious illogicality or repetition.

A play that relied upon sophisticated audiences who could detect its lyrical, symbolic subtext was steeped by Chekhov in the devices of coarse vaudeville: people falling downstairs or being hit over the head with a stick, gluttony, conjuring tricks, etc. After the highly emotional speeches that are given to almost every character—even down to Gayev, Pishchik, Dunyasha, and Firs—there immediately follows a farcical deflation, then the lyrical note returns, enabling us to understand the character's emotional state, and again his self-absorption turns into mockery of him (this is how Lopakhin's famous speech in Act III, "*I* bought it! . . . ," is constructed).

To what conclusions does Chekhov lead us by these untraditional routes?

A. P. Skaftymov has argued that in *The Cherry Orchard*, Chekhov is not portraying individual characters so much as the way in which life itself is arranged and organized. In contrast to the works of ear-

lier dramatists, in Chekhov's play man is not responsible for his failures, nor can the ill will of other persons be blamed. There are no
guilty people; "it is the actual arrangement of life that is the source
of this sad distortion and bitter sense of dissatisfaction."⁵

But is Chekhov really absolving his characters of responsibility
and transferring it to some "arrangement of life" existing outside
their ideas, actions, and relations? One recalls what Chekhov said
after visiting the convict island of Sakhalin about each person's responsibility for the existing order and general course of things: "We
are all guilty." Not *"There are no guilty people"* but *"We are all guilty."*

This "arrangement of life," which influences the fates of
Chekhov's heroes, must necessarily include the false, illusory, and
bankrupt nature of their ideas and guidelines: their conflicting,
"mixed-up" personal truths, interests, and convictions; their unwillingness or inability to see things from another person's point of
view, to listen carefully, to grasp, or to respond; and the confidence
that each of them has in the absolute nature of his own "truth."
These truths vary in their value, and the author certainly does not
lapse into caricaturing a valuable truth any more than he is unable
to see the complicating factors in a comically absurd, illogical truth
and to evoke sympathy for it, albeit briefly. He sometimes makes
use of obvious, instantaneous ways of revealing illogicalities, and
sometimes resorts to the "irony of life," when a wrong, unintelligent, or conceited opinion is overturned by the course of time, by
the logic of reality.

The most enigmatic aspect of Chekhov's divergence of opinion with
the Art Theater over its production of *The Cherry Orchard* is the insistence with which Chekhov pointed to Lopakhin's role as central
in the play.

In his letters from Yalta to Moscow he insisted that Stanislavsky
should play Lopakhin. On several occasions he stressed that
Lopakhin's role was "central," that "if it doesn't come off, that

5. A. P. Skaftymov, *Nravstvennye iskaniya . . .* , p. 375.

means the whole play will be a flop," that only a first-class actor, "only Konstantin Sergeyevich," could play the part. It would be too difficult for a merely talented actor, who would either "make Lopakhin very pale or coarsen him," turning him into "a little kulak. . . . After all, he's not a merchant in the vulgar meaning of the word, one must appreciate that."[6] Chekhov was warning against a simplified, trivial interpretation of a figure who was evidently dear to him.

Let us try to grasp what is in the play to support Chekhov's conviction that Lopakhin's role is central.

The first point, though not the only or main one, is the importance and singularity of Lopakhin's personality. Clearly, this is not the traditional merchant figure of Russian literature. A businessman, and a very successful one, Lopakhin also has "the soul of an artist." ("And when my poppies flowered, what a wonderful sight that was!") His remarks about Russia sound like a declaration of love for his native country. Nor should one forget that the most heartfelt words relating to the cherry orchard—"the most beautiful place in the world"—are spoken by Lopakhin.

In this figure of a merchant with the soul of an artist, Chekhov incorporated features that were characteristic of a small number of Russian entrepreneurs who left a significant mark on Russian culture at the turn of the twentieth century—men like Stanislavsky himself (known outside the theater as the factory owner Alekseyev); the millionaire Savva Morozov, who put up the money for building the Art Theater; Tretyakov, Shchukin, and Soldatenkov (all of whom created art galleries) and the publisher Sytin. Artistic sensitivity and a disinterested love of the beautiful were strangely combined in many of these merchants with features more typical of money-grubbing businessmen. Lopakhin was not based on a particular individual but given characteristics that were common to many of these businessmen-artists.

There is a certain parallel between Trofimov's final assessment of the man who would seem to be his opponent ("All the same, I'm

6. See *Letters*, 11:282–291.

still fond of you. You've got fine, sensitive fingers like an artist's. You've got a fine, sensitive soul. . . .") and Gorky's tribute to Savva Morozov in a letter to Chekhov: "When I see him standing in the wings, covered in dust and all of a dither for the play to succeed, I am willing to forgive him all his factories, which he doesn't need anyway, and I'm fond of him, because his disinterested love of art is something almost palpable in his peasant, merchant, money-grubbing soul."[7] Stanislavsky was anxious that future exponents of the role of Lopakhin should give him "the broad scope of a Shalyapin."[8]

Breaking up the orchard into plots for summer residences—the idea that obsesses Lopakhin—in his mind does not simply mean cutting down the cherry trees, but creating in place of the old estate a new cherry orchard that would be, as it were, universally accessible. Lopakhin's new orchard, scaled down and available to anyone for a modest payment, bears the same relation to the previous splendid orchard (that served only the few) as the democratic urban culture of Chekhov's epoch does to the wonderful country-estate culture of the past.

Chekhov was presenting an obviously untraditional figure for whom audiences and readers were not prepared, who broke all the fixed literary and theatrical rules.

The basic plot line of *The Cherry Orchard* is connected with Lopakhin. On this occasion the play's course of events is constructed not around a discovery but a peripeteia. Something anticipated and prepared for in Act I (saving the orchard), as a result of a number of circumstances, turns out exactly opposite in Act IV (the orchard is cut down). To begin with, Lopakhin makes a genuine attempt to save the orchard for Lyubov Andreyevna, but in the end he "accidentally" takes possession of it himself.

Having achieved success, Lopakhin is shown, however, by Chekhov to be anything but a victor. The whole content of *The Cherry Orchard* reinforces his own words about our "unhappy,

---

7. M. Gorky and A. Chekhov, *Perepiska, stat'i, vyskazyvaniya* (Moscow, 1951), p. 81.
8. K. S. Stanislavsky, *Collected Works*, vol. 1, p. 276.

disjointed life" which "goes by regardless." In fact, the one person capable of making a genuine assessment of what the cherry orchard stands for, is going to have to destroy it with his own hands (the realization of his plan is going to lead, after all, to the disappearance of everything that was valuable about the old estate). With unflinching honesty, Chekhov in *The Cherry Orchard* demonstrates the fatal divergence between a person's good personal qualities and subjectively kind intentions, and the consequences of his social activities.

Nor is Lopakhin granted any personal happiness.

At the start of the play he is obsessed by the idea of saving the cherry orchard, but nothing works out right. He fails to save the orchard for Ranevskaya, and his success makes a mockery of his best hopes: precisely because he has taken possession of the orchard, Ranevskaya is going away for good, to her ruin. Why this happens, Lopakhin cannot grasp, nor can any of the people around him explain it.

Thus Lopakhin embodies one of Chekhov's basic and earliest creative themes: that of life's hostility, insuperable complexity, and incomprehensibility for the ordinary ("average") Russian, whoever he may be. Many of Chekhov's main characters struggle equally unsuccessfully with the mysteries of life, whether it be a doctor, coffin-maker, shopkeeper, civil servant, or peasant ("The Wife," "Rothschild's Fiddle," "The Murder," "The Lady with a Little Dog," "The New Dacha"). Characters shown to be just as lonely, suffering, and at the mercy of hostile circumstances as Lopakhin include a millionaire, a factory owner, and a capitalist's daughter ("Three Years," "A Woman's Kingdom," "A Case History"). In the figure of Lopakhin, Chekhov remained faithful to this theme until the end: he is the last in a long line of such Chekhov characters.

*"A distant sound, as if from the sky, the sound of a breaking string, dying away and mournful"* . . . the thud of an axe heralding the death of the orchard . . . and the image of the orchard itself—these were understood by Chekhov's contemporaries as richly meaningful symbols.

Chekhov's use of symbols differs from that of the symbolists, for whom visible reality was only "a spider's web of phenomena" (Andrei Bely), entangling and concealing another—higher and mystical—reality. For Chekhov, no other reality exists except the one in which his characters live; even the most mysterious sound does not come from the sky but "as if from the sky."

It is not only that Chekhov leaves open the possibility of a natural explanation ("it must have been a bucket falling somewhere in a mine shaft. But a very long way off"). The characters may explain the sound wrongly, but there is no need to invoke the unreal or mystical here: the mystery is an earthly one, even though the characters fail to penetrate it.

Chekhov's symbols extend our horizons but do not take us away from this world. His symbols of happiness, beauty, the future, the eternal, and the higher aims of existence, and, conversely, of the terrifying real world, deepen the impression of what is being described. The degree of mastery and comprehension of the everyday world in Chekhov's works is such that the existential, general, and eternal shine through them.

The mysterious sound, referred to twice in *The Cherry Orchard*, was one that Chekhov had in fact heard in childhood.[9] But in addition to this real-life antecedent there was also a literary one: the sound that the boys hear in Turgenev's story "Bezhin Meadow." "Everything went silent. Suddenly, far away, a sound was heard, drawn-out, ringing, and almost like a moan, one of those unintelligible nocturnal sounds that sometimes emerge in the midst of deep silence, increase in volume, hang in the air, and in the end float slowly off, as if dying away." The parallel is reinforced by the similar situation in which the unintelligible sound is heard, and by the moods it evokes among the characters in both story and play: one shivers and is scared, another becomes reflective, a third reacts calmly and rationally.

In *The Cherry Orchard*, Turgenev's sound has acquired a new

9. See *O Chekhove. Vospominaniya i stat'i* (Moscow, 1910), p. 249.

note and come to resemble the sound of a breaking string. In this, Chekhov's last play, it combines symbols of life and of Russia, the homeland: it conjures up her vastness and a sense of time sweeping past. It is a familiar sound that will be heard forever above the Russian expanses, accompanying the countless comings and goings of successive generations.

Chekhov's wisdom, his conception of life and people, is not to be found in any of his characters' speeches. Distinctly, unambiguously, and at full volume it is to be heard in the way his works are arranged and his characters correlated, in his art of individualization and in how he combines the comic and the serious—in other words, in the language that Chekhov uses to communicate with his readers and audiences.

In his last play Chekhov captured the moment in Russian social history when only a short distance divided a state of universal disunity and listening only to oneself, from one of total breakdown and universal hostility. He called upon people not to be taken in by their own ideas about truth, not to regard as absolute the many "truths" that turn out to be "false conceptions," and to recognize each person's guilt and the responsibility of each of us for the general course of things—all of which was very difficult to grasp, as subsequent events indicated. Chekhov's depiction of Russia's historical problems made it possible for humanity to see problems that concern everyone at any time and in any kind of society.

# General Index

# Index of Works

# A NOTE ON THE AUTHOR

Vladimir Kataev has been professor of Russian literature at Moscow University since 1989, and head of the Chekhov Commission of the Russian Academy of Sciences since 1996. His many books and articles include *Chekhov's Prose: Problems of Interpretation*, *Chekhov's Literary Connections*, and *The Complexity of Simplicity*.


# A NOTE ON THE EDITOR

Harvey Pitcher, a British writer and translator, is the author of *The Chekhov Play: A New Interpretation* and *Chekhov's Leading Lady*, a biography of Olga Knipper. He has also translated *Chekhov: The Early Stories* (with Patrick Miles) and *Chekhov: The Comic Stories*.

APR 2003